A DAY ESTIVALL

◊

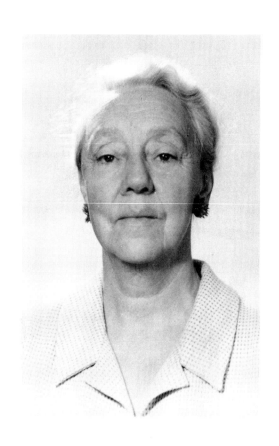

Dr Helena M. Shire
photograph: Shire family

A DAY ESTIVALL

Essays
on the Music, Poetry and History
of Scotland and England
&
Poems
Previously Unpublished

in honour of

HELENA MENNIE SHIRE

◊

edited by

Alisoun Gardner-Medwin & Janet Hadley Williams

ABERDEEN UNIVERSITY PRESS

First published 1990
Aberdeen University Press
Member of Maxwell Macmillan Pergamon Publishing Corporation
Text © The Contributors 1990
Illustrations © Jane Boyd 1990

British Library Cataloguing in Publication Data

A Day Estivall: essays on the music, poetry and
history of Scotland and England & poems
previously unpublished: in honour of Helena
Mennie Shire
1. Poems in English
Gardner-Medwin, Alisoun   II. Williams,
Janet Hadley
III. Shire, Helena M. (Helena Mennie)
780.9

ISBN 0 08 040914 8

Printed in Great Britain by BPCC-AUP Aberdeen Ltd. A member of BPCC Ltd

PREFACE

The summer flowering—the 'day estivall'—of literature and music in early Renaissance Scotland and England is here celebrated.

One of the first to recognise the potential of material surviving from this period was Helena Mennie Shire. Indeed, her pioneering work included the publication of previously unknown texts, which she had recovered from manuscript or inaccessible old print. The volumes of Helena Shire's Ninth of May series, together with her perceptive commentaries upon the literature and her lively exchanges of ideas with colleagues, engendered in this century a flowering of interest that produced a crop of scholarly achievements in these fields.

In grateful appreciation of Helena Shire's major contribution to this harvest, and with respect and affection, this posy of essays and poems is prepared in her honour. It is presented in June 1990, in which month Helena Mennie Shire enjoys her seventy-ninth summer.

◊

ACKNOWLEDGEMENTS

Many people gladly gave assistance to the book's production. Some gave financial help and others help of a practical nature, or in kind; all listed are most warmly thanked by the editors: M.I. Anderson-Smith, Kathleen Austin, Alec Bolton, Jane Boyd, Brian and Christine Bromwich, Sebastian Carter, Jean Clark, David Daiches, Margaret Dent, David and Alisoun Gardner-Medwin, Merle and Jim Hadley, Elizabeth and Michael Jeffreys, Iseabail Macleod, J. Derrick McClure, Ian A. Olsen, the Saltire Society, Tom and Becky Shankland, John Shire, R.H. van Dijk, The Warden and Fellows of Robinson College, Cambridge, Tony Weir, and Ian S. Williams.

Jane Boyd's designs for the divisional half-titles were especially prepared for *A Day Estivall*. Page one prefaces the Memoirs with a design on the theme of growth towards maturity, the process of using up and laying down. On page thirteen, before the Shire Bibliography, is a portrait of Helena Shire. Page nineteen introduces the Essays with a design on the opening up of ideas by Helena Shire. Preceding the Poems, on page one hundred and sixty-seven, is a spiral representing the development in arts subjects.

◊

CONTENTS

Frontispiece   ii
Preface   v
Acknowledgements   vi

MEMOIRS

1 From Helena's Childhood: Her Elder Brother Remembers
   DUNCAN M. MENNIE, University of Newcastle-upon-Tyne   3

2 Helena Mennie Shire: Portrait by a Friend
   DINA GARDEN, Aberdeen   5

3 Helena Mennie Shire, Doctor of Laws, *honoris causa*
   J.C. LAIDLAW, University of Aberdeen   9

4 Helena Mennie Shire: Scholarly Contributions   15

ESSAYS

5 *Ane Satyre of the Thrie Estaitis*: The First Edition and its
   Reception
   MARIE AXTON, University of Cambridge   21

6 Spenser's 'faire hermaphrodite': Rewriting the *Faerie Queene*
   RICHARD AXTON, University of Cambridge   35

7 'Th'old broad way in applying': John Donne and his 'Litanie'
   DOMINIC BAKER-SMITH, University of Amsterdam   48

8 The Commonplace Book of John Maxwell
   PRISCILLA BAWCUTT, University of Liverpool   59

9 The People Below: Dougal Graham's Chapbooks as a Mirror
   of the Lower Classes in Eighteenth Century Scotland
   ALEXANDER FENTON, National Museums of Scotland   69

10   A Ballad of the Battle of Otterburn: Scottish Folksong
     ALISOUN GARDNER-MEDWIN, Northumberland   81

11   'O Phoenix Escossois': James VI as Poet
     J. DERRICK McCLURE, University of Aberdeen   96

12   Dunbar in Paraphrase
     ALASDAIR A. MacDONALD, University of Groningen   112

13   *The Thre Prestis of Peblis* in the Sixteenth Century
     SALLY MAPSTONE, University of Oxford   124

14   'A Sober and Peceable Deportment': Court and Council Books
     of Dumfries 1561-1661
     MARION M. STEWART, Dumfries Archive Centre   143

15   David Lyndsay's 'Antique' and 'Plesand' Stories
     JANET H. WILLIAMS, Canberra   155

POEMS

16   My Grandmama
     HELEN BROMWICH, University of Bristol   169

17   A Gift from Helena
     JANET CAIRD, Inverness   170

18   The Antagonism
     THOM GUNN, San Francisco   171

     Index   173

◊

MEMOIRS

1

From Helena's Childhood:
Her Elder Brother Remembers

Duncan M. Mennie

Helena was predestined for literary studies. She was born on the twenty-first of June in the very week in which our father was completing the study of *A Midsummer Night's Dream* with his most senior pupils. Hence the Shakespearian form of her name being given in preference to the straightforward 'Helen', which Scottish custom almost insisted she should bear. But Marlowe had his say too. If Helena's childish features were ever disfigured by tears she could reckon on our father's gentle reproach: 'Is *this* the face that launched a thousand ships?' The weeping stopped.

One of Helena's major vexations when she was small was to be constantly mistaken for a little boy. She had very short, though curly, hair, and a tartan kilt with a knitted jersey which was the unisex winter wear of many Scottish children in World War I. On one classic occasion she was sent to deliver a 'bane tae mak' a suppie broth' to an elderly neighbour who could not face the elbowing mob in the local Co-op butcher-shop. To the grateful recipient's opening gambit which would normally have led up to the presentation of a 'pan-drop': 'What a nice little boy!', Helena apparently replied somewhat sharply: 'Not a little boy, a little girl. Here's your bone, and it's thrippence'. It was not the only time either that Helena put an abrupt end to a kindly-meant conversation. To another neighbour who asked her why she had not been seen playing at the front-door recently Helena replied laconically: 'I've had whooping-cough, chicken-pox and measles'. It was true, and the neighbour blanched and fled.

The 'mishanter' that I remember most clearly from Helena's early days happened in the hungry winter of 1917 when the milk in the tin pail was regularly frozen on the doorstep. A farming uncle had dumped on the landing a half-full sack of oatmeal for our mother to empty at her leisure into the meal-girnel. Helena jumped on the unfamiliar bulging sack in the vain hope that it would prove resilient and spilled over the precious gift a whole bottle of a very cheap scent, an eagerly solicited Christmas present from an over-indulgent aunt. The oatmeal thereafter smelled too pungently to make acceptable porridge and had to be used up slowly for baking oatcakes, which meant it and the strange aroma hung about the house for a long, long time.

Helena's predestination for literary studies suffered one serious set-back. In our father's absence on war-service our mother, also a teacher, took command and her main skills lay in drawing, painting and music. I have a vivid memory of Helena as a five-year-old carrying home her hand-blackboard with such a realistic chalk-drawing of a cow on it that her teacher had insisted she should 'show it to Mother'. Little did she know that it wasn't the first cow the apparent infant prodigy had drawn; Helena had been careful not to divulge at school that she had had her share of professional tuition.

That was where Helena was smart. She knew early in life when to keep her mouth shut and when to come out with this or that curious piece of literary, linguistic or musical information which she had snapped up at meal-times as our parents quoted Shakespeare, Burns, W.S. Gilbert, Scottish folk-song and the Scottish Metrical Psalms to and at one another, or I read aloud amidst a clutter of plates and spoons from the appropriate volume of the encyclopedia I had been sent to fetch from my father's study to clear up some disputed question of fact.

26 April 1989
Newcastle upon Tyne

Helena Mennie Shire: Portrait by a Friend

Dina Garden

'At fourteen, Helena would have eaten it.' The speaker, who was Helena's father and a headmaster in Aberdeen, said this with no boasting or relish—it was a plain statement of fact. The topic being discussed was Intelligence Testing— then new and debatable ground. I had brought on a visit to the Mennie home the paper inflicted on our group that day at Aberdeen Teachers' Training College.

I had first met Helena when I was in my third year and she in her first at Aberdeen University. We were introduced by Olive Fraser, a fellow-student, and became friends almost immediately.

When I think of Helena in her student days, I agree with her father that high intelligence was the first quality that attracted and stimulated her many friends. In memory, however, I see her not against the academic scene but in her home and with her family. Those of us who lived in lodgings in town—no residences or independent flats in the thirties—were thrilled in our early student days to be so liberated from home supervision and domestic tasks; later it was a privilege and refreshment to be a welcome visitor to such households as that of the Mennie family. It was warm, comforting, filled with laughter and wide-ranging chat. I think I was a little in love with the entire family. Possibly, the obtuse ego-centricity of youth prevented any doubts of my being always welcome; certainly that kindness, comfort and wisdom never failed is the best tribute I can pay to Helena's parents. That same warmth was part of her. What more? Humour always, a rich enjoyment of life, an appreciation of its comedies and possibilities—for we were not yet attuned to tragedy—enhanced the lives of her friends.

Helena came to Aberdeen University in 1929—having been head prefect and winner of the Dux Medal at the High School for Girls—and distinguished herself in her first year by winning the prize in the Short Story Competition, organised by the Literary Society and open to all students. Throughout her four years' Honours Course in English Language and Literature she was the top prizewinner and graduated in 1933 as first among firsts and Gold Medallist of her class. I was present at her graduation and was asked by an excited Helena to tell her parents that she had been awarded all the available prizes. It was the quaint custom of the time to keep all winners ignorant of their success until just before they entered the hall in procession when envelopes were placed in the appropriate hands. I have never found out why the ceremony, why the secrecy.

The next step was Newnham College, Cambridge: her lively letters describing her life there as a 'richer, rarer version of our time at King's' and giving witty vignettes of a growing circle of friends gave no hint of the homesickness suffered on occasion but admitted only very much later. She went on to take her degree with distinction in 1935 and to obtain for the years 1935-37 a Research Studentship at Newnham. In 1936 she married Edward Shire, a Fellow of King's College, later its Vice-Provost and University Reader in Physics.

It was the first marriage in the circle of my University friends, a thrill in itself and memory gives the clearest picture of Helena, in a classically-cut cream silk dress, looking endearingly, cheerfully happy. A few months later, four of us, all Aberdeen graduates, visited Cambridge in the course of a motoring trip. Edward and Helena invited us to dinner and we spent a wonderful evening, my admiration for Helena's cooking being surpassed only by that for Edward's charmingly warm welcome and total poise in face of this invasion from the north.

Marriage and, in due course, three children and the addition, after the death of his wife in 1941, of her father-in-law, made a household sufficient to absorb any woman's energies, but Helena continued to work in both teaching and research. She became a member of the English Faculty in 1940. When war brought students from the University of London to Cambridge, she taught them Mediaeval Literature and English to a Polish group evacuated from the London School of Economics—the latter enterprise producing many lasting friendships. Interestingly, her father, Mr John Mennie, was teaching a similar group of Poles in Aberdeen. She has continued to supervise, directing studies for King's and Fitzwilliam Colleges and, in 1974, was elected a Foundation Fellow of Robinson College.

To her teaching career she added literary reasearch, perhaps the most demanding of all, and over the years produced impressive results. The periods which engaged her interest were the Middle Ages and the Renaissance, involving the language, literature, music and dance of Scotland, France and England. The music and poetry of the Scottish Court became a particular theme. The adjective 'unhappy' so long has been the compulsive one to set beside the House of Stewart, justified indeed by the tragedies, wars—civil and religious—and personal betrayals of the Royal House and Scotland itself. There was, however, the part played by the Stewart sovereigns in encouraging with success, works in literature and music, to provide a bright counterpart to the darker mood.

In 1957, Helena, in collaboration with Kenneth Elliott, published the *Music of Scotland 1500-1700*, important and pioneering work in this field. In 1960 and 1961 came the editions of the poems and songs of Alexander Montgomerie and Sir Robert Ayton. Awarded (1961-63) a senior Research Fellowship by the Carnegie Trust, both tribute to work done and aid to further research, she published in 1969 *Song, Dance and Poetry of the Court of Scotland under King James VI* which has become a classic in the field. The range of skills and knowledge, especially in this major work, proclaims itself in its production, but special tribute is due to the energy, enthusiasm and self-discipline that fuel the engine, and the taste and style that polish the final product. It must be remembered also, that this busy life was carried on against frequent spells of debilitating illness and, on occasion, major surgery.

Outside her special field two books remain to be mentioned: the excellent *Preface to Spenser* in 1978 and *The Pure Account*, a selection of poems by Olive Fraser, our friend of Aberdeen University days. Now, in 1989, has been published an edition of Olive's work, as complete as could be made, with an introduction which tells the moving story of a tragic life. Helena and I were in touch throughout the years devoted to piecing together the fragments known and bridging the many gaps; I was impressed again and again by the patient thoroughness, the sheer amount of detective work, involving many journeys and contacts and correspondence, the perceptiveness that led from inspired guesses to solid fact to give an understanding of Olive's life, personality and difficulties. To this are added a sensitive appreciation and illuminating analysis of the poetry that enhance the reader's pleasure.

One special aspect of Helena's skills I must say something of—her powers as a Lecturer. Helena's mother died in 1941, but she continued to pay regular visits to Aberdeen until her father's death in 1957. So we knew how the family progressed, heard of her researches and enjoyed the books, but, naturally, were not acquainted with her work as lecturer or tutor. In 1978, however, my husband's interest in Scottish literature took us to Strasbourg, to the second of a series of conferences on 'Scottish Mediaeval and Renaissance Literature'. Helena was on the list of speakers and for the first time I listened to her giving a public lecture and was delighted. She combined an informal approach with the ease that comes from full knowledge. There was clarity in exposition and diction and a pleasing absence of unnecessary jargon. Above all, her enthusiasm for her subject carried her audience with her. We were pleased, informed, entertained. One proof of her success was the offer from a representative of an Australian University of a month's lecture tour in Australia, which she accepted and much enjoyed.

Her husband's shockingly sudden and unexpected death later that same year was a blow from which she did not easily or quickly recover but she did go on, to continue her roles as teacher, scholar, writer; as mother and grandmother, and to keep in touch with friends.

Memory gives me many portraits of Helena, as lively student, happy bride, young mother gazing with anxious pride at her first born, and one composite picture illustrative of a busy life that remains vividly with my husband and myself—ourselves in Cambridge, walking round the garden, accompanied by the two elder children, engagingly articulate, grandpapa in one corner keeping an eye on the baby, and Helena, meanwhile, giving an hour's coaching to one of her students. The most recent in the gallery was a special pleasure, when in 1988 she was given the honorary degree of Doctor of Laws by Aberdeen University. It was a dignified and moving ceremony and provided a beautiful portrait of Helena in the scarlet and blue of her doctoral gown and decoratively capped with her snow-white hair.

3

Helena Mennie Shire,
Doctor of Laws, *honoris causa*

J.C. Laidlaw

Vice-Chancellor. I present to you, for the award of the degree of Doctor of Laws, *honoris causa*, Helena Mary Mennie Shire.

Vice-Chancellor, learned Doctors and Masters, my Lords, Ladies and Gentlemen, it is always an honour to be asked to promote a distinguished scholar for an honorary degree. It is a rare pleasure when that scholar is also a friend of many years' standing.

Helena Mennie Shire was born in Aberdeen, the daughter of John Mennie, graduate of this university and a headmaster, and of Jane Rae. Many years later Mrs Shire made clear how much she owed to those enlightened parents, dedicating to them one of her most important books. It was to them that she owed her love of Scottish song, having learned the words from her father and the music from her mother. It was surely from them also that she acquired that love of language and of learning which has characterised her subsequent career.

Mrs Shire entered the university in 1929 from Aberdeen High School, and thus studied here during the years of the Depression. 'We were happy,' she was to write later, 'though it was 1929 into 1930 and of the last batch of our Honours graduates not one had a job.' Her student life was organised and busy: she served for two years on the SRC, representing women students in Arts; she played a prominent part in the Literary Society, reading papers on such diverse authors as Andrew Marvell, Marcel Proust and J.B. Priestley, and became President of the society in her final year. All these things are recorded in *Alma Mater* from which I quote the following pen-portrait published in February 1933. (The piece is in the best traditions of student journalism, being telegraphic, prejudiced, perceptive and allusive—not to say elusive):

> Although a product of the High School, Helena has nearly lived that down. A clever girlie this, for she won the short story competition for the second time and her Presidential Address was a marvel! Recently retired from public life for finals reasons, but is still sometimes seen, like the glowworm o' nights. Was a ringleader in the rebellion against the suppression of Free Speech in King's Library.

After graduating *summa cum laude* in 1933, Helena Mennie went to Cambridge where she read English at Newnham, again with distinction, and was elected to a Research Studentship in 1935. That she would remain in Cambridge became assured the following year when she married Edward Shire, a Fellow of King's College, and later its Vice-Provost and University Reader in Physics. Although Cambridge is where Mrs Shire has lived for over fifty years, it is not her only home. It is noteworthy how many of her books are signed 'Cambridge and Aberdeen'.

Marriage and the birth of her three children were not for Mrs Shire a signal to give up teaching and research. While today's generation may think it normal for a woman to combine marriage with a career, it was neither so obvious nor so easy a decision in the 1930s and 40s. She supervised in English in Cambridge, and became a member of the English Faculty in 1940. During the war she taught mediaeval literature to students of the University of London when their colleges were evacuated to Cambridge. She has continued to supervise, directing studies for King's and Fitzwilliam Colleges, and she was elected a Foundation Fellow of Robinson College at its inception in 1974. Mrs Shire is an excellent teacher, as generations of Cambridge students will testify, stimulating and stretching the bright, and coping firmly with the laggards, even when, as happened on one memorable occasion, the long promised essay turned out to be a brace of pheasant. She has also been unstinting in the time she has given to students and researchers who were not her particular responsibility, as I can testify from the many helpful conversations which I have had with her over the years, ever since I arrived in Cambridge myself as a raw undergraduate from North Britain.

Mrs Shire's research has centred on the Middle Ages and the Renaissance, taking in the language, music and dance of England, France and Scotland. She has long been fascinated by the distinctive and important musical and lyrical tradition developed by the Scottish court during the sixteenth century. That period has tended to be associated above all with political and religious turmoil, with Flodden, Mary Queen of Scots and John Knox. What has been less well understood is that it was also a time when the Scottish court was characterised by short but brilliant periods of literary and musical creativity. To understand that century requires a special range of skills and sensibilities. Let me quote from Mrs Shire herself:

> Scotland's remoteness made it retentive of old style. Its windows open on the ancient Celtic culture of the far west, its turbulent history, its uneasy relations with its island neighbour, England, together with its strong ties of affinity with France—all these laid down a pattern of politico-cultural relations in which the making and development of its courtly part-song may be traced in bright threads.

That quotation is taken from *Song, Dance and Poetry of the Court of Scotland under King James VI*, which Mrs Shire published in 1969. The detailed research which underlies that volume had been greatly helped by the Senior Research Fellowship which the Carnegie Trust awarded to her between 1961 and 1963. *Song, Dance and Poetry* drew on and developed another equally important and pioneering work, *The Music of Scotland 1500-1700*, which Mrs Shire published with Kenneth Elliott in 1957. And we must not forget the editions of the poems and songs of Alexander Montgomerie and Sir Robert Ayton which appeared in 1960 and 1961. (Montgomerie and Ayton both owed much to the patronage of James VI.)

Mrs Shire's research depends on a special range of skills and sensibilities, as I said just now. Understanding of mediaeval and Renaissance Scots *and* English language and literature, two distinct but complementary traditions, knowledge too of Renaissance France, for the works of Marot and the Pléiade were widely read in Scotland. Equally important, a deep love and appreciation of the secular and sacred music of the period. Only someone with those skills could have illuminated so clearly the tradition of song at the Scottish court, could have shown how essential it is to consider words and music together as an artistic whole, and not separately, as has so often been the case.

The field in which Mrs Shire has worked is an important one but one which had been neglected for too long, partly because in this age of specialists there are few who combine Mrs Shire's skills in literature and music. Her research has not always been given the recognition it deserves, and perhaps particularly in Cambridge. But, whether in history or in literature, Cambridge tends to think of Tudors and Stuarts in that order, forgetting that the Stuarts not only preceded the Tudors but survived them. Vice-Chancellor, inter-disciplinary research is one of today's watch words. In that field Mrs Shire has been a pioneer.

Let me close, by referring briefly to two other books. In 1981 Mrs Shire published the *Pure Account*, an anthology of poems by Olive Fraser, a friend and class-mate at King's. Haunting poems 'of severity and command, but also of tenderness and illumination' which she edited as a labour of love and friendship and which she introduced with great sensitivity and perception.

I have left until last *A Preface to Spenser*, published in 1978. I could elaborate on its qualities, indicating how well conceived it is, how it serves the needs of students at all levels, how it is properly allusive, avoiding the temptation to tell all. But I will not. I close with Spenser because it contains a characterisation of the poet which, *mutatis mutandis*, is equally applicable to Mrs Shire. Let me misquote:

among the attitudes and qualities we find in her writing are: enthusiasm for the widely educated and finely trained individual, respect for discipline and self-discipline, faith in the English and Scots tongues in all their varieties, an eager ambition to produce illustrious works, and a zealous patriotism.

Vice-Chancellor, I ask you to confer the Degree of Doctor of Laws *honoris causa* on Helena Mennie Shire.

7 July 1988
University of Aberdeen

This address was first published in *Aberdeen University Review* LIII, 1, No. 181 (Spring 1989), 69-71 and is reprinted here by kind permission of Professor J.C. Laidlaw and the Aberdeen University Alumnus Association.

4

Helena Mennie Shire:
Scholarly Contributions

BOOKS

Song, Dance and Poetry of the Court of Scotland under King James VI.
Cambridge: Cambridge University Press, 1969.
A Preface to Spenser. London: Longman, 1978.

EDITIONS

(With Kenneth Elliott.) *Music of Scotland 1500-1700. Musica Britannica XV.*
London: Stainer and Bell, 1957.
Alexander Montgomerie: A Selection from his Songs and Poems. Edinburgh:
Saltire Society, 1960. Reprinted 1985.
Poems from Panmure House. Cambridge: The Ninth of May, 1960.
Poems and Songs of Sir Robert Ayton. Cambridge: The Ninth of May, 1961.
*The Thrissil, the Rois and the Flour-de-lys: a sample book of state poems and
love-songs showing affinities between Scotland, England and France in the
sixteenth and seventeenth centuries.* Cambridge: The Ninth of May. 1962.
(With Kenneth Elliott.) *Music of Scotland 1500-1700. Musica Britannica XV.*
2nd edition, revised, 1964. 3rd edition, 1975.
(With Marion Stewart.) *King Orphius, Sir Colling, The Brother's Lament,
Litel Musgray.* Cambridge: The Ninth of May, 1973.
The Sheath and the Knife or Leesome Brand. 1974. A broadside sheet.
The Pure Account: Poems by Olive Fraser (1909-1977). Aberdeen: Aberdeen
University Press, 1980.
The Wrong Music: The Poems of Olive Fraser 1909-1977. Edinburgh:
Canongate, 1989.

ARTICLES

'Scottish Song-Book, 1611.' *Saltire Review*, I, No. 2 (1964), 46-52.
(With Alexander Fenton.) 'The Sweepings of Parnassus: Four Poems
transcribed from the Record Books of the Burgh Sasines of Aberdeen.' *Aberdeen
University Review*, XXXVI, No. 112 (Spring 1955), 43-54.

(With Kenneth Elliott.) 'Pleugh Song and Plough Play.' *Saltire Review*, II, No. 6 (1955), 39-44.

(With Kenneth Elliott.) 'La Fricassée en Ecosse et ses Rapports avec les Fêtes de la Renaissance.' *Les Fêtes de la Renaissance*. Ed. Jean Jacquot. Paris: Centre Nationale de la Recherche Scientifique, 1956. Pp.335-45.

'Musical Servitors to Queen Mary Stuart.' *Music and Letters*, XI, No. 1 (1959), 15-18.

'What Song did Dame Sensuality Sing?' *The Scotsman*, 12 September 1959, p.10.

'Robert Edwards' Commonplace Book and Scots Literary Tradition.' *Scottish Studies*, V (1961), 43-9.

'Alexander Montgomerie: The oppositione of the courte to conscience. "Court and Conscience walis not weill".' *Studies in Scottish Literature*, III, No. 3 (1966), 144-50.

'A Scots Poet Rediscovered?: R. Allane.' *Scottish Literary Journal*, I, No. 2 (1974), 5-14.

'The Lyric and the Renaissance.' *The Old World: Discovery and Rebirth. Literature and Western Civilization*. Ed. D. Daiches and A Thorlby. London: Aldus, 1974. Pp.147-75.

'Olive Fraser's Poetry in Scots: Known and Unknown.' *Lines*, No. 82 (1982), pp.5-12.

'Amour, mariage et transgressions: admonition au roi dans la poésie d'Ecosse à la fin du Moyen Age.' *Amour, Mariage et Transgressions au Moyen Age. Actes du colloque des 24-27 mars 1983*. Ed. Danielle Buschinger and André Crépin. Göppingen, Kummerle Verlag, 1984. Pp.465-70.

REVIEWS

Ballatis of Luve: The Scottish Courtly Love Lyric 1400-1570, ed. John MacQueen (Edinburgh, Edinburgh University Press, 1970). *Medium Aevum*, XLI, No. 2 (1972), 180-4.

The Kingis Quair of James Stewart, ed. M. P. McDiarmid (London: Heinemann, 1973). *Scottish Literary News*, III, No. 4 (1974), 45-7.

TRANSLATION

Jeromoki, *The Castle Looks Down*. Translated into Scots, and performed as a play reading, Saltire Society, Cambridge Branch, 1964.

SELECTED LECTURES AND PAPERS

'Words for Music perhaps Poetry in Seventeenth Century Scotland', Saltire Society lecture, Cambridge Branch, 1954.

'Fairs and Festivals of early Scotland', Saltire Society lecture, Cambridge Branch, 1961.

'Douglas's *Eneados*: Form and Meaning', First International Conference on Scottish Language and Literature (Medieval and Renaissance), University of Edinburgh, 10-16 September 1975.

'Style King James V', Second International Conference on Scottish Language and Literature (Medieval and Renaissance), University of Strasbourg, 5-11 July 1978.

'Music, Dance and Poetry at the Court of King James Fifth of Scotland', Waning of the Middle Ages Conference, The Australian National University, 7-11 August 1978.

'The Case of Colonel Cleland', Third International Conference on Scottish Language and Literature (Medieval and Renaissance), University of Stirling, 2-7 July 1981.

'Some Foreign Influences on Lyric and Song in King James VI Court Reconsidered', Fourth International Conference on Scottish Language and Literature (Medieval and Renaissance), Johannes Gutenberg Universität Mainz in Germersheim, 26-31 July 1984.

'Scots Language in Three Modern Poets of the North-East', First International Conference on the Languages of Scotland, University of Aberdeen, 26-29 July 1985.

'Images of Monarchy: Three Royal Stewarts', Fifth International Conference on Scottish Language and Literature (Medieval and Renaissance), University of Aberdeen, 3-8 August 1987.

RECORDING

Alexander Montgomerie (c. 1545-1611): Poems and Songs. Selected, introduced, and read (with Jack Aitken). Scotsoun Makars Series, SSC 060 1981.

ESSAYS

5

Ane Satyre of the Thrie Estaitis:
The First Edition and its Reception

Marie Axton

Did the fame of Sir David Lyndsay's play in the sixteenth century rest chiefly on handed-down memories of its performance? It was acted in the open air at Cupar in Fife and in Edinburgh before huge audiences at least twice before Lyndsay died in 1555, but what happened after that? When the first edition of his *Warkis* was printed in 1568, *Ane Satyre of the Thrie Estaitis* was not included. Yet in his epistle to the reader Henry Charteris, publisher of the collection, recalls how the Catholic clergy were stung by the play:

> This play did enter with sic grief in thair hartis, that they studyit be all menis to be auengit thairof....thay ʒeid about to haue his haill warkis condempnit, for hereticall, and cessit not, in Kirk and market, publictlie and priuelie, to rage and rayll aganis him, as ane Heretike.

The only surviving sixteenth-century text of the play was made for private use, also in 1568. The prosperous merchant copyist, George Bannatyne, omitted some passages because the clerical abuses they excoriated had been thoroughly reformed in Knox's Scotland. From 1602 there survives a quarto text and there is every reason to believe this is the first to have been printed. Douglas Hamer, Lyndsay's very thorough modern editor, suggested that printers in Scotland after the Reformation dared not print plays for fear of incurring the wrath of the Kirk. So it seems that Lyndsay, alive or dead, had little encouragement from the old or the new Scottish church; whereas Catholic prelates had opposed the matter of his play, the reformed church (which Bannatyne and Charteris considered Lyndsay to have fostered) was hostile to dramatic form itself. Lyndsay's collected works were frequently reprinted by Henry Charteris until his own death in 1599, and yet the play, praised in the preface, is always conspicuously absent. What then prompted Charteris's son, Robert, when he took over the family printing business at the turn of the century, to print the play in slim quarto?

Hamer suggests that the small flurry of play printing in Edinburgh at the beginning of the seventeenth century was a part of James VI's successful campaign to free the arts from the frosty opposition of the Kirk:

...from about 1590 onwards James VI began his magnificent stand against the elders to restore to the people, if it were not too late, some measure of liberty in games and festivals, while in the 1590's occurred his own quarrels with the elders regarding English players he himself had invited to Edinburgh. He did not give way, and some three or four years later we find the Edinburgh printers issuing four or five printed editons of plays ....[1]

Helena Shire has recreated for us that hopeful re-awakening of royal interest in poetry and drama in Scotland of the 1580s. Her history of James VI's 'Castalian band' of courtier-poets provides a stimulating context for further exploration. She suggests that the creativity of this coterie sprang from their lively appreciation of the great tradition of Scottish classics. Lyndsay's *Satyre* was among these 'classics':

> The Scottish court of the early 1580s was retentive of old style in the patterns of poetry it enjoyed....The pedigree of *Scottis Poesie* included...David Lindsay's 'The Dreme' and his 'Satyre of the Thrie Estaitis'.[2]

But did these practising poets know a text of Lyndsay's play or did their inspiration come from performance tradition or from reports of performance? Where did the printer, Robert Charteris, obtain his copytext (which is 1253 lines longer than the one Bannatyne transcribed for himself in 1568)? One possibility is that King James supplied the printer with a copy, and there is evidence of the king's interest in some of the publishing ventures of the last decade of his residence in Scotland. Until Peter Blayney's history of printing in the 1590s fills in the picture perhaps a few individual observations on the subject may be useful. Since there was apparently no tradition of play printing in Scotland, the choice of model for the design and presentation of this old and famous play is a matter of interest. The book itself, its type, paper, ornaments, evidence of the printer's intended market and of the book's reception all deserve some comment.

Lyndsay had been a close friend and adviser to James V, a poet, an envoy and a herald. This final distinction is perpetuated on Charteris's title-page. All the Charteris editions from 1568 onwards recall his official sobriquet: 'Schir David Lyndesay of the Mount, *Alias* Lyoun King of Armes'. As foremost herald of Scotland, named for the realm's symbol: the red lion of Scotland, he was the arbiter of the titles of Scottish monarchs and their nobility.

The physical aspects of the printed play may be thought of as the clothing in which Lyndsay was dressed for the early seventeenth-century reader. He appears in roman type, not in the black-letter textura of his earlier poetic *Warkis*. He is sent forth in two distinct kinds of paper. He makes two separate entrances: 1602 for the Edinburgh home market, then he was issued two years later in London, where he was bought and annotated. Considered together, these factors can tell us quite a lot about the circulation and reception of Lyndsay's play in England.

Seven copies of Robert Charteris's first printed edition are known. All have the colophon: 'Printed at Edinburgh/ be Robert Charteris /1602'. Of these, five bear on their title-page the printer's device, a woodcut of Justice and Religion (McKerrow: device 307), below them the date 1602. A further copy has lost its title-page. One copy of the 1602 edition was reissued with an entirely new title-page in English dated 1604; here this unchanged Scottish text of the single play is introduced as: 'The/ VVorkes of the/ Famous and worthy Knight, Sir Da-/ vid Lindsaie of the Mont, / Alias Lyoun King of Armes'. This copy is now in the British Library. On its 1604 title-page Robert Charteris is styled for the first time as 'Printer to the Kinges most excellent Maiestie'.[3] Instead of his printer's device, there is a recent woodcut of the royal arms to which James was entitled as King of England: a quartered scutcheon displaying his inherited rights, circled with the Order of the Garter *Honi soit qui mal y pense* and surmounted by the closed imperial crown of Britain. Directly below the king's arms we read that copies of this volume are to be sold in London by the English stationer, Nathaniel Butter, 'at his shoppe neare S. Austens Church in the old Change'. Thus, so far as is known, there was no actual 1604 edition of Lyndsay's *Workes*.[4] This curious title-page repays careful examination. The wording of its title and description of the poet repeat almost literally the title-pages of earlier Charteris editions of the *Warkis*; but the royal arms are new. This visual juxtaposition of the royal arms of James I with Lyndsay's official sobriquet, Lyoun King of Armes, implies public approval of the herald of the Scottish Reformation by England's new Protestant king. Coming from the newly styled king's printer the title-page holds out reassurance to an English readership that there will be no return to the Catholicism of James's mother, Mary Queen of Scots.

At least, this is how an Englishman interpreted the matter in the early seventeenth century. The British Library's *Satyre* has been carefully annotated by a man with legal training; his motives were to learn Scots, to compare Lyndsay's programme of church reform with the Anglican settlement of his day, and to find out about theatres in Scotland. These annotations are full enough to merit separate treatment, which is forthcoming. Before looking in detail at a selection of the notes, however, there is more to be learned from the physical appearance of the book itself.

Charteris did not send his most perfect sample to London. The copy owned by our English reader contains an average share of printer's errors. Comparison of his London re-issue with the six other known exempla of the 1602 edition shows that all extant copies originate from a single type-setting, but that the printer made corrections to his formes of type in the course of printing.[5] He kept sheets printed early from his uncorrected type and used some of them in putting together all the extant copies. Only the British Library's title-page in English was freshly set for 1604.[6] Surprising to a reader accustomed to English plays of the same era is the absence of a list of players and of preliminary information about where the play has been performed. Moreover, the new London title-page is not peculiar in being a single leaf sewn in; in all of the complete copies the play's title-page is a single leaf.[7] We might expect from the rest of the book's regular quarto format that Charteris had originally planned an A sheet with the usual preliminary matter, but of this there is no trace. The first speech of the play is printed on leaf B1 of the first complete gathering of four leaves.

It appears, then, that Charteris deliberately avoided any of the typographical hallmarks of a play. In contrast to Bannatyne's manuscript heading 'Schir David Lyndsayis Play', the printed edition doesn't call a spade a spade. The preference may indicate fashion or prestige: 'Satyre' not 'Play'. There is no word, either, of father Charteris's glee at the discomfiture the play caused among the Catholic clergy. But one cannot speculate further about what Charteris did not or could not print simply on the evidence of format.

The Charteris edition of *Ane Satyre* survives on two kinds of paper. It may be pure coincidence that a leaf of good white paper was used for the single title-page of the 1604 re-issue, and nineteen and one quarter sheets for the entire volume of the most completely corrected copy of the edition (Bodleian Library: Gough 221).[8] Textually Gough 221 is the most perfect copy, so it is curious that it does not carry on its title-page the words which guaranteed with royal authority the printer's right to print his text. *Cum privilegio regis* is the phrase common to all the other complete volumes of the 1602 issue, all of which were printed on what Hamer called 'coarse' paper. This 'coarse' paper rewards close examination and has an interesting, if obscure, history.

Until the end of the eighteenth century (and the application of chlorine bleach) the colour of paper was the colour of the rags from which it was made. Fine white linen made fine white paper. The dull grey brown paper of the *Satyre* when held up to the light reveals traces of vegetable matter and husks; chain-lines are not easily discerned in its thick, darkened texture. Patience is rewarded, however; in quire T of five of the copies there appears part of a distinctive watermark in the spine margin: 'I R 6' (Jacobus Rex VI).[9] At this point in the play Falset is about to be hanged and an unusually vivid stage direction explains how: 'Heir sal he be heisit vp, and not his figure, and an Craw or ane Ke salbe castin vp, as it war his saull' (T1[v]).[10] Flatterie, stripped of his disguise as a friar, escapes to a hermitage. Then Foly enters and offers hats to everyone he meets. Spying the King, he exclaims: 'The King, quhat kynde of thing is that?/ Is ʒon he with the goldin Hat?' (T3).

The watermarks in quire T are a reminder of another aspect of the king's encouragement of the book trade: his patronage of the earliest Scottish paper-making venture. The 'I R 6' watermark resembles one found on a Scottish Privy Council paper dated 1589 (reproduced by Robert Waterston in his pioneering study of early Scottish paper-making).[11] Systematic measurements are needed to establish how many different moulds bore this mark, and a rough chronology of use. However, the variant watermark in quire T of the Lincoln Cathedral copy is more easily datable; carrying the initials of James and Anne of Denmark, it has a *terminus ad quem* since they married on 20 August 1589. The initials, 'IR AR' are surmounted by a crown, thistle and cross.[12] Waterston has shown that Mungo and Gideon Russell, of Edinburgh, converted their corn mill at Dalry on the Water of Leith and, with the assistance of German paper-makers, were supplying paper to Edinburgh printers in the 1590s; he suggests that King James encouraged the manufacturing venture. It is hard to suppress the suspicion that some of the grain chaff has achieved immortality in the pages of Lyndsay's *Satyre*. Some mills used their water-power for both grinding grain and pounding rags for paper pulp.

Scots paper was certainly bought and used by Edinburgh printers in the final decade of James's residence there. When Henry Charteris died in 1599 an inventory of his goods shows: 68 reams of Scots paper at 28 shillings the ream, a bargain compared to his stock of French paper at 40 shillings a ream.[13] Henry Charteris had used some of his health-food Scottish paper to print the 1592 edition of Lyndsay's *Warkis*.[14] But he seems to have passed on rather a lot to his son. A systematic examination of the paper used in the late Charteris editions of Lyndsay might illuminate Robert Charteris's ambitions for a more inclusive edition of Lyndsay's complete works. We can already calculate roughly the cost of paper for each volume of *Ane Satyre*. Assuming Gaskell's estimates for a ream of paper at 480 sheets English and 500 sheets French,[15] the price difference is still noticeable: Scots paper (nineteen and one quarter sheets) 1 shilling 1 penny halfpenny; French paper: 1 shilling 6 pence halfpenny. If the Scots ream had 500 sheets the cost per book would have been about a shilling. *Ane Satyre* was valued at 4 shillings as we shall see. Waterston's evidence for James's interest in the paper venture is limited to a privilege granted in 1590.[16] Consideration of excise tariffs on imported paper may give a fuller picture of the financial protection afforded to the home product. There might have been other inducements. Perhaps it is only a coincidence that Charteris's health-food paper copies also bear the royal privilege on their title-pages.[17]

Scots paper was undeniably cheaper. Yet the quality of paper was only one factor in the price of a book. The prices of other books which Charteris sold in his 'buith on the North-side of the Gait at the West-side of the auld prouosts Clos head,' are listed in the detailed inventory taken when Henry Charteris died in 1599. Estimates are given for bound and unbound books and these figures, which provide the basis for comparison with his son's later play books, also enable us to gauge the rate of sale of the firm's 1597 black letter edition(s) of

Lyndsay's *Warkis*.[18]   Two years after printing there remained 788 'David Lindsays' at 8 shillings each; the entire lot reckoned at £315. Compare this with his stock of secular poetry and religious works. The bound Bibles were the most expensive:

> 1 folio Bible at £7
> 2 quarto Bibles at £5 each
> 23 copies of The Psalms in octavo at 29 shillings
> 22 New Testaments in Roman letter at 12 shillings each
> 545 Testaments of Cresseid at 4 pence apiece.[19]

Father Charteris's entire stock, including paper and printed books, as well as calfskins and sheepskins for binding, was worth a small fortune—£5,870.

Robert took over the business in 1599. His most notable innovation was printing plays; Lyndsay's *Satyre* (1602) was closely followed in 1603 by the anonymous comedy *Philotus*.[20]   Helena Shire has affirmed its author to be the Catholic courtier Alexander Montgomerie, whom James had dubbed 'the prince of poets in our land'.[21]   This comedy, too, bears the royal privilege on its title-page, and a woodcut of the royal lion of Scotland. The more complete first quire of preliminaries, including a cast list, may indicate Charteris's growing confidence in royal support for the printing of plays. From the colophon of *Philotus* it is clear that it was printed later than Lyndsay's play. This evidence helps us to steer through the inter-tidal zone between January 1 and March 24 1602/03—a period when a printer could avail himself of an old-style or new-style year date:

> The Printer of this present Treatise hes (according to the Kings majesties licence grantit to him) printit sindrie vther delectabil Discourses vndernamit, sic as are, Sir Dauid Lyndesayis play....

A likely date for *Philotus* is early in the year 1602/03, for the following reasons. Charteris's wife, Margaret Wallace, died on 1 February 1603. Her will was proved the last day of March 1603 and occasioned another inventory, providing further information about stocks and prices of books. At the time of Margaret's death the printing house held equal numbers of both plays: 500 'Dauid Lindesayis playis' at 4 shillings apiece and 500 'Philotus buikis' at 2 shillings. The amount of paper and labour is directly reflected in the relative valuation; whereas *Ane Satyre* has nineteen and one quarter sheets, *Philotus* uses only six. We have also some measure of Lyndsay's market; in the four years between August 1599 and March 1603 they had sold 188 of father Henry's collected 'Lindsayis' and had 600 left, now reduced from 8 to 7 shillings. Their Bibles and Psalms were not bound, showing that the great discrepancy in price between Henry's holy and his secular stock had, indeed, been due to binding. Robert had 300 psalms books 'with prose in the margin' at 6 shillings each (his father's bound octavo psalms cost 29 shillings).   There were 60 unbound Bibles at 40 shillings each (£2); his father's bound folio Bible had been £7, his quarto Bible £5.[22]

In the interval between the death of Mrs Charteris and the proving of her will on 31 March 1603, James VI became James I of England.   The woodcut arms of Scotland in *Philotus*, while wholly appropriate to the period January 1602/03 to March 24 1602/03, and which may have had continuing appeal for the Edinburgh market, were out of date by March 24 1603 when James became king of both realms; there was suddenly a new readership for Scottish books.[23]

Having no previous native tradition of printing plays, Scots printers seem to have looked for models to London, where playbooks had been staple fare for nearly a century.   Changing fashion in the choice of type is one factor. Lyndsay's *Warkis* had been printed in black-letter, but his play was issued in roman type.   In Scotland between 1600 and 1605 there was a cluster of books issued in roman; the works themselves are not Greek or Roman classics; rather their subject matter comes from court, implies proximity to the king.   In England a similar typographic shift happened a bit earlier.   Two printers from London, Thomas Vautroullier and Robert Waldegrave, who came to Edinburgh in the 1580s, had while still in London, influenced the change from black-letter to roman type.[24]   Waldegrave, an English printer of the Marprelate tracts, fled to Scotland for safety in 1589, had been welcomed by James VI and in 1590 made king's printer.   Waldegrave chose roman type for his Edinburgh imprint of the play of William Alexander, tutor to Prince Henry.   Alexander's *Tragedy of Darius* bears the date 1603 and Waldegrave is there styled 'printer to the King's Majesty'.

In English printing black letter (textura) had been the fount for plays and entertainments throughout the 1560s and 1570s.   However, beginning in 1578 with Thomas Churchyard's *A discourse on the queenes maiesties entertainment in Suffolk and Norfolk*, there is a new development.   Henry Bynneman printed narrative and descriptive passages in black letter but he gave the all-important speeches the lustre of roman.   He flaunts his connection with the court, styling himself 'servant to Sir Ch. Hatton'.   In the 1581 *The Fortress of Perfect Beauty*, Sidney's triumph before Queen Elizabeth and the French Ambassadors, black letter is used only for the descriptive portions; epistle, speeches, songs and marginal notes are in roman.   In the black-letter sections courtiers' names are in italic, in roman passages in contrasting small capitals.   This courtly entertainment had been printed in England by Robert Waldegrave before his Marprelate misfortunes.   John Lyly's *Sapho and Phao* and *Campaspe* (1584) are the first surviving English plays in roman type.   Their subjects are 'classical' but the printer may also be following recent fashion and signalling typographically the court connection.   By 1602 most English plays issue forth in roman type, so that the black letter of *Dr Faustus* in 1604 is by then a striking anomaly, perhaps even a deliberate sign of the tragedy's German ancestry.

The possibility of a calculated correlation between literary genre, subject matter, and format can be explored in Robert Charteris's output at the turn of the century. What survives from 1600-04 has mostly a political interest and emphasis. Of course, the use of roman type may indicate a more plentiful supply at hand, rather than a stylistic eye to readers' expectations—there aren't enough books to draw firm conclusions. But a tentative hypothesis would be that roman type announced works from the court.

1600   Roman:
Palinod of John Colvill penetently recant[ing]...that treasonous discourse lately made...against the vndoubted title of his dread Soveraigne...King James VI vnto the crown of England.
Gowreis Conspiracie...attempted against the kings maj's person...

Black letter:
Lyfe and actis of Wm Wallace...defender of the liberties of Scotland.

1603   Roman:
Latin works by Sir Thomas Craig & Adam King in praise of King James and Prince Henry.

Black letter:
Ane godlie dream...[of Elizabeth Melville, Lady Culross]
Philotus
Psalms...in meter

1604   Roman:
The Workes of Sir David Lindsay [ie *Satyre*]
De vnione Britanniae seu de regnorum Angliae et Scotie

1605   Roman:
The royal entertainment of the earl of Nottingham...ambassador to the king of Spain

In 1604 Nathaniel Butter, the London stationer at whose shop the London issue of Lyndsay's *Satyre* was sold, was just beginning his career; this is his first extant play. He came from a printing family and on 20 February 1603/04 was declared freeman of the Stationers Company. He made his name with newssheets, an output varied by occasional plays, and was immortalised by Jonson in *The staple of news*. Royal news was a family specialty; his widowed mother had published 'The True Report of the Baptism of the Prince of Scotland' on 24

October 1594. Her son continued to publish in the same spirit a selection of protestant volumes and royal chronicle plays of recent history:

1604-05:	Thomas Bell	*The downfall of poperie*
	Thomas Heywood	*If you know not me or the troubles of Queen Elizabeth*
	S. Rowley	*When you see me you know me...the historie of Henry VIII*
	Anon.	*The London prodigall*
1608:	William Shakespeare	*King Lear.*

Returning from the 'background' to the printing of Lyndsay's play, there are some puzzles about the actual printing. First, the state of the text: the absence of the preliminary 'Crying of the Play' and the thematically important episodes which form a prelude to the play's principal action (the Cotter and his shrewish wife, the braggart soldier, the Fool's wooing). These differences from the text of the Bannatyne manuscript have been reasonably explained by the survival of two distinct performance texts: Cupar 1552, Edinburgh 1554, and by Bannatyne's stated preference for jolly bawdry.[25]

Less easily explained is the curious absence of all stage directions in the first 808 lines of Charteris's edition. Thereafter these directions are printed in small roman type and are usually fuller than those in the Bannatyne manuscript. Yet a fifth of the play is over before these detailed directions begin. This same small roman type is used sparingly from the beginning of the play for centred speech-heads which indicate the first entrance speech of each character. Thereafter, change of speaker in dialogue is indicated by abbreviated speech-heads in standard size type illegibly flush with the left margin. It may be defective copy that caused this curious feature, but shortage of small type is a more plausible explanation, since full stage directions begin at a major division in the setting of the book. Sheets B, C, D have no indications of the stage business; the first direction occurs in sheet E when the young king emerges from offstage dalliance with his concubine: 'Now the King sall cum fra his chamber' (E2 808+). The printed text includes some stage directions not in the Bannatyne manuscript and these are sometimes very vivid in detailing how the play was performed: 'Heir sall the thrie estaits cum fra the pal3eon, gangand backwart led be thair vyces' (L2ᵛ 2315+). Sometimes a question of liturgical practice is at issue; Bannatyne had written: 'Heir sall thay sit doun and ask grace' (2727+). Charteris prints: 'Heir sal the Temporal stait sit doun on thair knies, & say' (N1 2706+). Sometimes the direction is more politically precise. Where Bannatyne writes: 'Heir sall thay imbrace the commoun weill' (2737+), Charteris prints: 'Heir sall the temporal staits, to wit, the Lords and merchands imbreasse Iohne the Common-weill' (N1 2716+). These directions give details of outdoor performance and staging; as Chastity flees from the enraged Edinburgh wives: 'Sho lifts vp hir clais aboue hir waist & enters in ye water' (G3ᵛ 1383+).

As has been mentioned, no cast list survives for Charteris's *Satyre*. This may have been one of the items planned for sheet A but never included.

In contrast, the slim text of *Philotus* ran only to 6 sheets in quarto and appears to have been more carefully designed. In layout it harks back to the English experiments of 1578 and the early 1580s. Predominantly set in black-letter, it has corresponding roman type for speech-heads and small roman for stage directions. But even so it is not advertised as a play. It is *Ane verie excellent and delectabill Treatise entitled PHILOTVS*. The Scottish printer was not printing for players, amateur or professional. The cast list is headed 'The names of the interloqvitors' and each character's first speech is indexed 'verse 1' or 'verse 169'; there are corresponding numerical markers in the text. Each page is bordered with printers' lace, making *Philotus* an ornament for study, a text to be read. Its stage directions summarise plot: 'The Macrell intends to allure the Madyn' (A4):

> Heir followis the Oratioun of the ʒonker Flavius to the Mayden, hir answer and consent, The convoying of her from her father: her father and the auld wower followis.... (C1ᵛ)

Finally, there is evidence of the reception of Lyndsay's *Satyre* in the notes made by the English reader. His linguistic interest was serious and reasonably methodical; he listed Scots and English vowel differences, working through his 'foreign' text at least twice. We can trace his progress in two distinct inks used to write idiomatic English glosses in the margins of the page for words and phrases which interested him:

> widdie wend **to the halter born** (T1ᵛ)
> chaipit this firie farie **escaped this hott brand** (T2)
> Hir arsse gaid evin lyke ane wind mill **was so full of winde as a windmill**
> (T3ᵛ)

Occasionally our annotator has something to offer the modern editor of Lyndsay. Hitherto 'bummillbaty' has been explained as a simpleton or booby; our annotator has glossed it as a melancholic. This makes better sense in the context where the unctuous courtier, Placebo, tries to tempt Rex Humanitas to take a mistress, and suggests that he ask my Ladie Prioress to tell him the truth: 'Gif it be sin to tak [ane] Kaity/ Or to leif like an bummillbaty' (C1 268). The annotator is fond of noting **'beware shrewish wives'**. Not content with the double bracket '[]' with which Charteris signals a bawdy passage, his pen records **'knaverie'**. Of Hameliness he writes approvingly **'a plain dealer/ no Daintie Dame'** (C1ᵛ); of Sensuality **'a good tractable wench'** (C4ʳ) further observing **'the mistress [for the] king the mayde for the servitors'**. There is a small clue for dating the darker ink annotations in the episode of the Pardoner's divorce of the

Sowtar and his wife. When the wife pleads as cause her husband's non-performance 'Becaus I gat na chamber-glew', dark ink records **'The sowtare wife like the L.C. Countesse'** (K4). If this is the notorious Countess of Essex, Frances Howard, who divorced her husband for impotence, this second series of annotations must have been made after Robert Carr was made Viscount Rochester in 1611 and might be called 'Lorde'.

Our Englishman read to understand Scotland and its ways: 'plackis' **'certain Scottish money'** (S1). He took delight in uplandish proverbs, relishing Falset's: 'Now let me bresse the in my armis:/ Quhen freinds meits harts warms' as **'a scottish proverb'** (D3); '[]Thou fein3eit Flatterie, the feind fart in thy face' is **'an odd scottish curse'** (M1). And he has a sure appreciation of vulgar idiom or euphemism: 'pillok' is glossed **'Wag Robin'** (T4ᵛ). More important, he has an exact knowledge of equivalent English and Scottish offices: 'Of this conclusioun Noter wee mak ane act': **'notayrice {c}larke of Parlament'** (O2ᵛ); 'Senature': **'counseylour of estate'** (R3ᵛ). He aligns himself with the pragmatic Sir Thomas Smith, ready to equate common weal with public weal: 'That is the caus that Common weill is cruikit': **'in regard of pr{iv}ate, publick wele is neglec{ted} naked and ungansom'** (R2). He is acute in matters of church practice and seems to be looking for reassurance that the Northern church be compatible with the Anglican settlement familiar to him. When the corrupt Pardoner laments that St Paul's words have reached the laity he translates: 'And als I wald his buiks:/ War never red in the kirk' as **'would also his booke had nev{er} byn published'** (K3). He highlights his approval of the proposal of 'one priest one benefice' by drawing a flower in the margin and penning: **'a good lawe at last'**. John the Commonweil's Acts of Parliament to reform abuses, proclaimed at the end of the play, are carefully annotated. Our Englishman writes of the fifth reform: **'A good Statute to/ those northern partes/ of Scotland. To ha{ }/ preachers & Juges/ sent amongst them'**; he adds a corresponding note about the English custom of justices of eyre. He has a strong interest in the details of administration noting that the Council for the North of Scotland **'shall have 16 Counsayl/ lours in addition to their Chancellours'** (R3ᵛ).

But perhaps the most valuable annotation comes in response to a stage direction. Our reader clearly was not accustomed to the traditions of large-scale outdoor playing where hill and stream formed part of the 'place'. When the Pauper challenges the Pardoner the following instructions are given to the actors: 'Heir sal thay fecht with silence and Pauper sal cast doun the buird, and cast the relicts in the water'. This calls forth the wondering comment: **'I think their Theater was the bare ground'** (L2).

The sense of cultural distance opened up here is both geographical and historical: Lyndsay's great play was, after all, written and performed a long way from London, in a tradition of pre-Reformation playing that had been virtually forgotten by London and which lingered on only in Cornwall and Cumbria. That there should be a reading public for the *Satyre* half a century after its last performance is first of all an index of the stature of the author himself, of his championing of the Reformation in Scotland (especially when viewed from after the event), and of his intimacy with James V of Scotland, grandfather of James I of England. The circumstances surrounding printing of the play in 1602 and the use of watermarked, Scottish-made paper suggest that James himself could have had a particular interest in publication. Elizabeth I's death and James's accession to the English throne on 24 March 1603 gave added point to the publication; the coincidental death of Waldegrave provided an opportunity for Charteris as printer to the king of two kingdoms, giving him the chance to issue the 1602 *Satyre* for sale in London to a much larger market. The Scots language, some half-century out of date, proved not to be much of a barrier.[26] At least, on the evidence of the notes in the British Library copy, there were well-educated Englishmen keen to understand the political and religious climate north of the border. By this time there was also in England some antiquarian interest in the old large-scale drama of the provinces (in particular at Chester); but BL's annotator was neither nostalgic nor patronising. He treats the text of Lyndsay's play as a record of recent and momentous change, as part of the Protestant credentials of the new King of England.

NOTES

1   Douglas Hamer, 'The Bibliography of Sir David Lindsay', *The Library*, 4th Ser. X, No. 1 (1929), 34-5.

2   Helena M. Shire, *Song, Dance and Poetry of the Court of Scotland under King James VI* (Cambridge, 1969), p.120.

3   Robert Waldegrave, the king's printer, went to London upon James's accession and died almost immediately thereafter; Charteris succeeded him.

4   *STC* 15664.7 is recorded as an edition of 1605 in the possession of the Marquis of Bute.

5   My re-examination of the variants listed in Hamer's edition (in vol. II of *The Works of Sir David Lindsay*, 4 vols, Scottish Text Society, 3rd Ser. 1, 2, 6, 8, Edinburgh and London, 1931-36) suggests that unless these are analysed by sheet and by inner and outer formes, only his broad distinctions stand. He helpfully distinguishes the two Bodleian copies both dated 1602, one containing a majority of uncorrected sheets, the other containing a majority of corrected sheets, (IV, 70-3). His evidence does not solve the problem of first and second issue for the volume which

has lost its title-page since *all* of the extant copies of Charteris's edition contain a mixture of sheets printed from corrected and uncorrected inner and outer formes. It follows that unless copies show identical states on all inner and outer formes they cannot be 'identical copies'. Sheets stacked after drying in whatever order they came from the racks, were gathered and bound up. This being the case the only certain confirmation that a volume belongs to the reissue in 1604 is the title-page. Hamer implies a typographical identity between the British Library 1604 and the untitled Lincoln copy which my examination does not substantiate. In Part I of the play corrected sheets C, E, F, H, are also shared by Bodleian (Gough 221), Huntington and Folger. Sheets I of both BL and Lincoln have been printed from an inner forme corrected for accidentals and pagination; BL has been printed from an outer forme corrected for accidentals; the outer forme used for Lincoln was not corrected. Sheet T confirms that in Charteris's shop correction for pagination and accidentals was carried out separately from correction of substantives: both copies have corrected pagination; the text of Lincoln's sheet T is corrected; the text of BL is not; together with the Folger copy BL preserves the uncorrected readings. For these reasons I do not think that the Lincoln copy should be esignated as part of the 1604 issue unless its title-page can be recovered. See Roderick Lyall, *Ane Satyre of the Thrie Estaitis* (Edinburgh, 1989), p.xliii for a different conclusion.

6   Charteris apparently kept his remaining stock of Lyndsay's play unbound; the new heraldic title-page was sewn in with the other sheets in place of the original 1602 title-page.

7   The rest of each quarto volume is made up of 19 sheets signed B-V, each folded and quired normally as four leaves: $A1$ B-V^4.

8   The watermark is a small post or column; the most complete one measures 19x18mm; it is on the foredge of *A1*, thus proving by its position that this title-page has been bound in as a single leaf, as W.W. Greg noted, *A Bibliography of the English Printed Drama to the Restoration*, 4 vols, Bibliographical Society (London, 1939-57), I, 192-3.

9   I have not yet examined the paper of the copy in the National Library of Scotland.

10   Quire T contains lines 4183-4429 in Hamer's edition, from which line numbers hereafter are cited.

11   'Further Notes on Early Paper Making Near Edinburgh', *Book of the Old Edinburgh Club*, XXVII (1949), 41. I am grateful to Professor Roderick Lyall for drawing my attention to this essay.

12   Robert Waterston, 'Early Paper Making near Edinburgh', *Book of the Old Edinburgh Club*, XXV (1945), Plate opposite p.40 prints a similar mark: IR AR crowned, but without the cross on top. Edward Heawood's No. 147 ('Sources of Early English Paper-supply: II. The Sixteenth Century', *The Library*, 4th Ser. X, No. 4 (1930), 427-54), also lacks the cross.

13   R. Dickson and J.P. Edmond, *Annals of Scottish Printing* (Edinburgh, 1890), p.354.

14   See BL C.39.d.40; this rough paper carries small clear watermarks of the king's initials: 'I R 6' measuring approximately 29x35mm on leaves B2, C2, R4.

15   Philip Gaskell, *A New Introduction to Bibliography* (Oxford, 1972), p.59. His figures are for the mid-seventeenth century.

16   Waterston, 'Early Paper Making', 53, 57.

17   *STC* does not seem to be correct; only Bodleian Gough 221 (printed on white paper) and lacking *cum privilegio regis* on its title-page can be certainly classed as 15681; the certain variants bearing *cum privilegio regis* are: Huntington Library copy 62230; National Library of Scotland; Bodleian 4° Z.3 Art. Seld; and Folger Library 15681; these should all be numbered *STC* 15681.5. Lincoln Cathedral copy Rr.6.13 has a modern printed facsimile title-page dated 1602 and therefore cannot be certainly designated either as variant or as first or second issue by this simple test. See note 5.

18   *STC* distinguishes two editions of 1597: 15664 headed 'Ane Prologue' [Durham and Yale] and the other 15664.3 'The Prologue' [National Library of Scotland and Folger].

19   Dickson and Edmond, ibid. pp.353-4.

20   *STC* 19888 collated A-F^4. There are three copies of this edition: in the British Library, Queens' College, Cambridge, and the National Library of Scotland.

21   *Song, Dance and Poetry*, pp.96, 115.

22   Dickson and Edmond, pp.491-2.

23   See F.S. Ferguson, 'Relations between London and Edinburgh Printers and Stationers (-1640)', *The Library*, 4th Ser. VIII, No. 2 (1927), 145.

24   See W.C. Ferguson, *Pica Roman Type in Elizabethan England* (Aldershot, 1989).

25   *The Bannatyne Manuscript*, Scolar facsimile, introd by Denton Fox and William Ringler (London, 1980), fols 177, 210.

26   See M.A. Bald, 'The Anglicisation of Scottish Printing', *Scottish Historical Review*, XXIII, No. 90 (1926), 107-15 and J. Derrick McClure, 'A Comparison of the Bannatyne MS and the Quarto Texts of Lyndsay's *Ane Satyre of the Thrie Estaitis*' in *Scottish Language and Literature, Medieval and Renaissance, Fourth International Conference 1984 Proceedings*, ed. Dietrich Strauss and Horst W. Drescher (Frankfurt am Main, 1986), pp.409-22 for expert discussion of Anglicisation and Scottish texts.

6

Spenser's 'faire hermaphrodite': Rewriting *The Faerie Queene*

Richard Axton

The image of lovers united as a 'faire hermaphrodite', which closed Book III of *The Faerie Queene* in the 1590 edition, presents a later reader with many puzzles. Not least is the status of such 'ghost text', since the five rapturous stanzas in which the mysterious creature is evoked were dropped from the poem in 1596. Although a strict respect for Spenser's 'final intention' might require the reader to suppress knowledge of that earlier and provisional cadence, the excision of the hermaphrodite stanzas from the expanded six-book Faerie Queene is obviously important evidence of what the poet had in mind as he responded to his own evolving creation. The implications of Spenser's second thoughts turn out to be far-reaching and they are traceable in almost every aspect of the work. I shall begin and end with the literal narrative and with what the reader is invited to imagine.

Britomart, the Knight of Chastity, has rescued Amoret from Cupid's Masque, a nightmare of ritual sadism and 'phantasies/ In wauering wemens wit', and leads her from Busyrane's palace, which has 'vanisht vtterly', through flames that have been quenched, to find Scudamour lying miserable on the cold earth. The perspective changes. Hearing Britomart's voice, he leaps up to clasp his Amoret:

> Lightly he clipt her twixt his armes twaine,
>   And streightly did embrace her body bright.
>   Her body, late the prison of sad paine,
>   Now the sweet lodge of loue and deare delight:
>   But she faire Lady ouercommen quight
>   Of huge affection, did in pleasure melt,
>   And in sweete rauishment pourd out her spright:
>   No word they spake, nor earthly thing they felt,
> But like two senceles stocks in long embracement dwelt.
>
> Had ye them seene, ye would haue surely thought,
>   That they had beene that faire *Hermaphrodite,*
>   Which that rich *Romane* of white marble wrought,
>   And in his costly Bath causd to bee site:
>   So seemd those two, as growne together quite,
>   That *Britomart* halfe enuying their blesse,

Was much empassiond in her gentle sprite,
And to her selfe oft wisht like happinesse,
In vaine she wisht, that fate n'ould let her yet possesse.

(1590, III.12.xlv-xlvi)[1]

Love's ecstasy is heightened by being seen through Britomart's inexperienced and half-envying eyes. Yet the image is cool and researched, deliberately monumental, paradoxical, grotesque, riddling. Spenser says the hermaphrodite he has in mind is 'faire' and speaks of 'that riche Romane' as if some particular archaeological find was common knowledge, yet what exactly is the reader to picture?

Three possibilities present themselves in Renaissance writing about the antique world. A bi-sexual nature deity was supposedly worshipped in the East and in Egypt, according to Plutarch, in the cult of Isis and Osiris. Statues of such 'effeminate' Dionysos-like figures were well known in Greek and Roman sculpture.[2] But such a figure is essentially single and sexually ambiguous; it is not a 'couple'. Most of the Elizabethan usages of the word refer disparagingly to such a monster of nature or, figuratively, to an effeminate man or a virile woman. 'Unnatural' creatures of this sort are certainly found in Spenser's sexual and political landscape, but seem quite inappropriate to the context here.

A second possibility is the grotesque hybrid mischievously—though with serious philosophical purpose—described by the character of Aristophanes in Plato's *Symposium* (189-91) and recalled by Ben Jonson's Lord Beaufort (*The New Inn* III.2.79-82). In the first of Plato's two myths of the origins of love, the hermaphrodite is said to have been the original and perfect third sex. Shaped in a circle with four hands and feet, a single head with two faces, two sets of genitals, it particularly enjoyed cartwheeling, until Zeus, out of envy for its self-sufficient happiness, split it down the middle. The two incomplete natures thereafter yearned to recombine, for, says Plato, all things desire total union with the object loved. This second hermaphrodite seems philosophically appropriate and literally possible, if visually incongruous in Spenser's scene.

But the hermaphrodite most readily familiar to Elizabethan readers was the son of Hermes and Aphrodite in Book IV of Ovid's *Metamorphoses*. Spenser's frequent indebtedness to Ovid makes it worth dwelling for a moment on the story. The youth Hermaphroditus was attracted to the clear fountain of the nymph Salmacis and, although he rejected her bold overtures (she was a defector from Diana's crew of huntresses), he could not resist her pool. Diving in after him, she clasped the struggling boy, praying that he was never to be parted from her. The gods granted both her request and his prayer that the pool should forever possess emasculating qualities. Ovid's concern with this disturbing tale is more aesthetic than moral; when Hermaphroditus enters the water he becomes an object of art. Spenser probably knew Arthur Golding's translation of 1567:[3]

> He clapping with his hollow hands against his naked sides,
> Into the water lithe and baine with armes displayed glydes.
> And rowing with his hands and legges swimmes in the water cleare:
> Through which his bodie faire and white doth glistringly appeare,
> As if a man an Ivorie Image or a Lillie white
> Should overlay or close with glasse that were most pure and bright.
>   The prize is won (cride *Salmacis* aloud), he is mine owne.
> And therewithall in all post hast she, having lightly throwne
> Her garments off, flew to the Poole and cast hir therinto
> And caught him fast between hir armes for ought that he could doe.
>   (434-43)

Metamorphosis of the unwilling lover is evoked in a series of images—the serpent coiled about the eagle, ivy round the tree bark, the branch grafted to the tree. Finally,

> They were not any lenger two: but (as it were) a toy
> Of double shape: Ye could not say it was a perfect boy,
> Nor perfect wench: it seemed both and none of both to beene.
>   (468-70)

Complete metamorphosis leaves us contemplating a human freak. Spenser's image holds back from the end product, emphasising instead the subjective nature of mutual experience. The visual suggestions of his description (the two bodies are 'grown together' like 'senseless stocks') suggest both metamorphosis and natural growth and relate directly to an emblem in the collection made by the Calvinist Barthélemy Aneau (*Picta Poesis*, Lyons 1552). In Aneau's woodcut the male and female bodies twine together forming a tree trunk (the legend runs 'Corpore sit duplicis forma Hermaphroditus in vno/ Vnaque sit facies foemina, & vna viri'); in the branches above birds are nesting. The emblem contributes to the Protestant view of married love as true chastity[4] and is headed 'Matrimonii Typus'.

The hermaphrodite has become a 'pagan mystery', expressing sacred Christian truths for Renaissance interpreters; it is a riddle inviting contemplation of a paradox ('two-in-one') or, in Lévi-Strauss's terms, mediating opposites (male/female, law/passion). Renaissance interpretation of the figure is not without appreciation of its grotesqueness. In Aneau's woodcut, to the left of the entwined couple the horned law-giver Moses pointing proudly to God's handiwork is balanced on the other side of the tree by a horned satyr gesturing derisively. However, Spenser's description seems oblivious of anything indecent in this particular 'mystery' (though he was later to bring an irreverent and disbelieving satyr into the orbit of Diana's sacred majesty); what wit there is in the paradox is gently subdued by feelings of passionate wonder and of Britomart's longing as she views the embrace.

Although Spenser cut out the narrative knot and with it the hermaphrodite image (leaving the lovers in a kind of cold storage), he nevertheless was fascinated by the hermaphrodite idea. Themes and possibilities which were concealed or 'in-folded' in the mysterious emblem of the 'faire hermaphrodite' are 'un-folded' later in the poem. This unfolding happens both in the story and in the monumental images. In tracing expansions of the hermaphrodite emblem I am conscious of a stimulating challenge thrown out by Helena Shire in her Cambridge lectures of 1961, and of following clues which C.S. Lewis offered in the lectures, shortly before his death, that we both attended.[5]

When our lover Scudamour tells how he won Amoret in the Temple of Venus, he describes an image or 'idol' of 'the Goddesse selfe' (*FQ* IV.10.xxxix-xl). The reader cannot be sure whether it is Venus herself or her life-like image that stands upon the altar of 'brickle glasse', superior in beauty to the workmanship of Pygmalion's sculptor. The allusion to the antique sculpture, as in the case of the 'faire hermaphrodite', cools warm flesh to wondering, inviting the reader to contemplate a mystery. Venus is veiled, because her own nature is mysterious; this mystery is elided with the mystery of her concealed sex:

> But covered with a slender veile afore;
> And both her feete and legs together twyned
> Were with a snake, whose head and tail were fast combyned.
>
> (IV.10.xl)

The snake, ancient symbol of wisdom, sexuality, and eternity, bites its own tail; the circle represents the eternal process of generation in a single androgynous figure. In the next stanza this mystery is further unfolded with the hint that Venus, herself an image or fiction of God the Creator, is herself both female and male.

> The cause why she was couered with a vele,
> Was hard to know, for that her Priests the same
> From peoples knowledge labour'd to concele.
> But sooth it was not sure for womanish shame,
> Nor any blemish, which the worke mote blame;
> But for, they say, she hath both kinds in one,
> Both male and female, both vnder one name:
> She syre and mother is her selfe alone,
> Begets and eke conceiues, ne needeth other none. (xli)

Similarly in *Colin Clout's Come Home Again*, when the shepherds sing the praise of their God of Love:

For him the greatest of the Gods we deeme,
Borne without Syre or couples, of one kynd,
For *Venus* selfe doth soly couples seeme,
Both male and female, through commixture ioyned .... (799-802)

Spenser's third—and probably his latest—unfolding of the hermaphrodite image in the *Faerie Queene* comes in 'Mutabilitie' with the statuesque figure of Nature, whose draped sex is indeterminate; her apparent womanhood seems like a veil of bright cloud covering the unseen maleness of God the Creator:

Then forth issewed (great goddesse) great dame *Nature*,
With goodly port and gracious Maiesty;
Being far greater and more tall of stature
Then any of the gods or Powers on hie:
Yet certes by her face and physnomy,
Whether she man or woman inly were,
That could not any creature well descry:
For, with a veile that wimpled euery where,
Her head and face was hid, that mote to none appeare.

That some doe say was so by skill deuized,
To hide the terror of her vncouth hew,
From mortall eyes that should be sore agrized;
For that her face did like a Lion shew,
That eye of wight could not indure to view:
But others tell that it so beautious was,
And round about such beames of splendor threw,
That it the Sunne a thousand times did pass,
Ne could be seene, but like an image in a glass. (VII.7.v-vi)

Nature radiates the pure light of the one God for whose sight the poet longs at the poem's end. That hidden male God is never seen in the poem, of course, and it is striking how often Spenser's images of perfected virtue or goodness are essentially female while hinting, like the hermaphrodite, at the qualities of both sexes.

Alastair Fowler, following Lewis, has called attention to this 'strain of cosmogonic myth' so that in the *Faerie Queene*,

a polarity of male and female principles characterises all natural processes and patterns of life....These mythological constructions display more than a mere predilection for certain bisexual images. It is not too much to say that the best parts of the poem express a sexual mysticism: a mysticism which perceives, in the most exalted forms of nature, even in nature's creator, a generative play of male and female.[6]

Less often observed, perhaps, is the congruousness of these mythological images with the literal stuff of the human narrative.

Returning to the lovers twined in 'senseless' union, like 'that faire hermaphrodite', it seems significant that we see them through the eyes of Britomart, champion of chaste marriage and a lady whom the reader knows to be on a quest to find her dream-knight. Yet for all that Scudamour and Amoret know, Britomart *is* a man. She dresses as a knight, rides and fights like one. Moreover, she has just rescued the lady-in-distress. What makes the cancelled stanzas so psychologically affecting as story is that Britomart shares in, but then is excluded from, the experiences of both man and woman. She is both rescuer and rescued. This is evident in the structure of the allegorical narrative and is clearly pointed in the dialogue, though whether there is any thematic significance in William Ponsonbie's printing errors in this context ('he' twice for 'she', 'him' for 'her', confusing Britomart with Busyrane) is doubtful.[7]   When Britomart first comes upon Scudamour lying helpless, his Cupid shield thrown aside, beating his head wilfully on the ground because he cannot pass the flames to Busyrane's palace, she offers to help and he replies: 'what couldst thou more,/ If she were thine, and thou as now am I?' (III.11.xix). Similarly, the slight wound that Britomart receives from Busyrane's knife 'into her snowie chest,/ That little drops empurpled her faire brest' links her in blood with Amoret, whose breast was 'entrenched deep with knife accursed keene'. The echo of the unfolded trauma indicates Britomart's susceptibility to an experience that can be read as hers but which she overcomes in her superior virtue. In a comparable way the heroine of Book III shares in the experiences of Florimel, Belphoebe, and the less attractive warrior-women of the poem.

Had Spenser finished his double *Aeneid*, it is possible he would have included a face-to-face portrait of the Faerie Queene herself, that elusive and transcendent spirit which touches and momentarily illuminates the lives of her worshippers. One might speculate, since thoughts of Gloriana seem inseparable in the poet's mind from thoughts of Queen Elizabeth, whether he would have had recourse to a hermaphroditic image of her perfection—like the well-known painting of Francis I, with the attributes of Minerva, Mars, Diana, Amor and Mercury.[8] However, he didn't. In the poem left to us, clearly Britomart comes closest to realising such female majesty—such a faerie queene. The secret of her success, both publicly in her achievements and political destiny, and in the sympathetic judgement of most readers of the poem, seems to me to have much to do with her hermaphroditic aspect.

The 'Polly Oliver theme' is familiar in Shakespearean comedy and in popular literature and festivity generally. Moreover, Spenser found the lady-disguised-as-knight ready-made in Ariosto and Tasso. But his treatment of the motif goes far beyond these models. Inconographically Britomart has often been seen as a

Venus in Mars' armour. At a naturalistic and domestic level, Britomart is introduced as a tomboy with a fine scorn for needlepoint and a passion for historical feats of arms. Her true appearance is certainly feminine, but it is only revealed at moments of epiphany, as she removes her knight's helmet and shakes loose those golden locks that 'raught unto her heele'. As she goes about in armour, her public presence creates an effect which is not only ironic for the reader, but also ambivalent to the fictional beholders:

> For she was full of amiable grace,
> And manly terrour mixed therewithall .... (III.1.xlvi)

This double aspect is directly responsible for the embarrassing though educative experience at Castle Joyous, when the wanton Malecasta slips into Britomart's bed 'all ignoraunt of her contrary sex'. When in mixed company Britomart evokes responses appropriate to both male and female. At Malbecco's castle, 'Yet euery one her likte, and euery one her loued' (III.9.xxiv). The Alexandrine, perfect in its rhetorical balance, expresses in miniature the harmony that is the key to Britomart's success. Interestingly, Spenser wrote a line of exactly similar metrical and rhetorical structure to describe his heroine as she first sets out: 'Ne euill thing she fear'd, ne euill thing she ment' (III.1.xix). The face she turns to the world is neither conventionally female nor male, but somewhere perfectly between.

Britomart's disguise is like the disguises of Viola and Rosalind, in that it allows the poet to treat a much greater variety of emotional experience in the one figure than would be possible with a simple 'lady' heroine: defeating in battle, and being defeated by, the man she loves; being the object of a man's aggressive jealousy and of a girl's worst fears; and so on. It is interesting to note, in trying to tie up the poem's stories with its emblems, that Spenser used a number of motifs and even speeches from Ovid's story of Iphis (*Metamorphoses* IX 668ff.), the girl brought up as a boy, who loves and is betrothed to a girl and rescued from the predicament on her wedding eve when the goddess Isis works an accommodating sex change.

Traditional sexual roles are frequently reversed in the narrative of the *Faerie Queene*, of course. Spenser's 'greater variety' includes an active Venus who 'reaps sweet pleasure' of a passively embowered Adonis, and a female rapist Argante. His men are perhaps less distinctly and variedly drawn, but they too undergo transformation. In particular, Britomart's lover Artegal, whose conspicuous and shaggy manliness makes him appear like some antique wodwos, and whose motto is 'Salvagesse sans finesse', finds himself softened by her love. Repetition of the story pattern shows how the same susceptibility in Artegal makes him vulnerable to the feminist tyranny of Radigund, as a result of which he is disarmed, dressed in a woman's smock and set like Hercules to twist linen twine, together with other captive knights 'spinning and carding all in a comely row'.   It is Britomart who rescues him from the laundry and re-establishes the 'lawful' relation of the sexes.   Spenser's bald statement of the doctrine of the subjection of women is disappointing, coming as it does after such suggestive narrative.   Moreover it is embarassingly two-faced, since his political theme necessitates qualifications to this view:

> But vertuous women wisely vnderstand,
> That they were borne to base humilitie,
> Vnlesse the heauens them lift to lawfull soueraintie.   (V.5.25)

Fortunately, the poem does not rest on such platitudes.   The suggestive exploration of the relationship of male and female power continues with the visit to Isis Church, which Britomart must visit before she liberates the enslaved and effeminated Artegal.   Here the mystery of justice is expressed in terms of sexual relation: 'doom' and 'clemency' are polarised in the Egyptian deities Osiris and Isis.   Leaving Artegal's iron man outside the temple, Britomart passes to the inner sanctuary of the lunar goddess, where she sleeps at the feet of Isis' statue and a disturbing and erotic dream bestows sovereignty on her.   In the secret inner life of the dream, under the protection of the moon goddess, the female rules.

It is time to return to the lovers left in cold storage and to look more closely at their destiny.   The final chapter of C.S. Lewis's *Allegory of Love* proclaims a bold and celebrated thesis:

> The last phase of that story—the final defeat of courtly love by the romantic conception of marriage—occupies the third book of *The Faerie Queene* and much of the fourth.   (p.298)

Lewis locates the scene of this climactic struggle in the 'sterility, the suffocating monotony' of Amoret's imprisonment in Busyrane's palace.

> When once Britomart has rescued her thence, the two lovers become one flesh—for that is the meaning of the daring simile of the Hermaphrodite in the original conclusion of Book III.   But even after this, Amoret is in danger if she strays from Britomart's side; she will then fall into a world of wild beasts where she has no comfort or guide, and may even become the victim of monsters who live on the 'spoile of women'.   (p.344)

Summarising the *significatio*, he concludes:

> Thus, in general, it is plain that Amoret is simply love—begotten by heaven, raised to its natural perfection in the Garden and to its civil and spiritual perfections in the Temple, wrongly separated from marriage by the ideals of courtly gallantry, and at last restored to it by Chastity—as Spenser conceives chastity.   (p.344)

The problem with so large and compelling a reading is not just the 'at last', in defiance of the literal text. It is also that, once you begin to look closely at the texture and tone of Spenser's continuation, the confidence seems unfounded. Moreover, Scudamour's contribution is left out of account.

The single most important thing about the 'hermaphrodite stanzas' remains: their cancellation in 1596. The reasons for the change and its consequences seem to me well worth pondering, because I think they indicate a new movement in Spenser's moral thought and new poetic strategies to accommodate the shift.

Clearly he needed a narrative link between Books III and IV. In the substituted stanzas which appeared in 1596 Scudamour despairs of Britomart's return and, when the ladies finally emerge from the vanished ruins of Busirane's palace, he has disappeared. In the first nine cantos of Book IV Amoret and Scudamour are kept apart by separate narratives up to the point (IV.9.xxxvii) where, logically, they ought to re-unite. Instead, Scudamour laments her loss and then responds to Britomart's request to tell how he won her first (IV.10). At plot level the broken thread is puzzling and it has widely been held as an example of Spenser's negligence or indifference to that sort of consistency. The puzzlement is greater in proportion to how far the reader has accepted Lewis's view of the significance of Amoret-and-Scudamour and is subconsciously trying to make them one flesh—in other words, to reinstate the hermaphrodite ending to their story. In fact there are plenty of signs that Spenser was developing a different view of their function.

The 'Second Part' of *The Faerie Queene* begins with the poet confessing that he has been criticised (almost certainly by Lord Burghley) for the eroticism of his poem:

> The rugged forhead that with graue foresight
>   Welds kingdomes causes, and affaires of state,
>   My looser rimes (I wote) doth sharply wite,
>   For praising loue, as I haue done of late .... (IV proem i)

He is particularly unhappy about the story of Amoret's 'hart-binding chaine' and says 'I...oftentimes doe wish it neuer had bene writ'. Modern readers are ill-disposed to take the sentiment at face value. Yet even as a 'rhetorical disclaimer' the lines must invite the reader to reconsider what had already been written, as indeed Spenser did. He could hardly call in copies that had been in circulation for six years, but he could rewrite the story of Amoret so as to provide some explanation for the traumatic captivity of III.12, by spinning new narratives which are retrospective. The most important episode, the Temple of Venus (IV.10), logically precedes the House of Busirane and it is the most substantial backwards narrative loop in the poem. It is further marked in that the whole canto (except for the final line, 'So ended he his tale, where I this Canto end') is related in the voice of Scudamour. Spenser's rewriting of Amoret-and-Scudamour, then, takes the form of retrospective analysis of episodes already experienced by the reader.

The process begins with excision of the hermaphrodite. The contrast between the old ending of Book III and the new beginning of Book IV could hardly be starker. For the hermaphrodite was an image of mutuality, losing of the self, so that 'they' become 'it', one flesh in marriage. The new beginning analyses the experience of the marriage day into its male and female aspects. Spenser can have written few stanzas uglier than the following, in which the casual, unthinking brutality of the male world where the woman is a mere appendage (object, or subject of merely passive verbs) is feelingly conveyed. Though the tonal surface is blandly approving, the choice of verbs and reiteration of the male pronoun are telling:

> For from the time that *Scudamour* her bought
> In perilous fight, she neuer ioyed day,
> A perilous fight when he with force her brought
> From twentie Knights, that did him all assay:
> Yet fairely well he did them all dismay:
> And with great glorie both the shield of loue,
> And eke the Ladie selfe he brought away,
> Whom hauing wedded as did him behoue,
> A new vnknowen mischiefe did from him remoue. (IV.1.ii)

The circumstances of Amoret's rape by Busirane and his maskers are delivered parenthetically, so that we seem to see and hear the grossness of the wedding guests provoking her terror:

> For that same vile Enchauntour *Busyran*,
> The very selfe same day that she was wedded,
> Amidst the bridale feast, whilest euery man
> Surcharg'd with wine, were heedlesse and ill hedded,
> All bent to mirth before the bride was bedded,
> Brought in that mask of loue which late was showen:
> And there the Ladie ill of friends bestedded,
> By way of sport, as oft in maskes is knowen,
> Conueyed quite away to liuing wight vnknowen. (IV.1.iii)

But it is not that her husband—or would-be husband—Scudamour provides a refuge from such male violence. On the contrary, when Scudamour finally tells how he battled for his shield of love and entered the Temple of Venus to claim his prize from the lap of Womanhood, the tone is boastful, the wit crude and aggressive:

> Whom soone as I beheld, my hart gan throb,
>   And wade in doubt, what best were to be donne:
>   For sacrilege me seem'd the Church to rob,
>   And folly seem'd to leaue the thing vndonne,
>   Which with so strong attempt I had begonne.
>   Tho shaking off all doubt and shamefast feare,
>   Which Ladies loue I heard had neuer wonne
>   Mongst men of worth, I to her stepped neare,
> And by the lilly hand her labour'd vp to reare. (IV.10.liii)

The 'courtly love tradition' does little to exonerate the hero. Even Jean de Meun's lover was not so forceful nor his Rose so unwilling. In Lydgate's *Temple of Glass* the lover pauses to ask permission from Womanhood. Scudamour, however, resorts to jocular violence:

> Thereat, that formost matrone me did blame,
>   And sharpe rebuke, for being ouer bold;
>   Saying it was to Knight vnseemely shame,
>   Vpon a recluse Virgin to lay hold,
>   That vnto *Venus* seruices was sold.
>   To whom I thus, Nay but it fitteth best,
>   For *Cupids* man with *Venus* mayd to hold,
>   For ill your goddesse seruices are drest
> By virgins, and her sacrifices let to rest. (IV.10.liv)

If one doubted the 'evidence of style' here, the iconography works to place Scudamour, Cupid's man. For the first time in the poem, his shield of love (unremarked when it was first seen thrown aside beside Busirane's repulsive flames) is described. The Cupid displayed is not one of Spenser's gentle, sportive, and amorous Cupids; he is deadly:

> With that my shield I forth to her did show,
>   Which all that while I closely had conceld;
>   On which when *Cupid* with his killing bow
>   And cruell shafts emblazond she beheld,
>   At sight thereof she was with terror queld,
>   And said no more: (IV.10.lv)

Despite struggles, prayers, and tears, Amoret cannot gain 'her wished freedome'. *Cosi fan tutte*, says the male critic with a smile, pointing out that Venus smiles on the endeavour. Strictly speaking it is Scudamour who claims the approval of Venus:

> Whom when I saw with amiable grace
>   To laugh at me, and fauour my pretence,
>   I was emboldned .... (IV.10.lvi)

Recalling the manifestations of Venus and Cupid already encountered in the poem does not simplify interpretation here. The amoral 'idole' of this overheated salon and the supervisor of biological creation in the Garden of Adonis are not the same 'character', merely aspects of the same life-force. We cannot therefore interpret Scudamour's behaviour as commendable nor see Amoret as resisting the necessity of nature. In the final words of his story Scudamour, boasting of his courage as he dragged Amoret past the Temple guards, likens himself to the fearless Orpheus who has rescued his Euridice. This unfortunate mythic comparison is apposite in confirming what the reader already suspects—that Amoret is to be lost forever. In fact, she is not heard of again in the poem. If a motto for the story of Scudamour and Amoret is needed, Spenser has already provided it in a lesson learned from Chaucer. The first speech of Britomart in *The Faerie Queene* is to rebuke knights fighting to enforce ladies' love. She quotes from Chaucer's Franklin:[9]

> Ne may loue be compeld by maisterie;
> For soone as maisterie comes, sweet loue anone
> Taketh his nimble wings, and soone away is gone.   (III.1.xxv)

Britomart, whose more complete virtue is shadowed in Amoret, complements and rebukes in her own experience the experiences of the lesser heroines; they are like graces moving at the edge of a dance which has her as its centre.

Spenser's continuation of the story of Scudamour and Amoret beyond the happy reunion provisionally commemorated in the hermaphrodite image turns out to be a bleak piece of rewriting. After publication in 1590 of Books I-III he appears to have pondered deeply the Ovidian experience of love in a traditional courtly mode which he had drawn prematurely into a marriage knot. As he prolonged the narrative lives of his lovers, so he recast Amoret's experience in the House of Busirane, expanding her fearfulness and developing Scudamour as a cruel captain of Cupid, whose service of Love is mere mastery. By analysing a traditional and literary courtly relationship in terms of 'maistrie' Spenser found the tenor for his larger imperial theme, and explored in the story of Britomart and Artegal the relationship between male and female qualities in the person of a 'governor'.

The strange image of sexual union as a single 'faire hermaphrodite' is thus at the very heart of Spenser's enterprise, a single paradoxical image of chaste marriage, the mysterious and perfect oneness of nature in *coincidentia oppositorum*, known by the experience of 'one flesh'. In his chosen form of allegorical romance all meaning is expressed through love, the love of a woman for a man, the love of a man for a woman. Marriage is the end of all stories, the knotting of all narrative threads in an ideal future. What is extraordinary about the story of Scudamour and Amoret, in view of its provisional ending in 1590, is that Spenser seems to have unpicked the thread of their future. If the reader is to imagine a future—and one might argue that Spenser's epic theory as outlined in the Letter to Ralegh requires the poem's action to be perfected by an act of 'fashioning' in the mind of the reader—then extrapolation of the narrative suggests a repetition of rape-and-rescue-and-loss, a perversion of Orpheus and Euridice, a travesty of true marriage. It is a story pattern whose seed was lurking in the wisdom of Spenser's master Chaucer:

> Love wol not been constreyned by maistrye.
> Whan maistrie comth, the God of Love anon
> Beteth his wynges and farewel, he is gon.

In rewriting the ending of Book III of his *Faerie Queene* Spenser replaced an iconographic puzzle with a narrative puzzle. Readers need to follow stories as well as to interpret emblems. But when we follow the story we come to a narrative black hole, into which Amoret has vanished. Peering down vainly, the interpreting critic finds himself unsettled by seeing the ghost of 'that faire hermaphrodite'.

NOTES

1   Quotations of Spenser are from *Poetical Works,* ed. J.C. Smith and E. De Sélincourt, 3 vols (Oxford, 1909-10).

2   See Marie Delcourt. *Hermaphrodite: mythes et rites de la bisexualité dans l'antiquité classique* (Paris, 1958), pp.65-103.

3   *Shakespeare's Ovid, Being Arthur Golding's Translation of the Metamorphoses,* ed. W.H.D. Rouse (London, 1961), pp.89-91.

4   Dominic Baker-Smith, 'Spenser's Triumph of Marriage', *Word and Image* IV (1988), 313.

5   The lectures appeared posthumously, ed. Alastair Fowler, *Spenser's Images of Life* (Cambridge, 1967).

6   Alastair Fowler, *Spenser and the Numbers of Time* (London, 1964), p.213.

7   Stanza 42 on p.588 of Ponsonbie's 1590 edition. The slip was noted in 'Faults escaped in the Print': '588 He she ibid. him her ibid.' but not corrected until the 1596 re-setting.

8   See Edgar Wind, *Pagan Mysteries in the Renaissance* (1958, rev. ed. Harmondsworth, 1967), Pl.80 and pp.213-4.

9   'Franklin's Tale', *Canterbury Tales* V 765-6.

7

'Th'old broad way in applying':
John Donne and his 'Litanie'

Dominic Baker-Smith

For the religious imagination love and fear must be finely balanced; let one gain undue predominance and there is a slackness or a tension, a complacency or an anguish, which stifles creative thought. Love, we might say, springs from that which is personal and under the control of the individual, while fear, or at least circumspection, derives from recognition of an external authority, a system or power that is distinct and unaccommodating. One direction leads through spontaneity to indulgence and presumption, unless it is checked by the second; and that, in its turn, may give rise to numbness and acquiescence. A vital interplay is the prerequisite of health, and Justice and Mercy will have to continue their dispute until the last trumpet has sounded. John Donne, who had such a dichotomous sense of things, was well aware of this fact, and the workings of his mind betray a constant struggle to come to terms with it.

One field in which this is evident is that of his ecclesiastical allegiance: fine adjustments of corporate obligation to personal conviction mark all the stages from his Catholic upbringing to his Anglican ordination. Much has been made of Donne's bad conscience in this matter, an apostasy which some have seen as a lasting burden on his awareness of self.[1] But there are alternative possibilities, and one does not have to endorse Donne's decision to recognise that he may not have read the situation in terms quite so fraught with guilt. It is impossible to pass judgement on such hidden motions, but at least there was an intellectual route by which he could move from the 'superfluous religion' of his Catholic family to the adiaphoristic poise of the English Church. That does not mean that self-interest did not enter into the transaction, or that his irenical assessment of the warring churches was not a fudging fear of matyrdom, but it does mean that we cannot presume to judge. One can at least recognise the plausibility of the position which he praised in Lady Danvers, 'Shee never diverted towards the *Papist* in undervaluing the *Scripture*; nor towards the Separatist, in undervaluing the Church'.[2] For present purposes, the important thing is that he worked himself into a position where spontaneity and structure, scripture and church, appeared to him to stand in a viable relationship.

If one can accept that Donne slipped imperceptibly away from Tridentine Catholicism, following arguments that would not seem unfamiliar to the fathers of Vatican II, then the process was an extended one. It was under way by the time he wrote 'Satire III' in the 1590s and continued until his ordination in 1615; in fact, it is of the nature of Donne's Anglicanism that it continued after that. What was clear was that a church was necessary: 'Take heed therefore of being seduced to that Church that is in one man'.[3] Donne's modest scepticism, whether it sprang from worldliness or weariness with controversy, demanded simple consensus with tradition,

> *quod ubique, quod semper*, those universall, and fundamentall doctrines, which in all Christian ages, and in all Christian Churches, have beene agreed by all to be necessary to salvation.

This minimal consensus provides the frame within which the believer must operate; there must be *concio, congregatio, coetus*, for 'God loves not singularity'.[4] As he would mockingly demonstrate in *Ignatius his Conclave*, innovation was the Devil's work, and it would later be his most serious charge against the Council of Trent, that it rendered 'Problematical things, Dogmatical; and matter of Disputation, matter of Faith; to bring the University into *Smithfield*, and heaps of Arguments into Piles of Faggots'.[5] The rather shrill wit of the climax should not distract us from the implicit concept of a church discipline in which questions are not all peremptorily closed; if, as has been said, Anglicanism is a religion for dons, then that is what Donne wanted.

This alertness to the relationship between group obligation and personal application coheres in Donne with a clear approval of liturgical acts, acts which declare public truths and nourish personal response. There must be established forms and outward decency, 'Rituall and Ceremoniall things move not God, but they exalt that Devotion, and they conserve that Order, which does move him'.[6] 'Order' and 'Devotion' adequately express those two aspects of religious life, the formal and the private, which a liturgy must aim to harmonise. The link between the two was clearly of some importance for Donne: if we leave aside certain of the Holy Sonnets, then his most successful religious poems are those which are occasional, which combine meditation on a Christian truth with its applications to personal circumstance. 'Goodfriday, 1613. Riding Westward' is the most obvious example, but it is striking that to four others which relate to specific events Donne has given liturgical titles. 'A Hymne to Christ, at the Authors last going into Germany' relates to his departure of 1619, and both the 'Hymne to God my God, in my sicknesse' and 'A Hymne to God the Father' have been associated with his grave illness in 1623. But there is also 'A Litanie', a much earlier work which Donne himself connects with an illness and which can be confidently dated in 1608. What is of interest is this combination of the liturgical with the personal, the formal with its private application. The point was not lost on his contemporaries.[7]

This sense that in 'A Litanie' Donne deliberately chose a canonical form to express his personal state of mind is reinforced by a letter which he addressed to his friend Sir Henry Goodyer; the letter is undated but is obviously connected with 'A Litanie' which can be dated in the autumn of 1608. He has been confined to bed by sickness and has made 'a meditation in verse, which I call a Litany', but is apprehensive that some may consider it inappropriate for a private individual to attempt such a public form,

> Amongst ancient annals I mean some 800 years, I have met two Letanies in Latin verse, which gave me not the reason of my meditations, for in good faith I thought not upon them then, but they give me a defence, if any man, to a Lay man, and a private, impute it as a fault, to take such divine and publique names, to his own little thoughts. The first of these was made by *Ratpertus* a Monk of *Suevia*; and the other by S. *Notker*, of whom I will give you this note by the way, that he is a private Saint, for a few Parishes; they were both but Monks, and the Letanies poor and barbarous enough; yet Pope *Nicolas* the 5, valued their devotion so much, that he canonized both their Poems, and commanded them for publike service in their Churches: mine is for lesser Chappels, which are my friends ...[8]

Quite apart from Donne's sensitivity to the issue, it is interesting to see how he reiterates the contrast of private and public in relation to his adoption of a liturgical form of prayer.

In his biography of Donne, R.C. Bald has suggested that the years 1607-10 were the most disturbed of his life. His secular career was derailed, his religious faith at the best unsettled, and in 1608 he wrote his defence of suicide, the unpublished *Biathanatos*. But it was a period that brought him into contact with Thomas Morton, Dean of Gloucester, whose *A Catholic Appeal for Protestants* (1609) provided a moderate defence of Anglicanism which must have been a balm for Donne. It has been suggested that Donne asisted Morton in his polemical investigation of Catholic writings and such a position would help to explain how he got access to continental books; one of the rare benefits of such public polemic between the churches was the stimulus it gave to the imported fruits of Catholic scholarship. One pertinent example is the *Antiquae Lectiones* by the Dutch canonist Henricus Canisius (1557-1610), who was professor at Ingolstadt. This massive collection of antiquarian materials was published in five volumes at Ingolstadt, 'ex typographia Ederiana', between 1601 and 1608, and it was in the *pars secunda* of Tomus V, which appeared in the latter year, that Canisius printed 'Epigrammata seu Hymni sacri illustrium virum antiquorum patrum monasterii S. Galli'. The signs are that Donne read this remarkably soon after its publication, and it is undoubtedly the source for the information he gives Goodyer about 'A Litanie' and its precedents. The 'Epigrammata' that Canisius prints are three litanies by monks from the Abbey of St Gall, Hartmann, Ratpertus and Notker the Stammerer (Balbulus), and with these is printed more or less the information which Donne gave to Goodyer. More or less, because Donne characteristically manages to get some details wrong.[9]

The important thing is that the details do establish the source of Donne's unexpected acquaintance with these early medieval poems. This in itself is not so surprising: an interest in medieval hymnology can be traced back at least as far as George Fabricius' *Poetarum Veterum Ecclesiasticorum Opera Christiani* (Basle, I. Oporinus, 1564). But obviously Canisius' volume struck a chord in Donne and quite possibly because of the note 'Ad lectorum', in which Canisius expresses his desire to print these hymns so that ancient spirituality might be of service to his own time. To Donne, aware of the need for a religious society but estranged from the certainties of recusant Catholicism, Morton's conception of a primitive Catholicism, stripped of its Roman accretions, must have been singularly appealing; so in these early writers—even if they were 'but Monks'— he could engage with a Church that might still be called patristic, innocent both of scholasticism and the Hildebrandine papacy.

The letter to Goodyer makes it clear that Donne claims the St. Gall litanies as precedents, not models; and his appeal to them is based simply on the fact that they are personal works which have been given canonical status. He makes no such claim for 'A Litanie', although in his later years, as Walton reports, when Dean of St. Paul's he caused 'A Hymn to God the Father' to be set to music, 'and to be often sung to the Organ by the *Choristers* of St *Pauls* Church, in his own hearing'.[10] In 1608 he was more reticent, and his invocatory meditation is designed 'for lesser Chappels', for the eyes of intimate friends rather than the ears of a congregation. Since Donne's other letters to Goodyer at this period suggest a common attitude on church allegiance, one in which purity of motive outweighs formal commitment, it might be supposed that Goodyer would appreciate Donne's play with public and private forms. Thus to suggest that 'A Litanie' is based on Cranmer's litany, as some have done, is to miss much of the force of Donne's idea: Cranmer simply adapted the *Litania maior*, the traditional Litany of the Saints as it appeared in the Sarum use, to fit Reformed theology.[11] His was not a personal work in the sense that Donne intends. Donne's poem certainly observes the requirements of a 'rectified devotion' in its attitude to the saints but, as his letter makes clear, this is to achieve just that kind of balance between the warring extremes which is characteristic of Morton's *A Catholike Appeale*,

> That by which it will deserve best acceptation is, That neither the Roman Church need call it defective, because it abhors not the particular mention of the blessed Triumphers in heaven; nor the Reformed can discreetly accuse it, of attributing more than a rectified devotion ought to do.

What it does not do, of course, is invoke the saints in their own right: the emphasis is on the operation of grace within them. The poem becomes a dramatisation of the process by which, through grace, the private does become public; and as such it has an an oblique reference to Donne's own intermediary position, adopting a devotional tradition but rectifying it by a reformed attentiveness to the absolute intitiative of grace.[12]

Thus, when we turn to the poem itself, it is striking that no saint is mentioned by name apart from Mary, and even she only by her role, 'that faire blessed Mother-maid'(37); rather we meet the traditional categories of sanctity, Patriarchs, Prophets, Apostles, Martyrs, Confessors, Virgins and Doctors, all seem as varying manifestations of grace in operation. The *Litania maior* lists a large number of saints who are invoked individually but they are also broken down into groups and it is these groups that Donne adopts. In the usual manner his litany opens with an invocation to God in the three Persons and in the Trinity (stanzas I-IV); then follows the invocation of the saints in their general categories (stanzas V-XIV), though Donne includes Angels as creatures of God concerned with the descent of grace on mankind, and here the notable feature is the suppression of direct invocation, 'orate pro nobis'. But it is not suppressed entirely and the saints are implicitly cast in an intercessory role which would not have pleased those who, in Hooker's words, 'measure religion by dislike of the Church of Rome'.[13] The supplications that follow closely match the standard form that Cranmer adopted into the Book of Common Prayer, praying for deliverance (XIV/XXII). and for audience (XXIII/XXVIII). What such a general account fails to indicate is the ingenuity of Donne's performance as he wrestles to particularise the broad outlines of the liturgical form.

The first stanza addresses the Father as creator, as father of the Son by whom all things were made: Heaven, its destined inhabitant mankind, 'and all else, for us'(2). But the cosmic focus narrows to the red clay from which Adam was shaped and which is evoked by the speaker's heart, linked by melancholy to the element of the earth, and red with 'selfe-murder'(6). So the scene is set for a new creation, that purging of 'vicious tinctures'(8) which promised resurrection. In its descent from the opening idea, the procession of the Son from the Father, the original of all creativity, to the plight of the sinner, the descendant of Adam, the stanza condenses the span of Christian history with remarkable force. Thus it provides the background for an important concept introduced in the second stanza, addressed to the Son: this is that of 'applying'(17) a term that recurs in line 80, 'Th'old broad way in applying'. 'Applying' means, of course the very process of relating a general truth or category to individual circumstance, the process that the poem itself enacts in its performance as a litany, a liturgical means of bonding private anxieties to the general economy of grace. So the prayer to Christ is a plea that the heart may also apply 'thy paine'(17), the passion, so focus on it and enter into it as to share in its fruits. To be 'Drown'd in thy blood, and in thy passion slaine'(18) is to be set to 'rise up from death'(9). It is by 'application' that the canonical text is rendered personal or, as Donne puts it elsewhere, made 'something fit for thy wearing'.[14] Then, in the third stanza, the individual is not only the temple of the Holy Ghost but 'Fire, Sacrifice, Priest, Altar'(27): the drama of man's relationship with God is recapitulated in what amounts to a private liturgy. The opening section, the 'Supplicatio ad Deum', concludes in the approved manner with a prayer to the Trinity, a mystery which may be but 'Bones to Philosophy'(29), but which offers milk, the food of infants, to faith; it is a mystery which Donne presents in a provocative image, that is the 'slipperinesse'(31) and 'entanglings'(31) of coiled serpents, the former suggesting distinction of persons and the latter their inseparability. Trinity of persons, figured in the attributes of power, love and knowledge, is fused with unity of nature to present a model for the believer,

> Give mee a suche selfe different instinct,
> Of these let all mee elemented bee,
> Of power, to love, to know, you unnumbred three.   (34-6)

The life of the Trinity is duplicated in the private self, realising that multiplicity in unity which is such a frequent preoccupation in Donne's writing.

We move next to the 'Invocatio Sanctorum', a section of particular interest, since it is that which Donne claims back from traditional Catholic practice, disregarding Anglican precedent. But, as one might expect, there is caution. In the Catholic litany the Saints are addressed directly, and Cranmer's earliest version retained this; Donne, however, follows the Book of Common Prayer in addressing God throughout, but there is no doubt that the saints have an intercessory function. Thus the stanza on (rather than to) Mary is in essence a prayer of thanks, 'For that fair blessed Mother-maid, /.../ Our zealous thankes we poure'(37,43): thanks, that is, for the necessary role played by 'That she-Cherubin'(38) in the drama of redemption. At the same time her continuing intercessory role in obliquely indicated,

> As her deeds were
> Our helpes, so are her prayers; nor can she sue
> In vaine, who hath such titles unto you.   (43-5)

In fact Donne's assertion that Mary 'unlock'd Paradise'(39) might even seem to allow her a dangerous initiative, were it not that the direct address to God serves to enclose all history within divine control. From the central truth of the incarnation the poem moves on to summarise that history in a succession of manifestations of grace, from the angels which are God's agents and the guardians of his children, through those particular offices, Patriarchs and Prophets, Virgins and Doctors, which have helped to construct a church, to 'this universall Quire'(118) which is its full realisation. Taken together these stanzas

(V-XIV) provide a reference system by which the working out of a providential scheme in history may be grasped.

The unifying element in all this is what we might describe as Donne's typological instinct, that sense which underlay his vivid image of the scriptures as a wardrobe stocked with garments, which the individual must put on. So each stanza celebrates a particular mode of holiness both in terms of past achievement, the canonised history of the saints, and by immediate application to the present of the reader. The Patriarchs,

> ...which saw
> More in the cloud, then wee in fire,
> Whome Nature clear'd more, then us grace and law, (56-8)

offer the basis for an ironical reflection on their virtues, achieved when redemption was only a shadow in the future, and the faltering performance of those illumined and supported by Christ and his Church. But the controlling prayer of the stanza is that these 'great Grandfathers, of thy Church'(56), who, 'in Heaven still pray'(59), may be at one with the Church in the present: 'And let thy Patriarches Desire /.../ Be satisfied, and fructifie in mee'(55, 61). Here the word 'still' marks the transition to a present application: the Patriarchs intercede now, and their desires fructify now. The Prophets, too, 'thy Churches Organs'(65), are the faithful but uncomprehending instruments of the Holy Ghost, harmonising by their anticipation of Christ the Old Testament with the New. Here Donne uses typology in its purest sense, but one is aware all through this section of the poem that there is an intense interrelation of the parts, one which is based on the mediating figure of Christ and establishes a unity of purpose and almost of identity between the different roles performed by God's servants, even down to the poet. Not only does the section comprehend the historical scheme of salvation, but the application which concludes each stanza recapitulates the collective drama in the struggle of the individual believer. In a particularly witty turn on the Confessors, those saints whose sufferings have been mental rather than actual, Donne declares,

> Tentations martyr us alive; A man
> Is to himselfe a Dioclesian. (98-9)

No one with an imagination need feel deprived of a tormentor, and if man is 'a little world made cunningly', as Donne puts it elsewhere in the 'Holy Sonnets',[15] then each believer is a little church.

From Donne's point of view these stanzas which commemorate the saints are of special significance since they embody the very kind of rectified use of tradition which seems to have appealed to him, and it can be no accident that they constitute the most effective section in 'A Litanie', offering an unusually dense but coherent field of reference. There is, on the one hand, that historical succession which demonstrates grace working through the community of God's people, the Church in its broadest sense, and then, on the other, there is that synchronic interdependence which is the communion of saints. The way in which each stanza addresses God is a tacit recognition that grace is his alone to give, but his agents, angels or saints, have their role in disseminating it through time. Hence the equal insistence in the poem on the continuing prayer of the saints: the Patriarchs 'still pray'(59); the Prophets 'in common pray'(70); the Apostles 'pray still'(79); the Martyrs, by their blood 'begge for us'(88); the Confessors both 'know, and pray'(95). Though the Virgins may have failed in one petition yet,

> Though they have not obtain'd of thee,
> That or thy Church, or I,
> Should keep, as they, our first integrity, (104-6)

it is clear that their role is to pray, even as the Doctors 'pray for us there'(113). What appeals to Donne evidently is this sense of incorporation in a community which transcends time and place, and it is the liturgical function of a litany, particularly in its older, pre-Edwardian form, to absorb private petitions in the corporate prayer of the Church. This is the conception which underlies the transitional stanza XIV,

> And whil'st this universall Quire,
> That Church in triumph, this in warfare here,
> Warm'd with one all-partaking fire
> Of love, that none be lost, which cost thee deare,
> Pray ceaselessly,'and thou hearken too,
> (Since to be gratious
> Our taske is treble, to pray, beare, and doe)
> Heare this prayer Lord, O Lord deliver us
> From trusting in those prayers, though powr'd out thus.

The appeal to the saints reaches its conclusion in this comprehensive reference to the church triumphant and militant, 'in triumph' and 'in warfare here'. For obvious reasons Donne omits the Catholic conception of the Church suffering, that is in Purgatory, but the treble function of the church on earth, 'to pray, beare, and doe'(124), does account in 'rectified' terms for the older triple division of 'this universall Quire'(118). But for Donne, it would seem, there was psychological comfort at this difficult period in a mental scheme which could reconcile his personal doubt and insecurities with participation in a spiritual community that transcended those controversies which rent contemporary Europe. Hence, the particular intensity of wit in his invocation of the Saints, those instruments of God's care who provided through their varied roles a bridge between present frustrations and ultimate meaning.

The second part of stanza XIV, the middle of the poem, marks a transition to those prayers which traditionally followed invocation of the saints. The 'Invocatio ad Christum', with its pleas for deliverance *ab*, 'from', and *per*, 'through', is exactly matched by Donne: 'From being anxious or secure'(127), 'And through that bitter agonie'(163). What is striking in the remainder of 'A Litanie' is the emphasis given to issues that are highly self-conscious. The transition in stanza XIV is an example: we pray, but we pray that we may not trust in our prayers (125-6), but in God alone. This seems a particularly apt way, given Donne's concern to 'rectify' the litany, to round off an 'Invocatio Sanctorum' which has been addressed, contrary to Catholic practice, to God directly. The saints are celebrated as God's handiwork, no more and no less, and all initiative is reserved in the best reformed manner to God. But the caution, or sensitivity to controversial issues, is also involved in the self-conscious manner of the later invocations. Stanza XVIII points to a *via media* in which poverty is given a positive evaluation, but riches are allowed. The prayer is actually for a condition of indifference which is more subtle and individual than the traditional emphasis on avoidance of material wealth. Another example comes in the following stanza when Donne appears to allude quite openly to the controversial issue of equivocation (which Shakespeare had only recently touched on in *Macbeth*),

> Good Lord deliver us, and teach us when
> Wee may not, and we may blinde unjust men.   (170-1)

The point is that Donne's invocations do not follow the common patterns of public concern but relate to a personal attitude or state of mind, one expressed in acts of anxious discrimination, 'That our affections kill us not, nor dye'(243).

The remainder of 'A Litanie' is closely modelled on the traditional structure, so that stanza XXIV marks a switch to the 'Supplicatio pro variis necessitatibus', and the final stanza with its prayer to Christ the Lamb matches the 'Conclusio' of the *Litania maior*. In all this Donne runs parallel to Cranmer's version, but his eye, one suspects, is on the Latin form in the first place. In fact, it is not difficult to see what Donne was about when he decided to put his personal petitions in a canonical form. The whole of 'A Litanie' is marked by acts of individual adjustment or application, which are nevertheless relieved of quirkiness by their reliance on an ancient liturgical formula. There is a sense in which Donne might be said to be having it both ways, and careful reading of the invocations does suggest a highly individual attempt to escape from the burdens of individuality.

Which brings us round again to the question of the purposes which liturgical forms are designed to fulfil. 'A Litanie', with its roots in the ancient prayer of the Church, but rectified and adapted 'for lesser Chappels, which are my friends', is itself an image of that reconciliation of personal needs with public forms which is the purpose of the Church. Donne's drift towards Anglicanism was certainly influenced by friends like Morton and Lancelot Andrewes, who understood reform to mean rectification rather than abolition. As Edwin Sandys saw it, the English were 'the only nation that walke the right way of iustifiable reformation, in comparison of other, who have runne headlong rather to a tumultuous innovation'; in England 'the honour and solempnithe of the worde were not abused, the more auntient usages not cancelled'.[16] This was not, of course, a majority view, but it fits well enough with Donne's intellectual circle in the difficult years that preceded *Pseudo-Martyr*. Donne's attempt to salvage 'auntient usages' was an act of reassurance to himself, a literary artifact which projected the Church he so desperately needed. The retention of the 'Invocatio Sanctorum' dramatises that community into which the troubled individual could merge and find release, becoming the directed instrument of a greater voice,

Heare thy selfe now, for thou in us dost pray.   (207)

NOTES

1 Thus John Carey sees the amatory poems as an attempt to transfer religious infidelity 'to the relatively innocuous department of sexual ethics', *John Donne: Life, Mind and Heart* (London, 1981), p.38. I have argued for a less wrenched view in 'John Donne's Critique of Pure Religion', in *John Donne: Essays in Celebration*, ed. A.J. Smith (London, 1972), pp.404-32.

2 *The Sermons of John Donne*, ed. G.R. Potter and E.M. Simpson, 10 vols (Berkeley/Los Angeles, 1953-61), VIII, 90.

3 Ibid., II, 280.

4 Ibid., II, 279.

5 Ibid., IV, 144.

6 Ibid., VII, 429-30.

7 Lord Falkland in his 'Elegy on Dr. Donne' refers to 'Those Anthems (almost second Psalmes) he writ / To make us know the Crosse, and value it, /.../ Next his so pious Litanie, which none can / But count divine, except a Puritan; / And that but for the name ...', *The Poems*, ed. A.B. Grosart (London, 1871), p.35.

8 *John Donne: Selected Prose*, chosen by Evelyn Simpson (Oxford, 1967), p.131.

9 *Antiquae Lectiones*, tomus V, pars secunda, 725-46. In fact Nicolas III (not V) gave canonical status to the litanies by Hartmann and Ratpertus, not, surprisingly, to the more distinguished Notker. For details see Baker-

Smith, 'Donne's 'Litanie'', *Review of English Studies*, N.S. XXVI (1975), 171-3. Notker had been beatified by Leo X in 1512.

10   Izaak Walton, *The Lives*, (Oxford, 1966), p.62.

11   Helen Gardner, in *Divine Poems* (Oxford, 1952), p.83, notes that Cranmer's 1544 version included the categories of saints but these were expunged for good under Edward VI; so to Donne their inclusion would be a 'catholic' gesture. Barbara Lewalski seems to me to overstate his 'Protestant care', *Protestant Poetics and the Seventeenth Century Lyric* (Princeton, 1979), pp.260-3. All textual references are to the Gardner edition.

12   In the following year he writes to Goodyer, 'They whose active function it is, must endevour this unity in Religion; and we at our lay Altars ...must beg it of him: but we must take heed of making misconclusions upon the want of it: for, whether the Mayor or Aldermen fall out (as with us and the Puritans; Bishops against Priests) or the Commoners' voyces differ who is Mayor, and who Aldermen, or what their Jurisdiction, (as with the Bishop of *Rome*, or whosoever), yet it is still one Corporation', Simpson, *Prose*, p.137.

13   *Laws of Ecclesiastical Policy,* IV, viii, 2.

14   'This is *Scrutari Scripturas*, to search the Scriptures, not as though thou wouldest make a *concordance*, but an *application*; as thou wouldest search a *wardrobe*, not to make an *Inventory* of it, but to finde in it something fit for thy wearing' (*Sermons*, III, 367).

15   'Holy Sonnets' (1635), no. 2, in *Divine Poems*, p.13.

16   Edwin Sandys, *A Relation of the State of Religion*, (London, V. Sims for S. Waterson, 1605), sig. V3^v.

8

The Commonplace Book of John Maxwell

Priscilla Bawcutt

Most readers of early Scottish poetry are acquainted with the names of George Bannatyne and Sir Richard Maitland; far fewer, I imagine, are familiar with that of John Maxwell. The small collection of verse and prose that he assembled between 1584 and 1589 cannot compare, either in size or richness, with the Bannatyne Manuscript and the Maitland Folio. It does not feature in the standard histories of Scottish literature; only observant users of *A Dictionary of the Older Scottish Tongue [DOST]* will have noticed occasional citations from Maxwell and the presence of his manuscript in the 'Register of Titles of Works Quoted' (vol. III). Yet this small work of only thirty-six leaves deserves to be rescued from obscurity. It is a precious Scottish example of a commonplace book, in the sense of that term used by medievalists—a collection of highly miscellaneous material assembled for the interest, instruction, and amusement of its compiler. Many such compilations survive from late medieval and early modern England: one of the more famous is Balliol MS 354, which belonged to Richard Hill of London in the early sixteenth century; another that has recently been published in its entirety is the fifteenth-century commonplace book of Robert Reynes (Tanner MS 407).[1] Probably many similar collections were put together in Scotland during the same period, but few now survive. The Maxwell manuscript thus has scarcity value; and it also provides interesting testimony of a minor Scottish poet's literary tastes as well as specimens of his own writing.

The Maxwell Manuscript is now in the possession of Edinburgh University Library (Laing III.467). Its early history is obscure, but at the beginning of the nineteenth century it was owned by William Motherwell, the poet and ballad-collector. In 1828 he published an article in *The Paisley Magazine* (I, No. 8, 379-86), called 'Renfrewshire Poets: John Maxwell Younger of Southbar'; in the next issue (437-46) he printed a portion of the manuscript, containing 'Sum Reasownes and Prowerbes'. Later in the century the manuscript was owned in turn by several Scottish book-collectors, James Dennistoun, Adam Sim of Coulter, and the great David Laing; on Laing's death it passed to Edinburgh University. Two distinguished American scholars, M.P. Tilley and B.J. Whiting, displayed particular interest in the proverb collection; unfortunately neither knew of the whereabouts of the manuscript, and therefore depended solely on Motherwell's transcript. Equally unfortunately their labours seem to have been unknown to the only scholar who devoted much attention to the manuscript in recent years, M.L. Anderson. He made a transcript of the text for *DOST*, and provided it with a brief introduction, notes and glossary. This exists in typescript, but has never been published. All students of early Scottish literature are indebted to Professor Anderson—he made transcripts of other Scots manuscripts and also edited *The James Carmichaell Collection of Proverbs* (Edinburgh, 1957). But his edition of this manuscript, valuable though it is, is weakened by his uncritical assumption that almost all the verses in it were 'the original products of Maxwell's brain' (p.11).[2]

Although there are variations in style, the manuscript seems to be written in one hand, that of Maxwell himself. He was proud of his name, which, along with dates ranging from 1584 to 1589, occurs repeatedly in a variety of spellings—'Iohne Maxwall' (1a), 'Iohne Maxwell' (21b), 'Iohne Maxwald' (6a), and the Latinized 'Ioannes Maxwaldus' (16b). He devizes puzzles and verses to tell 'the authouris name': in one place its last syllable rhymes with *tald* and *wald* (8a); in another with *tell* and *sell* (30a). He also proudly announces: 'This wers he pennit of his awin hand' (30a).

Very little is known of Maxwell. The most precise information is provided by the inscription: 'Be me Maxwell of Southbar 3ounger' (21a); the Latin version runs *per me Ioannem Maxweldum Iuniorem de Southbarr* (20b). This title shows that Maxwell was heir to the estate of Southbar in Renfrewshire. Anderson has assembled a number of contemporary references to this branch of the Maxwell family in the last decades of the sixteenth century; he also identifies the compiler of the manuscript with the John Maxwell *Iuniore de Southbar*, who was a bailie of Renfrewshire in 1603, and who died in 1606. There exists one small piece of external evidence to suggest that Maxwell had some reputation as a poet. This is the dedicatory sonnet by an unidentified 'A.S.' to William Mure of Rowallan, which contains the following lines:

> Sprang thou from Maxwell and Montgomeries muse
> To let our poets perisch in the west?[3]

This coupling of Maxwell and Montgomerie is interesting. The manuscript contains a copy of Montgomerie's 'Can goldin Titan schyning brycht at morne' (21a), a complimentary sonnet prefixed to James VI's *Essayes of A Prentise in the Divine Art of Poesie* (1584). The two poets were of the same generation and both came from the south-west of Scotland, but whether they were closely acquainted we do not know. Anderson suggests that Maxwell was 'on the side of the Reformers' (p.6), but there is no conclusive evidence for this. The manuscript contains little that is overtly Catholic, but there is a prayer to Mary, *Mater dei memento mei* (26b). It is perhaps significant, however, that his copy of the Beatitudes (7b) exactly follows the wording of the Geneva Bible (Matt. 5, 3-12).

There still remains much to be discovered about Maxwell's life and career; my chief concern, however, is with the contents of his manuscript. These are highly miscellaneous, in a manner typical of commonplace books. Some items are in Scots, some in Latin; some in prose, some in verse; there are exercises in penmanship (6a), puzzles or riddles (1a); a list of classical gods and goddesses (22b); historical memorabilia (25a); and short satirical squibs on contemporaries, such as the earl of Glencairn, 'bayth fals and gredie, et nunquam leill' (25a). But the part of the manuscript that most interested Motherwell and later scholars was a group of 232 'reasownes and prowerbes' (30b-36b). Motherwell printed this not only in *The Paisley Magazine* but in the Preface he supplied to Andrew Henderson's *Scottish Proverbs* (Edinburgh, 1832), pp.xxxiv-xliv. Anderson placed a similarly high value on this section, calling it 'the earliest known collection by a Scot' (p.1). What Motherwell and Anderson failed to realise, however, was that Maxwell culled the bulk of these sayings from two English works then immensely popular, George Pettie's *A Petite Pallace of Pettie his Pleasure* (1576) and John Lyly's *Euphues* (1578). [It is interesting that copies of the former were in the stock of two Edinburgh printer-booksellers, Thomas Bassandyne (died 1577) and Robert Gourlaw (died 1585).][4] The evidence for this is conclusively set out in M.P. Tilley's *Elizabethan Proverb Lore in Lyly's Euphues and in Pettie's Petite Pallace* (New York, 1926), especially on pages 4-6 and 357-82, and needs no repetition.[5]

One brief illustration of Maxwell's method may suffice. A famous passage in *Euphues* reads:

> althoughe yron the more it is vsed the brighter it is, yet siluer with much wearing doth wast to nothing, though the Cammocke the more it is bowed the better it serueth, yet the bow the more it is bent & occupied, the weaker it waxeth, though the Camomill, the more it is trodden and pressed downe, the more it spreadeth, yet the violet the oftner it is handled and touched, the sooner it withereth and decayeth.[6]

Maxwell deconstructs this into a set of self-contained aphorisms:

> Yrne the more it is wsed the brychter it is.
> Siluer with muche wearing doith waist to no thing.
> The cammocke the more it is bowed the better it serueth.
> The bow the more it is bent & occupyed the weaker it waxeth.
> The Camomill the more it is troden & pressed downe the more it spreadeth.
> The wiolet the ofter it is handeled and twiched the sooner it withereth & decayeth. (36a-b)

Lyly's mannered prose was parodied by Shakespeare (in I *Henry IV*, II.iv), but much admired by other Elizabethan writers. Maxwell was one of the first to display an interest in what we now call euphuism—particularly in its sententious subject-matter—and to link together Pettie and Lyly. Tilley found his response highly significant: 'The association of the proverbial contents of the two books in the mind of a contemporary poet may, I believe, be accepted as evidence of the literary importance of this element in Lyly's day' (p.6).

Maxwell was clearly interested in proverbial wisdom from all sources, and in various languages. B.J. Whiting has demonstrated that another small group of proverbs, numbers 171-80 (35b), which interrupts the larger collections from Pettie and Lyly, derives from a Scottish work, John Rolland's *The Sevin Seages* (Edinburgh, 1578).[7] Most of these come not from the narrative of *The Sevin Seages* but from the appended *Moralitates*—a part of the text unlikely to be read so attentively today. There is one proverb in this collection—'All erdlie plesure finisseth with wo' (no.170)—for which neither Tilley nor Whiting could find a definite source. Such a commonplace is perhaps untraceable. But the collection is in other respects so literary that it seems likely to have originated in Maxwell's reading. The closest parallel known to me is Gavin Douglas's 'All erdly glaidnes fynysith with wo' (*Eneados*, Prol. II, 21). The manuscript also contains a collection of Latin proverbs and 'reasownes', arranged according to the alphabetical order of their first words (12b-16b). Despite the heading *a Salam*, 'from Solomon', these are not all scriptural in origin—item D6 (13b), for instance, is the last line of Horace's Ode IV.12: *Dulce est desipere in loco*. After the Latin proverbs comes the rubric,

> Heir followis the expositiowne and declaratioune of the foir said lateine prowerbis in Inglis, liuelie interpreted according as thay ar written ... (16b)

The style of this strongly suggests a printed source (as yet unidentified); the vernacular translation unfortunately is incomplete, breaking off at the letter C (18a).

Several adages or sententious sayings are attributed to well-known classical authors, such as Seneca (3b and 11b) and Ovid (19b and 26b). Ennius is credited with *Amicus certus in re incerta cernitur* (19b). This had become proverbial, but it is indeed said to be by Ennius in Cicero's *De Amicitia* (17, 64). 'Propertius sayth' introduces reflections on the 'warld of gold'—

> For gold thow salbe lowed and set aloft,
> For gold thow sall ane verteows man be thocht,
> For gold is lowe & honowr also gotten,
> For gold is fayth, for gold the lawes ar broken. (26b)

This is a free rendering of Propertius, III, 13, 48-50. Perhaps the most interesting piece of Latin origin is the short, unattributed dialogue between two 'huiris' (9a). In it Syra exhorts Philotis to be ruthless to men—'quha so ewer thow finde, thow mot spolȝe him, mank him & rywe him'. Anderson queried whether this was 'an attempt at drama'. It is, in fact, a translation of the first eight lines of Terence's *Hecyra*, or 'The Mother-in-Law'. One regrets the brevity of this particular piece.

Maxwell includes many short pieces of verse in his manuscript. Of these Motherwell said:

> I do not consider them as *all* emanating from his own 'ingyne', but as being in some measure a mere register of certain popular rhymes which were current in his own day, or perhaps transcribed by him from some then known collection of homely truths. Many of them are familiar to us yet, and are traditionally preserved among children. Others seem very foolish and trivial; but it is worth while to be able to fix even the antiquity of such prattlings.[8]

Anderson objected to this assessment, yet to me it seems both perceptive and accurate. The manuscript provides better evidence for Maxwell the collector than for Maxwell the poet. The boundary between metrical proverbs and sententious verses is not easy to define: Maxwell liked both. Several short pieces are extracts from larger compositions. 'Quha wald be riche haif ee to honowr ay' (10b), for instance, is a seven-line stanza from the anonymous *De Regimine Principum*. This stanza seems to have been popular: other copies exist in the Bannatyne Manuscript (no. 119) and in a manuscript of Quintin Kennedy's *Ane Litil Breif Tracteit*.[9] Another interesting example is:

> Ane fwill he is that puttis in dainger
> His lyfe, his honowr, for ane thing of nocht.
> Ane fwill he is that will nocht glaidlie cownsall heir
> In tyme quhen it awaill mocht.
> Ane fwill he is that na thing hes in thocht
> Of thing that efter quhat may him befall
> Nor of his end hes no memoriall.   (11b)

This is a very corrupt version of a stanza from Henryson's *The Preaching of the Swallow* (*Fables*, 1860-66); another copy of the stanza occurs in Bannatyne (no. 117).

The manuscript contains other short pieces that also occur in Bannatyne's 'Ballatis of moralitie'. Denton Fox noted that 'He that thi frende hes bene rycht lange' (19b) represents Bannatyne, no. 112. But there are several other unnoticed instances: 'Befoir the tyme is wisdome to prowyde' (19a) corresponds to Bannatyne, no. 101; and 'Grounde the in pacience' (19a) corresponds to Bannatyne, no. 91. This latter also appears twice in a manuscript (Laing 447) containing pieces often attributed, probably erroneously, to Montgomerie.[10] 'Eit thy meit merelie' (12a) is a version of Bannatyne, no. 90. The commonplace books of Richard Hill and Robert Reynes both include variants of this very popular set of 'rhymed precepts in -*ly'*; Whiting gives it proverbial status.[11]   Another quatrain closely corresponds to Chaucer, *Wife of Bath's Prologue*, 655-8, which is treated by Whiting as proverbial:[12]

> Quho so biggeth his hous all of swalowis [*sic*=salowis]
> And pricketh his blind hors ouer the falowis
> And sufferth his wyfe to seik halowis
> Is wordie to be hangit on the galowis.   (22a)

Another piece can be traced back to the fifteenth century at least: this is the epigram on the paradoxes of the Incarnation, 'Belief is ane wonder that man tell can' (22a), that was well-known in both England and Scotland.[13]

The Maxwell manuscript contains many other 'popular rhymes'; some, but not all, of these I have identified. There is space to discuss but one further example:

> In my defence god me defende
> And bring my saull to ane guid ende,
> Out of this warld quhen that I wende
> Sum succour to my saull to sende.   (20a)

Several other versions of this quatrain are known: one occurs on folio 21b of this manuscript; others are found on folio 45a of the Gray manuscript (Adv. MS. 34.7.3) and folios 150a and 177b of a Latin Bible thought to have belonged to St Giles' kirk (Adv. MS. 18.1.2). Yet another is said to be inscribed on the inside of the vellum cover of a book that once belonged to Colin Campbell, third earl of Argyll—Guido delle Colonne's *Historia Troiana* (Strasbourg, 1494):

> In my defens god me defend
> And bring my soull to ane gud end
> In tyme of velth think on our distres
> He that this vret god send him grece.
>   Per me Andrew Mallis [?][14]

No versions of the quatrain are so far known from England.[15] The one fixed element in these verses seems to be the first line, which also occurs independently, sometimes as a motto linked with the royal arms of Scotland;[16] the rest of the quatrain varies both in wording and in metrical shape. Sometimes the same rhyme is preserved throughout; sometimes the verse divides into two couplets. It is not therefore surprising that the first couplet also occurs independently, 'liberally sprinkled on flyleaves, margins and blank sheets' of Scottish manuscripts from the sixteenth to the eighteenth century.[17] The form of the verse may vary slightly—in a way characteristic of popular and oral transmission—yet its function is constant. It is a formula whose recital or inscription may preserve the individual (such as John Maxwell or 'Andrew Mallis') from adversity, a mixture of prayer and good-luck charm. Its literary merit may not be high, but it has great human interest.

Maxwell called himself an 'authour', but it is difficult to be sure precisely which of the many verses he 'pennit' he also composed. I think it most likely that he was himself responsible for the various short pieces with a distinctive metrical shape that he himself called 'rowndales' (5a) and that we today usually term triolets—quatrains characterised by a triple repetition of the initial phrase:

> I die for lwife of sweit Susanna,
> But rest or rwife I die for lowe.
> I wald remowe & ʒit I canna,
> I die for lowe of sweit Susanna. (20b)

This delightful love song—it sounds singable, although not accompanied by music—is followed by another roundel:

> O Sara sueit, the lord mot blis the,
> Wis & discreit, o Sara sweit,
> Eit thow thy meit and I sall kis the,
> O Sara sweit, the lord mot blis the. (20b)

One wonders if this was addressed to a child.

Dunbar seems the first Scottish poet to have used this form, in *The Dregy*, and Montgomerie also employs it effectively in the first round of his *Flyting* with Polwart: 'Polwart, ʒe peip like a mouse amongst thornes'.[18] Polwart, using the same term as Maxwell, disparages Montgomerie's verse as 'ragged roundels'. Maxwell also uses the form for invective:

> Lytill foull aipe, quhy sayis thow sa?
> Iis brek thy skaipe, lytill foull aipe,   [scalp]
> Thowis nebbit lyk ane quhaipe & schankit lyk a ka,   [curlew]
> Lytill foull aipe, quhy sayis thow sa? (20a)

Elsewhere he seems to voice the sarcastic complaint of someone who has been robbed of his sword and cloak:

> I had ane sword & a clewk first quhen I come in,
> With ʒowr leif honest foik, I had a sword & a clewk,
> & now I stand lyk a goik & deill afurth can win,
> I had a sword & a clewk first quhen I come in. (6a)

Maxwell seems to have found the form congenial—Anderson lists 38 instances in the manuscript (p.6)—and puts it to a variety of uses, chiefly light, humorous or satirical. He explicitly says that he devised 'Thir rowndales schoirte' for his own 'spoirte'—'Me to comforte quhen I was fainte' (5a). In another snatch of verse he speaks of writing, in order 'to exerce my awin ingyne' (23b).

The notion of sport and 'play' is certainly strong in the following:

> Schiris we ar cum heir, the trewth for to tell,
> Na man for to deir, schiris we ar cum heir,
> Nor ʒit for to weir ocht amang our sell,
> Schiris we ar cum heir, the trewth for to tell.
>
> Send it is for play that we ar cum heir,
> Guid schiris I ʒow pray, send it is for play,
> Let na man affray, as it war for weir,
> Send it is for play that we ar cum heir.
>
> Schiris, play all fair, for that is best,
> Nocht ower sair, schiris, play all fair,
> Ilk man his skair, & syne tak rest,
> Schiris, play all fair, for that is best. (5b)

This is ritualised 'play', and the tone is communal and public. It would be interesting to know the occasion for which these verses were written; Motherwell said that they sounded 'very like some rymes that are sung by children in their games' (p.382).

The Maxwell manuscript has interest for historians of the Scots language, but its evidence needs to be treated with circumspection. The proverbs extracted from Pettie and Lyly preserve the inflections and vocabulary of their source; the spelling alone is given a light Scottish dress. The 'Inglis' rendering of the other group of proverbs is full of 'inkhorn' terms—'amicitie' (17b) or 'ignominie' (18a)—which derive from their Latin source.   At the other extreme, linguistically, are the 'rowndales': these, despite their ingenious metrical patterning, seem closest to the Scots vernacular. The flyting, 'Lytill foull aipe', for instance, preserves the Scots pronunciation of *sa* in its rhyme with *ka*; it also employs the distinctive 'cuttit' form, *Iis*, rather than *I sall*, that James VI recommended for flyting.[19] Perhaps one of the most interesting items, linguistically, occurs in another snatch of verse:

> Gwide schiris, I ʒow praa,
> Tak dewchane dorus or ʒe gaa. (5a)

Dewchane dorus represents Gaelic *deoch an dorus*, 'drink at the door', or 'stirrup cup'. The phrase is familiar in later Scots usage, but it is not recorded in

DOST. This occurrence in the Maxwell manuscript seems to anticipate those recorded in dictionaries, such as *The Scottish National Dictionary* and *The Concise Scots Dictionary*, by at least a century.

This brief study of John Maxwell and his manuscript is designed to be introductory rather than definitive. It must be conceded that the manuscript contains no long-lost poetic masterpieces; we may also regret that it included no ballads or indeed any narrative poems. Bannatyne's anthology is far more wide-ranging. Maxwell's taste was primarily for short pieces of writing. As a poet he seems to have made a speciality of writing roundels; and as a collector he selected proverbs, axioms, and short poems on a variety of topics. The manuscript reveals some interesting contrasts in Maxwell's reading: Terence, Pettie and Lyly jostle with Rolland and Montgomerie; Latin with English and Scots; recently printed books with poems that had been in popular circulation for a couple of centuries. The manuscript has thus importance of a wide cultural kind, as Motherwell recognised. It would be far-fetched to depict Maxwell as a sixteenth-century forerunner of the Opies; yet he was interested not only in some of the most modish books of his time but also in 'traditionally preserved' rhymes and fragments of verse. To sophisticated readers many of the latter may appear trite, or 'foolish and trivial', yet they provide fascinating clues to the everyday beliefs, values, and preoccupations not only of Maxwell but of many other people living in late sixteenth-century Scotland.[20]

NOTES

1   See *Songs, Carols and Other Miscellaneous Poems from Balliol MS 354*, ed. Roman Dyboski, EETS Extra Series 101 (London, 1907); and *The Commonplace Book of Robert Reynes of Acle*, ed. Cameron Louis, Garland Medieval Texts, No. 1 (New York and London, 1980).

2   References to Anderson are to his edition, available in the *DOST* office; my citations from the text are taken from the manuscript. The foliation is modern.

3   Anderson quotes in full this and another sonnet by A.S. (from Laing III.454) in an Appendix to his Introduction. See also *The Works of Sir William Mure of Rowallan*, ed. W. Tough, Scottish Text Society, First Ser. 42 (Edinburgh and London, 1898), p.xi.

4   See *The Bannatyne Miscellany II*, ed. D. Laing, Bannatyne Club (Edinburgh, 1836), pp.200, 210 and 214.

5   For further information about early Scottish proverb-collections, see B.J. Whiting, 'Proverbs and Proverbial Collections from Scottish Writings before 1600', *Medieval Studies*, XI (1949), especially 123-5; and Coleman

O. Parsons, 'Scottish Proverb Books', *Studies in Scottish Literature*, VIII, No. 3 (1971), 194-205.

6   *The Works of John Lyly*, ed. R.W. Bond (Oxford, 1902), I, 195-6.

7   See 'John Maxwell's *Sum Reasownes and Prowerbes*', *Modern Language Notes*, LXIII (1948), 534-6.

8   *Paisley Magazine*, I, 381.

9   For poems from the Bannatyne Manuscript I employ the numbering used in the Scolar Press facsimile, edited with an Introduction by Denton Fox and William A. Ringler (1980). The manuscript of the *Tracteit* has been inserted within a print of Kennedy's *Compendius Tractiue*; it is on deposit at the National Library of Scotland (T.D. 313).

10   I owe this information to Anderson's note on the poem.

11   For fuller information, see Carleton Brown and Rossell Hope Robbins, *The Index of Middle English Verse* (New York, 1943) [*IMEV*], no. 3087; B.J. and H.W. Whiting, *Proverbs, Sentences and Proverbial Phrases from English Writings mainly before 1500* (Cambridge, Mass., 1968), G 259; and Cameron Louis, *Commonplace Book of Robert Reynes*, pp.392-6.

12   *Proverbs*, H 618.

13   See further, Bawcutt, 'Dunbar and an Epigram', *Scottish Literary Journal*, XIII, No. 2 (1986), 16-19.

14   On the *Historia Troiana*, see J. Durkan and A. Ross, *Early Scottish Libraries* (Glasgow, 1961), p.136; the book's present location is unknown, but the quatrain is printed in A. Rosenthal, *Catalogue V* (Oxford, 1944), p.11. I owe this information to Denton Fox.

15   *IMEV*, no. 1509, has only Scottish examples.

16   See Bawcutt, 'Dunbar's Use of the Symbolic Lion and Thistle', *Cosmos*, II (1986), 90-91.

17   My quotation comes from a private communication by Marion Stewart of Dumfries Archive Centre.

18   *The Poems of Alexander Montgomerie*, ed. James Cranstoun, 3 vols, STS First Ser. 9, 10, 11 (Edinburgh and London, 1886-7), I, 59-60.

19   *Reulis and Cautelis*, published in *Poems of King James VI*, ed. J. Craigie, 2 vols, STS, Third Ser. 22, 26 (Edinburgh and London, 1955-8), I, 75-6.

20   I am very grateful to Dr John Durkan for making me aware of this manuscript.

9

The People Below:
Dougal Graham's Chapbooks as a Mirror of the
Lower Classes in Eighteenth Century Scotland

Alexander Fenton

Dougal Graham, the most popular chapbook writer in Scotland, was both a literary pedlar and for a time the 'skellat' (handbell) bellman of Glasgow. He was, therefore, well used to public performance both *viva voce* and on paper. What is known of him is summed up, and on occasion speculatively filled out, in George MacGregor's two volume edition of Graham's collected writings.[1] The data for the following notes come from this edition.

Graham was probably born near Raploch in Stirlingshire about 1724, as the son of a Scottish Highlandman and a Yorkshire wench—if we are to believe his *History of John Cheap the Chapman*, which is thought to be autobiographical. In early life he was a servant to a farmer near Campsie, but having a deformed body and possibly lacking strength for heavy work, he soon became a chapman.

Like all good chapmen, he had a taste for the novel and unconventional, and a sense of the dramatic occasion whether in personal life or in national politics, allied with an ability to present these graphically to avid audiences. The '45 Rebellion gave Graham an outstanding opportunity. Aged about 21, he joined the Young Chevalier's army on 13 September 1745 and followed the seven month long campaign, claiming to have been an eye witness of the events from the Ford of Frew to Culloden, including the march to Derby and the retreat upon Inverness. He told the story of these events in a lengthy rhyming chronicle, the *History of the Rebellion*, first published in Glasgow five months after Culloden in September 1746.

Graham thus became a poet of passing events. He moved from Stirling to Glasgow, and is said to have become a printer of broadsides and chapbook ballads. He certainly ran some kind of small business, since the second edition of the *History* in 1752 calls him 'Dougal Graham, merchant'. Only oral tradition marks his holding of the post of town crier, for the Glasgow Burgh Records nowhere record payments to him for this service. Of course a news- and publicity-conscious chapman might well have run his own service at times, for publicising, *inter alia,* his own wares.

His appearance may be judged from a woodcut in the third edition, 1774, of the *History of the Rebellion.* Strang, in his book on *Glasgow and its Clubs,* described him on the basis of this illustration:

> fancy a little man scarcely five feet in height with a Punch-like nose, with a hump on his back, a protuberance on his breast, and a halt in his gait, donned in a long scarlet coat nearly reaching the ground, blue breeches, white stockings, shoes with large buckles, and a cocked hat perched on his head ....[2]

He is said to have died on 20 July 1779, at the age of 55 or 56.

So much for the man, whose story and description already point to the place and time and social milieu in which he lived. Including the *History,* MacGregor ascribes nearly twenty works to Graham in this two volume edition. Most of the chapbooks were printed by J & M Robertson in the Saltmarket in Glasgow, though widespread and repeated printing also took place elsewhere. It may be that not all the works presented were entirely or even partly by Graham—it is indeed in the nature of chapbook literature to borrow, adapt, recycle, add and exclude as occasion demands—but authentication of authorship is irrelevant for the purposes of this paper, which are to consider the accuracy of representation of the ways of life of the lower layers of society during the second half of the eighteenth century.

In this context, statements have been made by a number of writers, some of them relating to the communicative qualities of chapbook material, and some to its reflection of the manners of the times. A publisher, George Caldwell of Paisley, said of Graham:

> A' his works took weel, they were level to the meanest capacity, and had plenty o' coarse jokes to season them.[3]

Motherwell wrote in 1829, at a time not too remote from Graham's period, that:

> To his rich vein of gross comic humour, laughable and vulgar description, great shrewdness of observation, and strong, though immeasurably coarse sense, every one of us, after getting out of toy books and fairy tales, has owed much. In truth, it is no exaggeration when we state, that he who desires to acquire a thorough knowledge of low Scottish life, vulgar manners, national characteristics, and popular jokes, must devote his days and nights to the study of John Cheap the Chapman—Leper the Taylor— Paddy from Cork—the whole proceedings of Jockie and Maggie's Court- ship—Janet Clinker's Orations—Simple John, &c, all productions of Dougald's fertile brain, and his unwearied application to the cultivation of

vulgar literature.   To refined taste Dougald had no pretensions.   His indelicacy is notorious—his coarseness an abomination—but they are characteristic of the class for whom he wrote.   He is thoroughly involved with the national humours and peculiarities of his countrymen of the humblest classes, and his pictures of their manners, modes of thinking and conversation, are always sketched with a strong and faithful pencil.   Indeed, the uncommon popularity the chapbooks above noted have acquired, entitles them, in many a point of view, to the regard of the moralist, and the literary historian.   We meet with them on every stall, and in every cottage. They are essentially the Library of Entertaining Knowledge to our peasantry, and have maintained their ground in the affections of the people, notwithstanding the attempt of religious, political or learned associations, to displace them, by substituting more elegant and wholesome literature in their stead.[4]

In this last sentence, we see the beginning of the moral pressures of Victorian times that led to the bowdlerising and cutting down of nineteenth century editions of chapbooks (and no doubt, as a result, to their fading popularity by the 1830s), but no writer casts any doubt on their authenticity as a mirror of society.   John Frazer, in his *Humorous Chap-Books of Scotland* (1873), went even further than Motherwell.   He noted that Graham had an advantage over the ordinary historian, in that:

the latter from his superior height and position seldom condescended to enter the huts of the poor, and when he did enter, the inmates were frightened into their 'Sunday clothes and manners' by his stately and majestic appearance.   But Dougal, being himself one of the poorest, introduces us into the most secret, domestic, and every-day life and thoughts of the lower classes of last century.   Nothing is hidden from him.   He is treated with a familiarity which shows that his hosts have no wish to hide anything.   Then, too, he made his reader familiar not only with their mode of life, but with the peculiarities of their dialect, and in this way shed a not infrequent light on philology.... Nor are his sketches wanting in dramatic power.   The characters are full of individuality and life, rendered more significant by a local flavour of demeanour and dialect.[5]

MacGregor himself, the Editor of the Collected Writings, also expressed the view that nowhere else was such a view to be found of the common people of the period; and that, in addition, the value of the chapbooks as affording illustrations of the folklore of Scotland was hard to overestimate.[6]

The only recent literary historian to have touched on Graham is David Craig. With his usual sharp sense of observation, he speaks of the overwhelmingly English nature of the prose of the period he is discussing (1680-1830), except for the chapbook prose, the 'vernacular of the still broad-spoken lower classes.' He sees the chapbook dialogue as:

> straight off speech, no printed standard intervening, and is thus a close transcript of contemporary spoken usage.... The dialogue...keeps close to a peasant speech whose rhythms, tones, forms, and vocabulary make up a medium quite distinct in character or whole physical entity from Standard English.[7]

To these points, syntax could be added.

There is, therefore, a strong body of agreement on the Bellman's faithfulness—within the limits dictated by the heightening or exaggeration of any form of popular dramatic presentation—to the manners and speech of his time. This now falls to be tested, especially in relation to the material culture of the times. There are other aspects previous writers have not mentioned directly that could be treated with profit also, especially forms of community life and personal attitudes, but these must wait for another occasion. Even as regards material culture, only a selection of points can be made here.

HOMES.   An engineer who fired a train of powder to blow up St Ninian's church in Stirling was himself blown up, landing first on the roof of a thatched house and sliding from there to a midden-head:

> He first fell on a thatched house,
> Next on a midden, with a *souse*. (I, 143)

This thatched house in the town, even if a midden lay adjacent to it—as was normal—was certainly more elegant than the seasonally-used fisherman's hut in the Western Isles (the isle of 'Euirn') where the Prince had to hide:

> An old hut, like a swine's stye
> Which fishers us'd to occupy:
> They had no bed but heathry feal,
> The hut's roof cover'd with the sail (I, 175)

—or a cottage in Benbecula, possibly with a fire in the middle of the floor, and with a door so low that entry was by crawling:

> On feet and hands they *crawled* in,
> Sowre was the smoke their eyes to blin':
> Then Edward Burke digg'd down the door
> And made the entry somewhat more. (I, 176)

Thatching was so general in the Highland areas, as in the countryside everywhere and to a great extent in towns, that jokes could be made when John Highlandman was faced with blue-slated houses in Glasgow:

> For a' the houses that be tere
> Was theekit wi' blue stane,
> And a stane ladder to gang up,
> No fa' to break her banes.   (I, 257)

The stone forestair was obviously also a matter of wonder.

Jockey and Maggie's Courtship shows how a farmhouse could be extended when a son married. When Jockey married, his mother was to 'big a twa bey to her ain gavel to be a dwelling house to me and my wife', and he was to get 'the wee byre at the end o' the row' to hold his cow and two colts, as well as half of the barn (II, 12). The two bays of the house extension probably indicate a room whose roof was supported by a pair of cruck frames. Horses and cattle apparently shared the byre. In the existing house, there was a clay 'hallen', an inner partition wall, no doubt of uprights linked by clayed wattle-work, above which was a 'hen-bauk' or beam on which the hens roosted. These were knocked down during the celebrations of Jockey's wedding night (II, 16).

In the Glasgow area, Leper the Taylor visited a house where cows and people lived in one apartment. This may have been a long-house or byre-dwelling, but whether or not here, such sharing was a widespread practice that lasted well beyond the period of Dougal Graham. John Falkirk tells a story that indicates a similar situation. A lass was got with child in a byre, by the cow's stake. The elder investigating this sin on behalf of the Kirk Session asked how far it was between the byre and the house. She answered, 'just butt and ben, up and down twa steps of a stone stair' (II, 160). Here too, the one roof-tree seems to cover byre and living space. The practice of using upright stakes in byres for tethering the cattle (without partitions between the beasts), also appears in *Jockey and Maggie's Courtship*, where Jockey's mother was unable to hold her cow, 'meikle Riggy', up to her own stake to tie her (II, 9), and has survived in parts of Scotland, for example, Peeblesshire and West Lothian, into our days.

SLEEPING.   Sleeping accommodation is a matter of some interest. It was to a great extent more casual than now, with beds being made up on the kitchen floor or in an outhouse, at least for visitors, as need arose. As noted above, the fleeing Chevalier slept on heathery sods in a Hebridean fishermen's hut. In *Jockey and Maggie's Courtship*, we learn that Jockey slept in the byre-bed with the herd boy, and his mother's servant lass 'in the little lang sadle at the hallen end', that is, on the long wooden settle by the partition wall (II, 28), this being a characteristic item of furniture that served for sitting by day and sleeping by night.

When John Cheap the Chapman was on his rounds near Old Kilpatrick, he sought lodging at a farm. The goodman told him:

> Indeed lad, we hae nae beds but three, my wife and I, and our sells twa, and the twa bits a little anes, Willy and Jenny lies in ane, the twa lads our twa servant men Willie Black and Tam, lies in anither, and auld Mags my mither, and the lass Jean Tirram lies the gither, and that fills them a' (II, 91).

In this way eight people shared three beds. At another farm south of Dalkeith, John Cheap was given a shake-down on the floor beyond the fire. In the same room, there were three women sharing a bed (II, 100). Lying 'heeds an' thraws' was clearly a common custom (II, 15).

There seem to have been box-beds or press-beds at the time also, for at a farm near Glasgow, Leper the Taylor stole a piece of meat laid on a shelf within the bed of the farmer's wife (II, 112).

SANITATION.   Sanitation is an associated factor.   At the social levels under discussion, even chamber pots were luxuries. What were the other options? It was certainly the habit of both men and women to go out last thing at night (if they did not use the byre), which no doubt explains why it was better to wait till daylight before moving about, 'whan well (we'll) ken a turd by a stane' (II, 31). When John Cheap visited a farm at Old Kilpatrick, he observed the goodwife coming out in the dark to sit against a stone at the end of the house to make water (II, 90).   In the fishing village of Buckhaven, men eased themselves amongst the kail in the kailyard (II, 224). And the three women in the one bed in the farm-kitchen south of Dalkeith simply made use of the ash-pit beneath the coal-burning grate (II, 100). This kind of point is not generally touched on in polite literature, but it is a solution to a problem, and leads us to remember that ash-pits were not uncommon in kitchen-floors, both with grates in hearths set against a wall, and with central hearths.[8] Pits in floors go back to prehistoric times.

GOODS AND GEAR.   The domestic picture is completed by references to a range of furnishings, utensils, equipment, produce and stock. A great amount of information could be extracted. It will be enough for the moment, however, to take some grouped samples. When Jockey was courting Maggie, he listed for her the goods his father had left him:

> fifty merks, two sacks, two pair of sunks (straw pads for horses' backs), the hens, an the gawn gear was to be divided between me and my mither, and if she died first, a' her gear was to come amang mine...she is to gie me Brucky an the black mare, the haf o' the cogs, three spoons, four pair o' blankets an a can'as....

Maggie in turn recited what her father was to provide as a dowry on her wedding night:

forty pund Scots,...a lade of meal, a furlet of groats, auld Crummie is mine since she was a cauf, and now she has a stirk will tak the bill e'er beltan yet, I hae two stane o' good lint, and three pocfu's o' tow a good cauf bed, two bousters and three cods, with three pair o' blankets, an' a covering; forby twa pair to spin, but my mither wadna gie me crish to them, an ye ken the butter is dear now (II, 12).

On the male side, there was an outdoor emphasis; on the female, it was indoor, with food and covering playing a leading role.

TEXTILES.   Spinning equipment for both flax and wool is often mentioned. As Maggie indicated, butter ('crish', grease) was used on the fibre in spinning. A round heckle was kept in a kist in the house of Jockey's mother, and a 'rippling kame' was used to help prop up the broken marriage bed; both of these are for cleaning fibres and laying them straight prior to spinning, some of which was done on 'rocks' (distaffs), as an evening job for lasses 'that rins between towns (that is, farmtowns), at een', spreading tittle-tattle. In the *Haverel Wives,* the dialogue is conducted by two old women at their distaffs. Spun yarn was wound on a four-cornered 'yarn winnle' (II, 12, 16, 17, 19, 26, 133).   At Slamannan, John Cheap was in a farm kitchen where the 'Jennies' gathered with their spinning wheels, and indeed the ability to card and spin, like milking kye, mucking byres and keeping cows from the corn-rigs (II, 148) were amongst the desirable attributes of a good country wife.

The preparation and spinning of wool was very much a domestic craft carried on by women.   The next stage, weaving, usually moved into the male domain as a more professionally conducted craft.   Simple John was a coarse country weaver, who made 'nothing but such as canvas caff-beds, corn and coal-sacks, druggit and harn was the finest webs he could lay his fingers to'.   As a sack-weaver, he had a loom and a pirn-wheel for winding yarn on to bobbins.   When his father-in-law furnished a house for him, he set it up with 'the bed, loom, heddles, treadles, thrums, reeds and pirn-wheel' (II, 207-8, 211).   Though John's was not high-class work, it was essential, for there was a great and continuing need for covers for chaff beds and even more for sacks as containers for corn. Some sacks were of value enough to be included in the inventories for dowries and testaments, marking a real community need.

Some textiles, like coloured napkins and garters, were got from chapmen, along with bone combs (with close-set teeth to cope with lice), thimbles, needles, leather-laces and other small accessories.   Tailors were also well known. John Cheap did business with a tailor:

The next house I came into, there was a very little taylor, sitting on a table like a t-d on a truncher, with his legs plet over other, made me imagine he was a sucking three footed taylor. (II, 106)

'Leper the Taylor', brought up near Glasgow, has a chapbook to himself. As an apprentice, he had to endure a static learning time, but as a journeyman and eventually master tailor, he was free to move around, staying in various houses where the goodman wanted to have a suit made, getting board and lodgings and a small sum of money, and gathering and dispensing news as a special bonus. Dressmakers to serve the women's needs would come on the same principle.

FOOD.   A subject of major importance in the chapbooks is food. Both everyday and festival foods are touched on, and a reasonable picture of the eating patterns of the period can be put together. In the *History of the Rebellion*, Charles had to live off the country. Travelling north of the Forth, he found that though sheep and cattle had been driven away, eatables to be found on the farms were 'milk and butter, kirns and cheese'. At Bannockburn, he got 'bread and ale', 'brose and kail'. The English view of the Scottish soldiers was that:

> they can feed
> On drinking water and eating bread:
>
> ...
>
> Beef or pudding they never mind:
> Them Scots can live on *snuffing wind*. (I, 93, 95, 107)

A potato-bed and potato-field are mentioned in relation to the Stirling area, in terms that imply the lazy-bed form of planting, with alternating beds and trenches (I, 137-8), which is likely enough in 1747. Apart from this, however, the potato is conspicuous by it absence.

When the Prince and his companion put to sea in the Hebrides:

> For store they had four pecks of meal
> A pot they brought for making kail,

and after a storm forced them to land on Benbecula, they lit a fire in an old byre,

> Shot a cow and did her boil,
> And made fine brochan of her oil. (I, 170-1)

On setting off for Orkney on a later occasion, they did rather better:

> For store they got two pecks of meal,
> Brandy, beef, butter and ale. (I, 174)

There was meat on occasion, as in Benbecula, and in Clan Ranald's house, the Prince himself was found roasting a sheep's pluck on a wooden spit. Later, when he came to Lochaber:

> They had kill'd a cow the day before,
> Kept a pudding feast, you may be sure,
> Part of it roast, part of it sodden:
> But here no bread was to be gotten ... (I, 188, 212)

In this rhyming source, cereal- and milk-based products predominate, except where meat was taken on the hoof for food without a by-your-leave, or where a chief was providing hospitality. In the prose texts, meal-based dishes are frequent. In a domestic quarrel, Maggie told Jockey how she gripped her enraged father's hands 'till yence my guidame plotted him wi' the broe that was to make our brose' (II, 9-10). Evidently, brose, made by pouring water or the liquid from boiled kail or turnips into oatmeal, was here a fairly wet mixture. When Jockey's mother was ill, she asked for a 'cogfu' o' milk brose, an' a placks worth o' spice in them', to avoid constipation (II, 38). Sammy, however, in the *Young Coalman's Courtship,* sited near Edinburgh, took thick brose to his breakfast. Through the day he had baps and ale, and when he was able to afford it, 'bought an oven farl and two Dunbar weathers (whitings or haddocks), or a Glasgow magistrate (herring, mainly from Loch Fyne), which fishwives ca's a waslen herrin'. The creel-wife's daughter, who had an eye to Sammy, encouraged him with:

> fat, fat brose out o' the lee side o' her kail pot, there was baith beef and paunches in't, od they smell'd like ony haggies, an' shin'd a' like a gou'd lac'd waistcoat, figs I suppit till I was like to rive o' them, an' had a rift o' them the morn a' day; when I came out, I had a kite like a cow in' ca'f.
>
> (II, 49-50)

Brose, therefore, was eaten in a great variety of forms, not only as a standard food but sometimes also as a medicine. Even the great George Buchanan, when entertaining a bishop, chose to give him a 'great bowl full of milk-brose', with a great ram's horn spoon to sup it. 'Well, says the bishop, and how do you call that scalded meal? says George, we call it Scots brose' (II, 269).

John Cheap found a weaver near the Pentland Hills with a plate of hot 'pottage' on the inner side of the window to cool. On a farm near Falkirk, when the breakfast porridge was ready, the farmer's wife collected about a mutchkin of it for the chapman from the wooden cogs of the others present (II, 104).

In the chapbooks, porridge plays a lesser role. This may simply be an accident of what the chapbooks tell. On the other hand porridge takes longer to prepare as it is boiled in a pot, and requires stirring and attention. The time factor, and above all the need for more equipment, may have made porridge less common at the lowest social levels.

The third in the trio of gruel type dishes is 'sowens' or flummery, made of the flour of meal deposited out of soaked (and sometimes slightly fermented) husks. John Cheap got the job of stirring the pot of sowens one evening over the fire on the Falkirk farm on another visit (II, 104). The housekeeper at a gentleman's house visited by Leper the Taylor had 'supper-sowens' also (II, 117). It was seen as a supper dish; but as often happens with common-place foods in several countries, it was also integrated into the system of festival foods, being prepared as a dish at Yule (II, 31).

Some details of the times of meals come from Leper the Taylor's jocular responses to 'Mess John', who had accused him of being a drunkard:

> I a drunkard! you have not a soberer man in your parish:... In the morning I take a choppin of ale, and a bit of bread, that I call my morning; for breakfast I generally take a herring and a choppin of ale, for I cannot sup brose like my lads; the herring makes me dry, so at eleven hours I take a pint; at dinner another pint; at four afternoon my comrades and I join, sometimes we are a pint and sometimes three choppins; at supper I take a bite of bread and cheese and a pint, and so I go to bed. (II, 123-4)

Leaving aside the liquid content, it is evident that a three-meal system was in operation, besides morning, forenoon and afternoon extras. The system may be accepted as realistic, even if Leper was making the most of things, and the routine was not followed in its fullness by everybody.

Festivals and personal occasions, however, gave opportunities for eating and drinking, as far as possible to excess. What else should an occasion be for, as an island in the everyday sea of little-varying cereal- and milk-based dishes, with kail from the kail-yard as the main legume?

Jockey and Maggie's wedding dinner must have been memorable in this way. In preparation, Jockey's mother killed a dry ewe, three hens and a cock. Five pecks of malt were brewed in the 'meikle kirn', and thickened and sweetened with a pint of treacle. Five pints of whisky were prepared with garlic and spice, 'for raising o' the wind, an the clearing o' their water'.

After the wedding in the kirk, and the homeward procession interrupted by stops for the drinking of healths at every change house, they had the dinner in the house:

> his mother presented to them a piping hot haggies, made of the creish of the black boul horn'd Ewe, boil'd in the meikle bag, mixt with beer meal, onions, spice and mint: this haggis being supt warm. (II, 14).

For the blithe meat, a thanksgiving after the birth of a child, bread and cheese was the usual fare. The bread, in the form of 'three nucket scons', was carried in on the corn riddle, and the cheese was cut in good thick slices (II, 19, 41).

At the New Year, Jockey and his wife and mother had Yule sowens, and there was a great cog of brose for breakfast, made from the cheek of an old cow's head that had hung in the big pot over the fire all night. Added to the brose was 'a chappen o' clean creish like oil, which made a brave sappy breakfast for Jockey and his mither, and Maggie got the cog to scart' (II, 31).

The Haverel Wives also reminisced about Yule and Fastern's E'en (Shrove Tuesday),

> when we got our wames fou o' fat brose, and a sippet Yule sowens till our sarks had been like to rive, and after that a eaten roasted cheese and white pudding well spiced, O bra times for the guts. (II, 136).

Then, as now, Sunday was deemed a day that justified something different from week-days. Leper the Taylor and his master got a little bit of flesh on the Sabbath, the bones being kept and put in the pot to make broth during the week (II, 112).

This paper has concentrated on examining a selected range of aspects of the material culture of the second half of the eighteenth century, in particular the house, its fitments, crafts, textiles and the food people ate every day and on special occasions. The purpose was to test the authenticity of the data presented in the chapbooks. Other aspects of this data—for example, language, the roles of people within the communities, their attitudes to each other, to their social superiors and to the outer world, their beliefs and superstitions—remain to be analysed. It is, of course, necessary to be source critical, for it is in the nature of chapbooks to pick up curious tales and stories from everywhere and adapt them to suit particular scenes. We cannot be sure of the chronology of many of the points made. The Haverel Wives, for instance, appear to be harking back to a pre-Reformation situation, though this does not mean that the chapbook writer or compiler did not add data that was fully contemporary as far as he and his audience were concerned. The general conclusion, however, of the present sampling is that Dougal Graham's material is astonishingly authentic; that it is in itself an important source for social history provided it is properly and carefully interpreted; and that it reflects with great faithfulness the people below, about whom historians have been largely silent until within recent years.

NOTES

1   G. MacGregor, *The Collected Writings of Dougal Graham,* 2 vols (Glasgow, 1883).

2   Quoted in MacGregor, I, 27.

3   Quoted from Motherwell, *Paisley Magazine* (December 1829), in MacGregor, I, 17.

4   Quoted in MacGregor, I, 63-4.

5   Quoted in MacGregor, I, 64-5.

6   MacGregor, I, 67.

7   D. Craig, *Scottish Literature and the Scottish People 1680-1830,* (London, 1961), pp.251-2.

8   See A. Fenton, *The Northern Isles. Orkney and Shetland* (Edinburgh, 1978), pp.196-7 for the Northern Isles.

10

A Ballad of the Battle of Otterburn: Scottish Folksong

Alisoun Gardner-Medwin

The Border between England and Scotland was for centuries a cause of strife, and even after the line of the Border had been agreed between Henry III of England and Alexander I of Scotland in the early fourteenth century the lands either side continued to be disputed territory. The two royal powers attempted to keep peace in the Border counties by appointing Wardens, two or three on each side of the Border, who were supposed to work together, with regular international meetings. The two sovereigns were dependendent, however, upon the powerful noble families of the area to provide the Wardens, and family feuds sometimes prevented peaceful co-operation. In spite of the Wardens, from time to time the Border areas became troubled by raids from one country into the other, especially when there was political unrest in one country which gave the other the chance to cause trouble.

Such was the case in 1388, when the Scots, aware of political instability in England, where Richard II was king, took the opportunity to send two raiding parties over the Border. The larger went to the western marches, while the smaller, under James Douglas, got as far south as Durham, then turned north again, stopped briefly for a skirmish before the gates of Newcastle, and withdrew northward to Otterburn. Here, in August, at Lammastide, 'when the muir-men win their hay', the Scots were attacked by English forces led by Harry Percy, known as Hotspur, and through the moonlit night the English and Scottish forces under Percy and Douglas fought the battle of Otterburn. A steeply sloping field just west of the village, beside the modern road to Carter Bar and Jedburgh, is the traditional site for the battle.

The battle itself was not of great importance politically; it changed nothing in the relationships between the two countries, and fourteen years later the same Harry Percy fought a return match at Homildon Hill on the other main central route across the Border, this time defeating James Douglas's cousin Archibald. One reason why Otterburn became famous was that it was recorded by the contemporary French historian, Froissart,[1] whose work was frequently read and relied upon in the fifteenth and sixteenth centuries, especially after his history was translated into English by Lord Berners[2] in the reign of Henry VIII. A major reason why this battle was long remembered among all classes in both countries was because it was also recorded in song.

As a glance at the great collection, *The English and Scottish Popular Ballads,* by the nineteenth century American scholar, F.J. Child,[3] will confirm, the counties north and south of the Border were some of the richest sources of the ballads. A ballad is a song that tells a story, and among the many stories of the border marches recorded in ballads are many accounts of historical events, among them accounts of the battle of Otterburn. Child found four related ballads which mention a battle between Percy and Douglas, and published them in two groups of two, *The Battle of Otterburn* (Child 161) and *The Hunting of the Cheviot* (Child 162). The latter includes the ballad known popularly as *Chevy Chase* and it is this one which Addison called 'the favourite ballad of the common people of England'.[4] It is also probably this ballad of the four about which Sir Philip Sidney made his famous comment:

> Certainly I must confess my own barbarousness. I never heard the old song of Percy and Douglas that I found not my heart moved more then with a trumpet; and yet it is sung but by some blinde crouder, with no rougher voice then rude stile ....[5]

The ballad which is the subject of this paper is one of these four: Child 161, *The Battle of Otterburn* version C1 and other variants collected from oral tradition in Scotland from the mid-eighteenth century onwards. The relationship between the story as told in the ballad and historical fact, as far as it may be identified, is important, but also important is the emotional effect the song has upon the hearer.

A brief comment about the geographical and historical background is relevant. The Border crosses the country on a diagonal approximately from Berwick-upon-Tweed in the north east to the Solway Firth in the south west. For much of this distance the border follows the top of the Cheviot hills. There are many routes across the Border, even over the Cheviots. The main central route in medieval times followed the Roman Dere Street and the modern road by Carter Bar runs close to this near the village of Otterburn. The traditional site of the battle lies north of the River Rede between the Roman road and the village. The site is now marked by a late eighteenth century monument, which replaced the original 'battle stone'. This, usually a large boulder, was the traditional way of marking a battle ground; examples may be seen beside the route from Coldstream to Wooler, which skirts the eastern edge of the hills. The battles commemorated beside this road are Homildon Hill (1402), Yeavering (1414) and Hedgeley Moor (1464). This route by the eastern edge of the Cheviots opens into the area dominated by the Percy strongholds of Bamburgh, Alnwick and Warkworth, whereas the central route by Otterburn offers several ways to the

Tyne, either down the Rede and North Tyne valleys or across the flat plain to Newcastle. Since there were these four battles worthy of a 'battle stone' it is remarkable that only Otterburn seems to have been remembered in song. (In contrast, Percy's victory at Homildon is mentioned in Shakespeare's *Henry IV, Part II*.) Since Froissart's *Chronicles* end with the coronation of Henry IV in 1400, the question of any relationship between the ballad and the chronicle calls for consideration.

For Jean Froissart, historian of the wars of fourteenth century Europe, and advocate for the chivalric ideal, events of 1388 were contemporary. He had indeed, at an earlier time, travelled in the Borders, and had met James Douglas, then a boy. As a dedicated historian, Froissart sought the truth of what happened at Otterburn, and he quotes evidence from four men who had been at the battle.

Froissart records that in 1388, Douglas and his men formed one of two *chevauchées* which entered England to harry the country. Douglas's party rode south, crossing the Tyne west of Newcastle, and burned villages between the Tyne and Durham. The smoke could be seen from Newcastle, and Percy was sent for to defend that city. On their return northwards, the Scots took part in a skirmish outside Newcastle, where barriers, as was common, had been erected before the gates. Froissart comments on this skirmish:

> There were many proper feats of arms done and achieved: there was fighting hand to hand: among others there fought hand to hand the earl Douglas and sir Henry Percy and by force of arms the earl Douglas won the pennon of sir Henry Percy's, wherewith he was sore displeased.[6]

Percy was especially upset at the loss of the pennon, because it touched his honour, and he openly defied Douglas to carry the pennon out of England. There is a strong contrast between the Scots' behaviour south of Newcastle, where they 'began to make war, to slay people and to bren villages and to do many sore displeasures',[7] and the almost playful comments Froissart attributes to Douglas:

> Well, sir, come this night to my lodging and seek for your pennon: I shall set it before my lodging and see if ye will come to take it away.[8]

Here is in sharp contrast war as experienced by the ordinary people whose homes were burnt, and war between knights, who spoke to each other across national boundaries, and for whom war was a matter of honour, and in which defeat often meant ransom. The fighting outside Newcastle was only a scrimmage *escarmuche*, and what Froissart emphasised were the expert feats of arms, *appertises d'armes*.[9]

Dissuaded from rushing out to attack Douglas that very night, Percy waited inside Newcastle. Douglas withdrew, returning northwards, attacking Ponteland en route, and reaching Otterburn, where he encamped. Douglas stayed there, seeking double honour by attacking Otterburn castle and waiting to allow Percy time to come after the pennon, which he intended to prevent Percy getting. On learning where Douglas was Percy set off for Otterburn without waiting for reinforcements from Durham. There he arrived as the Scots were preparing to rest after spending the day attacking the castle. Although surprised by Percy, the Scots had time to arm, and to follow Douglas's strategy of attacking from behind a rise in the ground. Thus commenced a real battle, *la bataille felle et furieuse*.[10] Douglas, 'young and strong and of great desire to get praise and grace'[11] came forward crying 'Douglas', and Sir Henry Percy cried 'Percy'. He nearly got his pennon back, for the English fought so hard they 'reculed' the Scots, but two Scots knights defended the pennon so valiantly and 'did such feats of arms, that it was greatly to their recommendation and to their heirs' for ever.[12] In the battle Douglas was killed, but his death was not announced. Sir Hugh Montgomery attacked and defeated Henry Percy, and took him prisoner.

> This battle was fierce and cruel till it came to the end of the discomfiture; but when the Scots saw the Englishmen recule and yield themselves, then the Scots were courteous and set them to their ransom, and every man said to his prisoner: 'Sirs, go and unarm you and take your ease; I am your master': and so made their prisoners as good cheer as though they had been brethren, without doing them any damage.[13]

This is indeed chivalrous behaviour between the knights of both nations. It is in stark contrast to the fierceness of the battle which left numbers of young men to be buried beside the church at Elsdon, the next village. However, it is not my purpose here to consider how accurate Froissart's account is, but to point out the emphasis he laid upon chivalric behaviour between knights. Nonetheless it is relevant to consider whether the ballads follow Froissart either in the details of his account, or in this chivalric tone.

Ballads are part of folk literature. They are preserved by being sung, remembered and passed on to younger singers. They are therefore very difficult to use as historical evidence, since they may well not be written down until centuries after the event they are about, and during that time corruptions may occur. In England ballads were occasionally written into manuscripts before 1600, and in the sixteenth and seventeenth centuries a few were printed on broadsides for public sale, whereas in Scotland evidence from before 1700 is scarce, the eighteenth and early nineteenth centuries being the great period of ballad recording.

For the ballad under consideration, *The Battle of Otterburn* (Child 161 B, C), there is inevitably a long gap between the date of the event itself, 1388, and the first copies of the texts.   The earliest hint that we have comes from *The Complaynt of Scotland*, a prose work published in 1549.[14]   This was presented to Mary, Queen of Scots, and contains a list of the titles of pastimes of the shepherds, the common people of Scotland.   Among the song titles are 'the battel of the hayrlau', 'the hunttis of chevet' and 'the perssee & the mongumrye met'.   *The Battle of Harlaw* (Child 163) is a ballad known from North East Scotland, where the battle took place in 1411; the other two titles suggest the two ballads associated with Otterburn.   Since great emphasis is laid upon the single combat between Percy and Montgomery in the ballad under consideration, and indeed the phrase, 'The Percy and Montgomery met' occurs there (Child 161 C30 B9), it seems possible that this ballad was already current by 1549. However, in contrast to the other three ballads associated with Otterburn, which are all known from English manuscript sources before about 1650, the text was first recorded in 1776.   This was Herd's version, B; the fullest text, C, was published in 1833.

THE BATTLE OF OTTERBURN (CHILD 161 C)

1   It fell about the Lammas tide,
        When the muir-men win their hay,
    The doughty Douglas bound him to ride
        Into England, to drive a prey.

2   He chose the Gordons and the Graemes,
        With them the Lindesays, light and gay;
    But the Jardines wald not with him ride,
        And they rue it to this day.

3   And he has burned the dales of Tyne,
        And part of Bambrough shire,
    And three good towers on Reidswire fells,
        He left them all on fire.

4   And he marched up to Newcastle,
        And rode it round about:
    'O wha's the lord of this castle?
        Or wha's the lady o't?'

5   But up spake proud Lord Percy then,
        And O but he spake hie!
    'I am the lord of this castle,
        My wife's the lady gay.'

6   'If thou 'rt the lord of this castle,
        Sae weel it pleases me,
     For, ere I cross the Border fells,
        The tane of us shall die.'

7   He took a lang spear in his hand,
        Shod with the metal free,
     And for to meet the Douglas there
        He rode right furiouslie.

8   But O how pale his lady looked,
        Frae aff the castle-wa,
     When down before the Scottish spear
        She saw proud Percy fa.

9   'Had we twa been upon the green,
        And never an eye to see,
     I wad hae had you, flesh and fell;
        But your sword sall gae wi me.'

10   'But gae ye up to Otterbourne,
        And wait there dayis three,
     And, if I come not ere three dayis end,
        A fause knight ca ye me.'

11   'The Otterbourne's a bonnie burn;
        'T is pleasant there to be;
     But there is nought at Otterbourne
        To feed my men and me.

12   'The deer rins wild on hill and dale,
        The birds fly wild from tree to tree;
     But there is neither bread nor kale
        To fend my men and me.

13   'Yet I will stay at Otterbourne,
        Where you shall welcome be;
     And, if ye come not at three dayis end,
        A fause lord I'll ca thee.'

14   'Thither will I come,' proud Percy said,
        'By the might of Our Ladye;'
     'There will I bide thee,' said the Douglas,
        'My troth I plight to thee.'

15   They lighted high on Otterbourne,
        Upon the bent sae brown;
     They lighted high on Otterbourne,
        And threw their pallions down.

16 And he that had a bonnie boy,
  Sent out his horse to grass;
 And he that had not a bonnie boy,
  His ain servant he was.

17 But up then spake a little page,
  Before the peep of dawn:
 'O waken ye, waken ye, my good lord,
  For Percy's hard at hand.'

18 'Ye lie, ye lie, ye liar loud!
  Sae loud I hear ye lie:
 For Percy had not men yestreen
  To dight my men and me.

19 'But I have dreamed a dreary dream,
  Beyond the Isle of Sky;
 I saw a dead man win a fight,
  And I think that man was I.'

20 He belted on his good braid sword,
  And to the field he ran,
 But he forgot the helmet good,
  That should have kept his brain.

21 When Percy wi the Douglas met,
  I wat he was fu fain;
 They swakked their swords, till sair they swat,
  And the blood ran down like rain.

22 But Percy with his good broad sword,
  That could so sharply wound,
 Has wounded Douglas on the brow,
  Till he fell to the ground.

23 The he calld on his little foot-page,
  And said, 'Run speedilie,
 And fetch my ain dear sister's son,
  Sir Hugh Montgomery.'

24 'My nephew good,' the Douglas said,
  'What recks the death of ane!
 Last night I dreamd a dreary dream,
  And ken the day's thy ain.'

25 'My wound is deep; I fain would sleep;
  Take thou the vanguard of the three,
 And hide me by the braken-bush,
  That grows on yonder lilye lee.'

26   'O bury me by the braken-bush,
          Beneath the blooming brier;
     Let never living mortal ken
          That ere a kindly Scot lies here.'

27   He lifted up that noble lord,
          Wi the saut tear in his ee;
     He hid him in the braken-bush,
          That his merrie men might not see.

28   The moon was clear, the day drew near,
          The spears in flinders flew,
     But mony a gallant Englishman
          Ere day the Scotsmen slew.

29   The Gordons good, in English blood
          They steeped their hose and shoon;
     The Lindsays flew like fire about,
          Till all the fray was done.

30   The Percy and Montgomery met,
          That either of other were fain;
     They swapped swords, and they twa swat,
          And aye the blood ran down between.

31   'Now yield thee, yield thee, Percy,' he said,
          'Or else I vow I'll lay thee low!'
     'To whom must I yield,' quoth Earl Percy,
          'Now that I see it must be so?'

32   'Thou shalt not yield to lord nor loun,
          Nor yet shalt thou yield to me;
     But yield thee to the braken-bush,
          That grows upon yon lilye lee.'

33   'I will not yield to a braken bush,
          Nor yet will I yield to a brier;
     But I would yield to Earl Douglas,
          Or Sir Hugh the Montgomery, if he were here.'

34   As soon as he knew it was Montgomery,
          He struck his sword's point in the gronde;
     The Montgomery was a courteous knight,
          And quickly took him by the honde.

35   This deed was done at Otterbourne,
          About the breaking of the day;
     Earl Douglas was buried at the braken-bush,
          And the Percy led captive away.[15]

This version was published in the second edition of Scott's *Minstrelsy of the Scottish Border* in 1833. Of this ballad Scott said that it was an earlier version he had found thirty years before and that it had been completed by two copies 'obtained from the recitation of old persons residing at the head of Ettrick Forest by which the story is brought out and completed in a manner much more correspondent with the true history'.[16] Since Herd's version has the first three introductory stanzas about Douglas's raid into Northumberland, and then moves in stanza 4 to Douglas's death it is clear that much of the story has been lost. Scott is therefore giving the most complete version available to him from oral tradition of the Borders, Ettrick Forest being at the headwaters of one of the tributaries of the river Tweed.

Since Froissart's account of the battle had been published long before in French, and had been translated into English by Lord Berners during the reign of Henry VIII, the question of whether either of the Otterburn (Child 161) ballads took material from Froissart must be considered. Naturally, there are many similarities. All the accounts agree on the date and time of year.

> It fell about the Lammas tide
> When the muir-men win their hay,
> The doughty Douglas bound him to ride
> Into England, to drive a prey.

Both mention that Douglas burned part of the countryside, but the ballad speaks of parts of Northumberland, including Bambroughshire, which was too far east to be en route between Otterburn and Newcastle but which was open to attack by the Coldstream/Wooler route often taken by invading Scots. Froissart makes it clear that Douglas went swiftly without doing damage until he got south of the Tyne, and then he started burning villages near Durham.[17] Chronicle and ballads agree that the battle took place at night; the ballad is quite clear that the place is Otterburn. (Doubts have been raised by those who study Froissart about the the site of the battle, but to my mind the name he gives the place—Ottebourg—suggests the traditional site.) In Froissart Douglas was killed in the press of battle by an unknown person, while in the ballad Percy kills Douglas in hand to hand fighting, without knowing who he was, and the death of Douglas is concealed. Froissart tells of the burial of Douglas at Melrose, while the ballad says that Douglas was *buried* at the bracken bush. Both ballad and chronicle agree that Percy was captured by Montgomery. Froissart of course has a full account of the causes and events leading up to the battle, as he has also of events afterwards.. The ballad is more selective. For example, Froissart states that both the Percy brothers were captured, while the ballad ignores Ralph Percy altogether, and concentrates on the rivalry between Percy and Douglas, and Percy's own defeat after he had killed Douglas. It is in the heroic tradition of oral literature that Percy and Douglas fought hand to hand. In this Scottish ballad Douglas is the hero; he is called 'doughty Douglas', while

Percy is 'proud lord Percy'. The ballad mentions many Scottish family names, with praise, and the enemy are 'gallant Englishmen', whereas Froissart takes pains to be fair to both sides. This is the difference between the historian's account, inclusive and balanced, and the ballad's, selective and patriotic. This difference in approach, because of the different function, must be borne in mind when one considers whether the ballads can be used as historical evidence.

The capture of the pennon is an important piece of evidence. In the ballad, as in the chronicle, Douglas invades England and fights with Percy before Newcastle gates (stanzas 4-10). Douglas takes Percy's sword away from him. They promise to meet again (stanza 14) and it seems to be understood that this is a return match (stanza 9). None of the versions mention the pennon. I believe that the absence of the pennon episode supports the view of Sir Walter Scott as a genuine ballad collector, for we know that he possessed Froissart both in French and in two English translations, and if he had been in the habit of putting in non-traditional elements he would surely have put in the pennon. But he recorded and printed an incomplete version in 1803, and this much longer one later.

The ballad here may be used, I suggest, as historical evidence of a fairly general kind, to support Froissart in his account of the burning of the villages, because it is clear that burning and harrying is what the invaders always did. Place and time are the same, yet important details are different. Paradoxically, it is the mistakes, such as including Bambroughshire as being burnt and stating that Douglas was buried at the bracken bush, which reinforce the impression that the similarities between ballad and chronicle arise because both are about the same event, rather than because the ballad is derived from the chronicle.

Whatever the ultimate origin of this ballad, by the late eighteenth century it was clearly widespread in the border areas of lowland Scotland from where it was collected several times. It shows many features typical of traditional ballads. There are examples of formulae, set phrases or even whole stanzas, which may appear in several ballads, and there is repetition of the typical ballad type, which carries forward the action by alteration of a single aspect. In stanzas 15 and 16 there is repetition of this kind; stanza 16 is a set piece. Similarly, stanzas 21 and 30 describe the two single combats in nearly identical terms. Apart from the names, the stanzas are interchangeable; this kind of formula may be used in a ballad wherever it is needed, and indeed very similar stanzas appear in the parallel English ballad, Child 161 A, stanzas 50 and 54.

The structure of this ballad is held together by time sequence. The time starts by placing the event within the year, at 'Lammas tide', and then the challenge from Douglas to Percy demands fulfilment at the end of the traditional three days. The battle itself is framed by the single night. It starts as the Scots are settling their horses for the night, and continues through the night, when 'the moon was clear' until 'the day drew near'. The final action happened 'about the breaking of the day'.

The ballad is also held together by ironic comments which foreshadow the end. In stanza 6 Douglas says:

> For, ere I cross the Border fells,
> The tane of us shall die.

Again, in the ballad's most famous stanza, Douglas says:

> I saw a dead man win a fight,
> And I think that man was I.

In the next stanza he forgot his helmet, which gave Percy the chance to wound him on the brow. The dead man does indeed win the fight, by being hidden in the bracken bush, to which Percy is asked to yield.

Stanza 19 is only found in this ballad. The 'dead man' may clearly be taken literally, yet it may also have connotations, as of the walking dead man of Scandinavian and some British folk lore. The idea of second sight, or a premonition of one's own death, is not usual in ballads; possibly there is some influence here from Celtic sources. It may also be related to a traditional statement, as recorded by Hume of Godscroft.[18] Whatever its origins, this stanza is very powerful poetically; it is unique, and it is memorable like the hero's bitter comment in *Johnie Armstrong* (Child 169):

> To seik het water beneth cauld yce,
>   Surely it is a great folie;
> I haif asked grace at a graceless face,
>   But there is nane for my men and me.[19]

Douglas and Percy fight in single combat, as heroes traditionally do, but after the death of Douglas there is a second combat, in which the Scot Sir Hugh Montgomery is victorious. In this last section, the repetition of the phrase 'the braken-bush' echoes and re-echoes, especially when the song is sung, and reminds the audience that it is indeed the dead and hidden Douglas who wins the fight. This construction, based upon anticipation and repetition, is in the best of oral tradition.

Scott's version is supported by others, collected in the same period. One of these, published by Herd in 1776, has a different account of how Douglas was killed:

4   Out then spake a bonny boy,
  That served ane o Earl Douglass kin;
 'Methinks I see an English host,
  A-coming branken us upon.'

5   'If this be true, my little boy,
  And it be troth that thou tells me,
 The brawest *bower* in Otterburn
  This day shall be thy *morning-fee.'*

6   'But if it be false, my little boy,
  But and a lie thou tells me,
 On the highest tree that's in Otterburn
  With my ain hands I'll hing thee high.'

7   The boy's taen out his little *penknife*,
  That hanget low down by his *gare* ,
 And he gaed Earl Douglas a deadlay wound,
  Alack! a deep wound and sare.

This incident is most unlikely; it goes against all other accounts of Douglas's death, which seems to have occurred in the middle of the battle. (But there is a suggestion, in a tradition recorded by Hume of Godscroft and mentioned by Child,[20] that Douglas was killed during the battle by a discontented servant.) Moreover, the words which I have emphasised suggest quite a different situation. In the Scottish ballads generally, a *bower* was the place where the women lived, and a *morning-fee* was a kind of dowry given to a bride on the morning after her wedding. Again a *gare*, originally a strip of land or material, is part of a skirt, as in modern 'six-gored skirt'. In ballads a *penknife* was a gift from a man to a woman, and sometimes was used to avenge betrayal or seduction. A knife is clearly a symbol of sexual import, exemplified in *The Sheath and the Knife* (Child 16) and used by the Nurse in *Romeo and Juliet*. It seems quite out of place to have words with such feminine connotations in a ballad about a battle. I suggest that what has happened here is that in the process of oral transmission, the account of Douglas's death was forgotten, and to fill the gap a singer slipped in some stanzas and formulae about a killing. That these stanzas were felt to be inappropriate may be deduced from the same episode in Sharpe's version.[21]

8   O he hes staid at the Otter burn
  The space of days two or three;
 He sent his page unto his tent-door,
  For to see what ferleys he could see.

9   'O yonder comes yon gallent knight,
  With all bonny banners high;
 It wad do ony living good
  For to see the bonny coulers fly.'

10   'If the tale be true,' Earl Douglass says,
    'The tidings ye have told to me,
  The fairest maid at Otterbum
    Thy bedfellow sure shall she be.

11   'If the tale be false,' Earl Douglass says,
    'The tidings that ye tell to me,
  The highest tree in Otterbum,
    On it high hangëd shall ye be.'

12   Earl Douglass went to his tent-door,
    To see what ferleys he could see;
  His little page came him behind,
    And ran him through the fair body.

Aware of the uncomfortable connotations of *morning-fee, bower* and *gare,* this singer has given a more acceptable compromise, but kept in a feminine element. In these two versions may be seen how folk-singers alter their songs, sometimes by forgetting and putting in whatever comes to hand and sometimes by a thought out change, which nevertheless betrays what went before. Again, paradoxically, this flaw in two versions from tradition supports the view that this ballad was truly traditional in Scotland, that it was not created from a reading of Froissart, and that it records the Scottish view of the events of the battle of Otterbum. Returning to Scott's version, stanzas 17 to 20, we find the little page boy wakening Douglas 'For Percy's hard at hand'. Awakened from his sleep, Douglas then foretells his own death and victory. Curiously, the little page boy spoke 'Before the peep of dawn'. This phrase may betray that the aubade-like stanzas entered the ballad before the dream of foreboding, for it would be more natural for a bride to speak 'before the peep of dawn' than for the page on sentry duty who had seen Percy arriving in the evening, before the night-long battle took place. These varying forms are like a palimpsest in manuscript, but through them we can at least perceive that this ballad had been in oral tradition for a considerable time.

The usefulness of a ballad such as this as historical evidence is not great, for it is too slippery and too uncertain in interpretation. In this ballad the facts have been selected to make Douglas the hero, and as well there is a strongly chivalric tone. Percy yields ceremonially by sticking his sword's point in the ground, and his captor, 'a courteous knight', took him by the hand. This is of a piece with Douglas's actions in taking Percy's sword rather than killing him, and in the formal promises to meet again in three day's time. In this chivalric tone this version is reminiscent of Froissart's work. However, chivalry went in and out of fashion over the centuries. It seems really to have been practised between knights during Froissart's own time, to have faded over the next decades, to have been revived by Henry VIII at the Field of the Cloth of Gold (and perhaps also by Berners' translation of Froissart). Courtesy and chivalry between knights was upheld in the works of Malory, Sidney and Spenser, and was revived again in the romantic period, when Scott's own influence was great. So it is impossible to date the ballad from the chivalric tone.

Finally, since a ballad is a song, one should consider the melody also. Melodies of folksongs are notoriously difficult to keep track of, and various melodies, with various names, have been attached to the four Otterburn ballads, as may be seen in Bronson's *Traditional Tunes*.[22] When this ballad was first collected, melodies were not always taken, but two versions, Scott's of 1833 and Sharpe's, did have tunes with them. Sharpe's tune, according to Bronson, has 'the more archaic and plaintive character' and may be related to the second melody. The melody that appears in Scott's *Minstrelsy* with this ballad has an ancestry that may be traced back to the seventeenth century, but its clearest connection is with the *Lines* of the Marquis of Montrose, famous for his support of Charles II. The same melody appears in Stokoe's *Northumbrian Minstrelsy*[23] with the romantic Jacobite song, *Derwentwater's Farewell*, which of course must first have been written after 1716, and which Stokoe published in 1882. Perhaps, as was suggested to me by my colleague Ian Roberts, the Scottish traditional ballad revived in the eighteenth century and was sung to a melody chosen because it was already associated with the Stuart cause. The narrative takes for hero Douglas, a Scot who was tragically to die, and this nationalist and romantic slant would have been acceptable in some parts of Scotland in the years after the '45.

Whether or not the strongly Scottish interpretation of the events of August 1388 is a true account cannot be decided; what does appear is the national fervour, the artistic creation of a story in song, and, perhaps, some indication of the changes that a folksong undergoes as it is passed down the generations. The only melody I have heard this ballad sung to is not at all like Scott's, yet this ballad still has the power to hold an audience, and that, after all, is its function.

NOTES

1   *Oeuvres de Froissart,* ed. Kervyn de Lettenove, XIII (Brussels, 1871), 214-28.

2   John Bourchier, Lord Berners, *The Chronicles of Froissart*, ed. G.C. Macaulay (London, 1904). All quotations are from this edition.

3   F.J. Child, *The English and Scottish Popular Ballads*, 5 vols (Boston, 1882-98).

4   Joseph Addison, *The Spectator* (1711), No. 74, in *The Spectator*, ed. G. Gregory Smith (London, 1897), I, 264.

5   Sir Philip Sidney, *An Apologie for Poetry,* ed. Geoffrey Shepherd (Manchester, 1973), p.118.

6   Berners, 371.

7   Berners, 370.

8   Berners, 371.

9   Froissart, XIII, 211.

10   Froissart, XIII, 217.

11   Berners, 373.

12   Berners, 373.

13   Berners, 376.

14   *The Complaynt of Scotland*, ed. John Leyden (Edinburgh, 1801), pp.100-101.

15   Child, III, 299-301.

16   Walter Scott, *Minstrelsy of the Scottish Border* (Edinburgh, 1833), p.125 in the 1931 edition by Thomas Henderson.

17   Berners, 370.

18   As commented upon by Child, III, 295.

19   Child, III, stanza 22, 371 (spelling modernised).

20   Child, III, 294.

21   Sharpe's version was published by Child, V, 243-4.

22   Bertrand H. Bronson, *The Traditional Tunes of the Child Ballads*, 4 vols. (Princeton, 1959-72).

23   *Northumbrian Minstrelsy*. ed. J. Collingwood Bruce and John Stokoe (Newcastle upon Tyne, 1882), p.71.

11

'O Phoenix Escossois': James VI as Poet

J. Derrick McClure

In the great pageant of European royalty, King James the Sixth of Scots occupies a place all of his own. Not even the features of Henry VIII or Louis XIV can be more familiar than the oft-portrayed, very Scottish face of James, with its ungracious yet disconcertingly penetrating glower. By the mere fact of dying peacefully in his bed he attained to a distinction rare enough among Scottish kings; and by doing so after a long and on the whole successful reign lasting from his childhood he achieved a status unique in the annals of the House of Stewart. His political achievements, as King of Scots, King of England and an active player on the European scene, are by any standards remarkable; and his success in maintaining order in both his kingdoms, and exercising a powerful influence for peace in Europe, is all the more extraordinary through being achieved in defiance of almost unending criticism directed at—from different quarters and at different times of his life—his religion, his political theories, his nationality, his physique, his recreations, his drinking, his scholarship, his choice of companions, his artistic tastes, his personal hygiene, his sense of humour and much else. An idiosyncratic blend of political acumen and personal eccentricity, such as James displayed, is not so unusual among European monarchs; but James adds to this a truly amazing capacity for provoking diametrically opposite reactions, from his own time to the present, in each of his two kingdoms: Scottish accounts of James VI and English accounts of James I can scarcely be understood as referring to the same man.[1] All these factors make of James perhaps the most fascinating and (with the obvious exception of his mother) certainly the most controversial figure ever to occupy the Scottish throne: for the scholarly attempts at undercutting the heroic stature of Robert Bruce, in the first half of the present century, represent a passing aberration, now happily resolved, rather than part of an enduring debate.

Beyond controversy is the guid conceit which James had of himself; and no doubt his lasting fame would have pleased him greatly. Yet in one respect he has not had the attention which he would certainly have considered his due. As self-appointed head of the Castalian Band he exerted considerable influence on Scottish literature during a short-lived but interesting and distinctive phase, and his leadership has been acknowledged and discussed. But James, besides being an enthusiastic patron of poets, was—or at least tried to be—a poet in his own right. On poetic theory he wrote with sense and shrewdness: his *Schort*

Treatise, derivative though much of it is, is the work of a man who had not only studied but clearly understood the precepts and the practice of earlier poets and scholars. His prescriptions on 'the wordis, sentences, and phrasis necessair for a Poete to vse in his verse' are sound practical advice. More interesting are his observations on metre: his technical terminology is sometimes idiosyncratic and sometimes erroneous (though he can hardly be censured for a mistake as widespread, in the sixteenth century and much later, as the misleading use of *long* and *short* to mean *stressed* and *unstressed*; but a modern reader familiar with metrical theory can see beyond this to the fact that he had come much nearer to grasping the principle of stress-timing and the prosodic structure of English (and Scots) words than many of his contemporaries. His own poetic effusions, too, were widely remarked on in his time, often in terms of high praise.[2]   The complimentary sonnets prefaced to his *Essayes of a Prentise* need not, of course, be taken as the writers' true estimate of James's work: Montgomerie's fulsome eulogy in particular:

> Can goldin *Titan* schyning bright at morne
> For light of Torchis, cast ane greater shaw?
> Can *Thunder* reard the heicher for a horne?
> Craks *Cannons* louder, thoght ane *Cok* sould craw?

admirable though it is as rhetoric, must provoke some scepticism. (One should remember, however, that those poets were not only judiciously flattering their king but kindly encouraging a very young man of unmistakeable promise.) Much more significant is the tribute paid by Du Bartas in the dedicatory introduction to his translation of James's *Lepanto*:

> Hé! fusse-je vrayment, ô Phoenix escossois,
> Ou l'ombre de ton corps, ou l'echo de ta voix,
> Si je n'avoy l'azur, l'or, et l'argent encore
> Dont ton plumage astré brilliantement s'honnore,
> Au moins j'auroy ta forme; et si mon rude vers
> N'exprimoit la douceur de tant d'accords divers,
> Il retiendroit quelque air de tes voix plus qu'humaines,
> Mais, pies, taisez-vous pour ouyr les Camœnes.[3]

Du Bartas, perhaps, had appreciated James's enthusiasm for his own work (the young king, in inviting the French poet to visit his court, had expressed himself as eager to meet Du Bartas as Alexander to meet Diogenes)[4] and been pleased with the royal entertainment he received at Falkland: nonetheless, he was in no way dependent on James's patronage as the Scottish court poets were; and this dignified compliment is surely a genuine expression of regard.

Yet James's personal contribution to Scottish poetry, as distinct from his indirect influence on the development of it at his court, has rarely received the attention of critics: even by the standards of Scottish poets apart from the very greatest, he is a neglected figure.[5]   Assuredly he is no Montgomerie or Drummond, and—unlike his great ancestor James I—nothing can make his achievements in the poetic field seem comparable in magnitude to those in the political; but his poetry is at least of sufficient interest to warrant a serious assessment.

A difficulty in judging the work of a poet who is also a major historical figure with an exceptionally well-documented life story is that of considering his poems as poems and not as outcomes of events in his personal history or evidence regarding his thought or character. The song 'Sen thocht is frie', for example, is discussed by some historians as a revelation of the cunning and secretive cast of mind which James perforce acquired in early adolescence.[6] No doubt it is this; but it is also a very good lyric. The simplicity and clarity of the language (in several cases defying, but to no ill effect, James's later precept against filling a line with monosyllables), the regular but not inflexible metre, and the skilful matching of the clause and sentence structure with the lineation and rhyme scheme—a feature conspicuously lacking in much of James's later work—shows technical aptitude of a respectable order. One is tempted to wonder whether the boy who wrote this song, which not only unites thought and expression in a less contrived manner but has the ring of spontaneity to a far greater extent than many of James's more mature writings, might have developed into a really considerable lyric poet if he had not become so fascinated with reulis and cautelis.

In sharp contrast to this early effort, the *Essayes of a Prentise* are clearly the work of a practitioner who, in his own belief at least, had learned exactly what poetry was and how he was expected to proceed in writing it. The graceful apologia in sonnet form which James appended to the collection makes the entirely just point: these are the works of a mere beginner in the craft, and:

> Then, rather loaue my meaning and my panis,
> Then lak my dull ingyne and blunted branis. (13-14)

James's ambitions as a poet were lofty indeed, at any rate in his youth, but throughout his poetic career his meaning and his pains were very often in excess of his ingyne. The twelve sonnets which open his *Essayes* show this, at times all too clearly. The theme of these poems—a series of prayers to the various gods in turn, for the gift of poetry so inspired that readers will think they see and hear the gods' own works—could only have suggested itself to a man whose imagination was capable of being profoundly stirred by poetry; and his youthful eagerness cannot fail to arouse the sympathy, at the very least, of any reader. And in the last sonnet of the series if nowhere else, his ambitions are stated with real dignity:

> I shall your names eternall euer sing,
> I shall tread downe the grasse on *Parnass* hill
> By making with your names the world to ring....   (7-9)

The couplets in these sonnets are in some cases so weak as to suggest that James did not even realise the necessity to the sonnet form of a decisive conclusion; but this poem ends with firmness:

> Essay me once, and if ye find me swerue,
> Then thinke, I do not graces such deserue.   (13-14)

James knew well what poetry can do: his sonnet sequence is in effect a catalogue of traditional poetic themes (the stories of the gods, the changing seasons, the sea and voyages, heroic tragedy, warfare); and his technical competence is unfailing in the sense that he never writes a grossly unmetrical or cacophonous line.   Nor is the writing without some felicitous touches.   He can use alliteration judiciously, produce onomatopoeic lines such as:

> ...the whiddering *Boreas* bolde,
> With hiddeous hurling, rolling Rocks from hie,   (Sonnet 6, 5-6)

add colour to an address to Neptune by the use of technical terms from seafaring: 'That readars think on leeboard, and on dworce', (Sonnet 7, 3) and make a metrical list of sea creatures whose names (*seahorse, mersvynis, pertrikis*, that is, soles) or another feature ('*Selchs* with oxin ee') suggest the conceit:

> In short, no fowle doth flie, nor beast doth go,
> But thow hast fishes lyke to them and mo.   (Sonnet 8, 13-14)

The classical references, too, are sometimes turned to good effect: the cleverest instance, perhaps, being (from the same sonnet):

> As *Triton* monster with a manly port,
> Who drownd the *Troyan* trumpetour most raire ....   (3-4)

Bathos and vacuity intrude with distressing frequency, no doubt; and even the least practised of poets should not have been reduced to filling up a line with 'seasons dowble twyse' (2:8) (as likewise in the first two lines of a later *Sonnet to Chanceller Maitlane* he made twelve years into '...the space / That Titan six tymes twise his course does end'); making the phrase 'that be / Myle longs' cross a line break (8:9-10); comparing a smooth sea to *alme* for the sake of a rhyme with *calme* (7:14), or ending a sonnet with 'visited by him' (9:14).   Yet as juvenilia, these sonnets show promise, and occasionally more than this.

The sonnet form continued to entice James, and some of his later exercises show considerable improvement in technique and inspiration over this early sequence. Certain easily-recognisable faults he never outgrew: blatant padding of lines, feeble rhyming tags, lines ending bathetically on semantically unimportant words, failure to counterpoint grammar with metre resulting in distortions of word order or ineptly run-on lines, and a general tendency to peg entire poems on ideas or conceits of insufficient weight to sustain them. A sonnet with an arresting opening may lapse into disappointing banality: examples are the third of the *Amatoria* sequence:

> As on the wings of your enchanting fame
> I was transported ou'r the stormie seas (1-2)

and the 'Sonnet painting out the perfect Poet', where after the promising opening line, 'A ripe ingine, a quicke and walkened witt', the task of rendering as poetry a list of poets' qualities defeated James entirely. Sonnets which show a tolerable degree of competence throughout may be marred by a weak conclusion: the 'Sonnet against the could that was in January 1616', after a strongly alliterative lament on the baleful effects of the weather ends:

> Curst bee that loue and may't continue short
> That kills all creaturs *and doth spoile our sport.* (13-14)

The witty 'Sonnet on Sir William Alexanders harshe vearses after the Inglishe fasone' opens effectively with the parody-rhetoric of:

> Hould hould your hand, hould, mercy, mercy, spare
> Those sacred nine that nurst you many a yeare, (1-2)

proceeds to the deliberately jarring prosody of 'Bewray there harsh hard trotting tumbling wayne' (12), and then concludes with the solecism of making the Muses use a mixed metaphor: 'Our songs are fil'd with smoothly flowing fire' (14); and the fine line, 'Although that crooked crawling Vulcan lie' (*Amatoria* 5, 57), leads through a notably lifelike account of the fire spreading through 'the greene and fizzing faggots made of tree', only to fall flat in the hopelessly prosaic last line: 'I houpe Madame it shall not be for noght' (70). His poetic taste failed him much less often than his technique: the crass over-literalism of the second sonnet in the *Amatoria* sequence: 'I frie in flammes'—'my smoaking smarte'—'And all my bloode as in a pann doeth playe'— is a breach of decorum of which he is rarely guilty.

On the occasions when he is able to sustain his verbal technique throughout and match it with a thought or idea of sufficient content, however, James can produce sonnets fully worthy of preservation. The two associated with the *Basilikon Doron*, particularly the verse summary of the argument of the book, can hardly be faulted on any count. The second of the three sonnets 'When the King was surprised by the Earle Bothwell' effectively employs an unusually forceful vocabulary, a skilful weaving of alliteration within and across lines, and a striking anaphora in the last quatrain:

> How long shall Furies on our fortunes feede
> How long shall vice her raigne possesse in rest
> How long shall Harpies our displeasure breede
> And monstrous foules sitt sicker in our nest. (9-12)

The rhetorical catalogue, a frequent device, is turned to expert use in the sonnet which concludes the *Poeticall Exercises*, where the things of the created universe are listed in due order from 'The azur'd vaulte, the crystall circles bright' to 'the bounded roares and fishes of the seas'; and the same theme and method are applied in the second of his poetic tributes to Tycho Brahe, which summarises in imposing language the Christian model of the universe. The names of classical deities appear with monotonous frequency in James's verse and rarely suggest anything but the routine application of a stock poetic device; but the conceit of Minerva, Diana and Venus competing to bestow their favours on his queen results in an inspired and delightful sample of poetic wit (*Amatoria* 3). The attractive sonnet 'On the moneth of May' likewise turns classical allusions to good effect, including the memorable line 'Of sadd Saturnus tirrar of the trees'. Jack has pointed out the indebtedness of this poem to one of Desportes's,[7] but James's adaptation is very free: a much closer translation, resulting in another distinguished sonnet, is his rendering of Saint-Gelais's 'Voyant ces monts de veue assez lointaine' (*Amatoria* 5). His rather touching naturalisation of the poem by the change of 'ces monts' to 'the Cheuiott hills' is far from the most important of his modifications to the original. The French poem opens non-committally with 'Je les compare à mon long desplaisir'; James anticipates the result of the comparison in:

> The Cheuiott hills doe with my state agree
> In euerie point excepting onelie one. (1-2)

He elaborates on 'Haute est leur chef, et haut est mon desir' by introducing a contrast between the height of *cloudes* and that of *skies*, embellishes Saint-Gelais's 'grands vents' with a characteristic onomatopoeia by making them 'hurle with hiddeous beir', and relates the points of comparison in 'Ils sont sans fruict, mon bien n'est qu'aparence' at least somewhat more closely by his use of 'no fruicts...no grace'. And for once the use of a personal pronoun as a rhyme-word in the final couplet does not sound bathetic: in 'That snowe on them, and flames remaines in me', if anything the word-order renders the antithesis more strikingly than in the original 'Qu'en eux la neige, en moy la flamme dure'.

That James should have embarked on a project as ambitious as a translation from Du Bartas, even 'the easiest and shortest of all his difficile, and prolixed Poems', is a further measure of his youthful poetic ambition. Though the French poet has no longer the reputation, in his own country or elsewhere, which he had among his contemporaries, it is easy to recognise the qualities in his work that appealed to James: the devoutly Protestant orientation of his thought, his erudition and firmly intellectual approach, his grandiose choice of subjects. As a fluent speaker and reader of French, too, James would no doubt have been intrigued by Du Bartas's neologisms and linguistic experimentation. But little can be said in praise of James's *Uranie*. The movement of his pentameters is inflexible and plodding compared to the alexandrines of his original, and his use of couplets instead of Du Bartas's *abba* quatrains has a dismally confining effect on the expression of his thought. The translation is close, at times almost literal:

> Exerce incessament et ta langue, et ta plume
> Exerce but cease thy toung and eke thy pen   (108)

> Chacun reuereroit comme oracles vos vers
> Echone your verse for oracles wolde take   (183)

> Qui, sage, le profit auec le plaisir mesle
> Who wysely can with proffit, pleasure ming ....   (280)

The only instances in which he shows any degree of linguistic enterprise are the very rare cases where he simply adopts a word, until then not naturalised into Scots, from the original (such as *macquerel* or *mignarde*), or alters the meaning of *oweryere* (normally in Scots 'left over from last year') to make a calque on *surannée*, rendering *ces fables surannées* as 'those oweryere lyes'. Flashes of inspiration such as the rendering:

> Car il vaut beaucoup mieux n'estre point renommé
> Que se voir renommé pour raison de son vice

as:

> For better it is without renowme to be
> Then be renowmde for vyle iniquitie   (231-2)

—where the terser and blunter Scots considerably increases the force of the statement—are outnumbered by infelicities such as the rhyme of 'Parnass' with 'lyke as', or rhyme-enforced syntactic distortions like 'It that the hevinly court contempling bene' (56).

The fourteeners which James used for his second translation from Du Bartas, *The Furies*, at least move with greater fluency than his pentameters; but to counter this advantage they intensify the tendency to line-padding which constantly bedevils his poetry. 'Puisses-tu quelque jour reprendre ta couronne' becomes 'Mot thou win home thy crowne againe, *The which was reft away'* (Exordium, 43-4); and the exigencies of metre and rhyme compel him to eke out 'From Edens both chas'd ADAMS selfe And seed...' (11-12), rendering 'Bannit des deux Edens Adam et sa semence', with '...for his pretence' (in both versions the line rhymes with 'offence'). More creditable additions to the original are James's augmentations of Du Bartas's lists of mutually attractive and mutually antipathetic beings with examples of his own: this piece of esoteric learning clearly aroused his interest.

An examination of James's translations of Du Bartas suggests, rather oddly, a great opportunity lost through the accidents of spatio-temporal contiguity. Du Bartas is a fascinating and highly individual representative of the exuberant literary and linguistic efflorescence which French, like English but unlike Scots, was enjoying in this period; and his verbal inventiveness—his use of technical terms, onomatopes, new compounds and derivations, Gasconisms—is in principle characteristic of a gifted poet consciously participating in a new and lively movement in his national literature. The finest Scottish poets of the reigns of James III and IV, and of the present century, made enthusiastic and effective use of all these devices. And Du Bartas's fondness for lists and catalogues, the precision and detail of his visual and other sensual images, his combination of factual and scientific knowledge ostentatiously displayed with a pervasive sense of numinous awe and delight, all are features which have a habit of recurring in Scottish poetry. If this French poet had been translated by Douglas, or MacDiarmid, what masterpieces of Scots verse might the sympathy of tastes and talents have produced! But alas, he only got James, who could render his meaning with unimpeachable competence, but whose language is barren compared to that of his model.

Of greater interest are the two original long poems in James's early collections, *Phoenix* and *Lepanto*. The former, if once again the poet's execution does not fully measure up to his intention, certainly is among his most competent works. The difficulty, already mentioned, of assessing James's poems apart from their known origins in events of his life is particularly pressing here, since much of the merit of the poem inheres in the careful allegorical presentation of Esmé Stewart's career in Scotland as the story of James's Phoenix; and the description of the bird's beauty, the emphasis on the cruelty and malice of her attackers, and the pathetic picture of her fleeing vainly for protection to the speaker of the poem, are undoubtedly made more poignant by the historical fact of the boy king's helpless grief and fury at the dismissal of his adored cousin. However, the poem has other commendable features. The carefully-balanced preliminary meditation, with its parallel listing of Fortune's blows and the consolatory reflections for each of them, is well-conceived as an

introduction, though not all readers would find particularly admirable the
sentiment of:

> For death of frends, althought the same (I grant it)
> Can noght returne, yet men are not so rair,
> Bot ye may get the lyke. (17-19)

The narrative flows steadily in unfailingly regular verse—lack of clarity is never
one of James's faults—enlivened by such touches as the account of the
Phoenix's glorious colours and the hyperbole:

> ...whill she did shame
> The Sunne himself, her coulour was so bright,
> Till he abashit beholding such a light. (61-3)

A moral point is effectively underscored by anaphora in:

> Lo, here the fruicts, whilks of *Inuy* dois breid,
> To harme them all, who vertue dois imbrace.
> Lo, here the fruicts, from her whilks dois proceid,
> To harme them all, that be in better cace
> Then others be. (127-31)

And James attains to real eloquence in the four apostrophising stanzas
beginning:

> O deuills of darknes, contraire unto light,
> In *Phœbus* fowle, how could ye get such place,
> Since ye are hated ay be *Phœbus* bright? (225-7)

The cumulative effect of the rhetorical questions and exclamations here is to
produce a passage of unusual power.

A more impressive poem, and one of the few in either of James's early
collections for which a reader does not have to make continuous allowance for
the poet's youth, is *Lepanto*. Prolix it is, and prone as always with James to
unsubtle and bathetic passages; but as a Protestant scholar-poet's narrative
account of one of the great battles of the sixteenth century it is a fine
achievement. The racy fourteeners bear the reader along at an exciting pace; the
story is competently told, incidents being selected, balanced and commented on
with considerable skill; the alternation of narrative passages with other material
(for example, the description of Venice (97-112), the classical 'autumn' passage
(345-56), or the list of artisans and their activities (431-40)) makes for an
interesting variety of tone. James's gift for onomatopoeia is again in evidence:

> Like thunder rearding rumling raue
>   With roares the highest Heauen: (621-2)

his insistence on the *noise* of the battle is indeed one of the most noteworthy features of his description of it. The simple language at times acquires an almost ballad-like quality, as these two examples show:

> With willing mindes they hailde the Tyes,
>   And hoist the flaffing Sayles.... (297-8)

> The foming Seas did bullor vp,
>   The risking Oares did rashe,
> The Soldats peeces for to clenge
>   Did shoures of shotts delashe. (305-8)

There is also evidence of careful structural arrangement. The poem opens with an authorial apostrophe, a scene in Heaven, and a scene in Venice; and concludes with a similar sequence in reverse order, mourning in Venice now giving place to rejoicing and hostile confrontation between Christ and Satan to an angelic chorus of praise. A further Heavenly episode occurs at a pivotal point in the story, before the joining of battle; shortly before it a speech by a Christian commander is quoted, shortly after it a speech by a Turk.   Authorial interventions are placed to mark new phases in the narrative: the short passage concluding the account of the sorrowing city of Venice, the introduction to the lengthy battle sequence with its engagingly honest disclaimer:

> No, no, no man that witnes was
>   Can set it out aright,
> Then how could I by heare-say do,
>   Which none can do by sight:
> But since I rashlie tooke in hand,
>   I must assay it now,
> With hope that this my good intent
>   Ye Readers will allow: (589-96)

and the dramatic interruption of the vigorous passage describing the wholesale slaughter:

> O now I spie a blessed Heauen,
>   Our landing is not farre:
> Lo good victorious tidings comes
>   To end this cruell warre. (769-72)

The fervour of religious partisanship in Scotland and all Europe at this period makes it natural that *Lepanto* should have provoked violent political and religious controversy, but the fact is that James's theological standpoint is stated as clearly as it could possibly be, and is admirably moderate and enlightened. The final *chorus angelorum* contains an extended series of variations on the theme expressed in the lines:

> For since he shewes such grace to them
>   That thinks themselues are just,
> What will he more to them that in
>   His mercies onelie trust? (969-72)

and the line put into the mouth of God:

> All christians serues my Sonne though not
>   Aright in everie thing (79-80)

could hardly be bettered as a concise encapsulation of a wholly respectable moral and religious position. In the present age, when the context of the poem is less likely to arouse strong feelings, the work itself can more easily be appreciated on its own merits; and the verdict must be that James has written a thoroughly good and enjoyable poem.

Another attractive poem in a different vein is *A Complaint of his mistressis absence from Court*. James's ability, on occasion, to write genuinely musical verse is in evidence here: the opening lines with their unusually intricate sound-patternings show a degree of technical expertise to which he rarely attained, and at other points in the poem, too, alliteration and vowel harmony are again skilfully applied:

> Inflam'd with following fortunes fickle baite... (9)

> The Sunne his beames aboundantlie bestowes... (16)

When the image of the sea voyage through sunshine and storm is dropped the quality of the writing flags somewhat; but interest is added to the latter part of the poem by the characteristic Castalian mannerisms: the quasi-correction in 'The like, ô not the like bot like and more' (43), the anaphora with its pointedly contrasting third element in 'Whose comelie beautie...Whose modest mirth...Whose absence...' (47-9), the sequence of similes in:

> The Court as garland lackes the cheefest floure
> The Court a chatton toome that lackes her stone
> The Court is like a volier at this houre
> Whereout of is her sweetest Sirene gone... (50-3)

complemented in the last line of the stanza by the ordered sequence 'Our light, our rose, our gemme, our bird' (56).

A dreame on his Mistris my Ladie Glammis is less felicitous as poetry: the relentless fourteeners, admirably suited for fast-moving narrative, are much less so for a meditative poem of this kind. Yet it is of interest in demonstrating James's propensity for expressing his knowledge in poetic form: the discussion of dreams, the extended account of the properties of the amethyst, and the interpretation of the tablet show at any rate considerable ingenuity in arranging the products of his learning and imagination into verse, and the poem can be read with pleasure as an interesting discourse. Perhaps the most extreme instance in all James's work of a poem written purely to display his knowledge in witty form is *A Satire against Woemen*, where, the title notwithstanding, the anti-feminist matter is restricted to two stanzas, preceded by no fewer than six in which every single line enumerates a characteristic of some living thing. This stichomythic bestiary is a minor literary tour de force.

The possibility has been raised that James might have been a better poet if his gifts had been less circumscribed by his own conception of how poetry should be written. To some extent this is supported by two of the few poems written in the latter part of his reign, the *Elegie written by the King concerning his counsell for Ladies & gentlemen to departe the City of London according to his Majesties Proclamation*, and the *Answere to the Libell called the Comons teares*. These are not 'poetic' in the conscious and prescriptive sense of most of his earlier work: they contain neither classical allusions (except a cleverly-applied reference to Caesar's wife) nor decorative language, and make no parade of learning. They are, however, pointed, forceful and at times witty compositions, expressing the king's argument in forthright fashion.

In the first, James gives free reign to his satirical propensities, employing such weapons as word-play, as in these two examples:

> & to be kept in fashion fine & gay
> care not what ffines your honest husbands pay (3-4)

> Visite the sicke & needy & for playes
> play the good huswifes.... (41-2)

He uses sarcastic overstatement: 'the world hath not a more deboshed place' (20), and understatement:

> your husbands will as kindly you embrace
> without your jewels or your painted face.... (37-8)

And the conclusion is menacingly epigrammatic:

> and ye good men 'tis best ye gette these hence
> least honest Adam pay for Eves offence. (49-50)

James in the second poem falls into his old habit of verbosity; but though the sentiments of the poem can hardly have been gratifying for those at whom it was directed, surely few kings have ever delivered so scathing a dismissal—through the medium of verse—to their critics:

> Kings walke the milkye heavenly way
> but you by bye paths gad astray.
> God and Kings doe pace together,
> but vulgars wander light as feather. (7-10)

There is no sign in this poem of the sad, senile figure that James had, by some accounts, become in the last years of his reign. The king who aimed such shafts as:

> Whereto you must submitt your deeds
> or be puld vp like stinkinge weeds (27-8)

> And to no vse were Counsell Tables
> if State affaires were publique bables (78-9)

was still the man who, in one mood, had written the *Basilikon Doron* with its unique blend of exalted pride in his God-given calling and shrewd common sense in the methods of putting it into practice, and in another had modestly but devastatingly demolished the vaunting even of 'Belouit sandirs maister of oure airt'.

A reading of James's poems and his observations on poetry in Scotland prompts the disconcerting question: to what extent was he aware of the great achievements of his compatriot makars of the earlier Stewart period? That some at least of the poetry and song of pre-Reformation Scotland had survived to contribute its influence to a poet such as Montgomerie has been clearly demonstrated, notably by the recipient of the present volume;[8] but the fact that the works of, say, Henryson or Dunbar were there for James to read does not prove that he had read them. His poetic models, as has always been recognised, were French and Italian rather than Scottish; and the one contribution which he by his actual example made to the subsequent course of poetry in Scotland was the introduction of the Petrarchan sonnet form. The only Scottish poet, other than his contemporaries, whom he mentions by name is David Lyndsay; and in more than one respect his writing suggests a curious ignorance, rather than mere ignoring, of Lyndsay's predecessors. Would the language of his seasonal descriptions have been so tame if he had modelled it on Dunbar or Douglas; would his *Schort Poem of Tyme* have been so banal if he had read Henryson's *The Preiching of the Swallow* or *The Testament of Cresseid*? (The line 'The mous did help the lyon one a day' is hardly evidence that the version of the fable he had in mind was Henryson's.) These questions can evoke nothing but guesses; but a much more definite one also arises: would he have argued with Hudson that Virgil was 'inimitable to vs, whose toung is barbarous and corrupted',[9] or proclaimed 'I lofty *Virgill* shall to life restoir' (Sonnet 12.10, in *Essayes*), if he had been acquainted with the *Eneados*? His reference in a letter to Du Bartas to his 'douleur que ce pais n'a esté si heureusement fertil que d'avoir produict un tel colosse ou arc triomphal'[10] is of course primarily an expression of his enthusiasm for the recipient's work; but would even this have taken the form of a direct denial of the existence of half a dozen Scottish poets of the late fourteenth, fifteenth and earlier sixteenth centuries whose merits are comparable at least to those of Du Bartas if he had been familiar with their works? The sentence in his *Reulis and Cautelis* 'Thairfore, quhat I speik of Poesie now, I speik of it, as being come to mannis age and perfectioun, quhair as then [the meaning of 'then' is not specified] it was bot in the infancie and chyldheid' is taken by Craigie[11] to be a contemptuous dismissal of his Scottish predecessors; but the present writer finds it inconceivable that a man possessing any degree of poetic sensitivity or patriotic pride—and James incontrovertibly had both—would have rejected the superb national poetic achievement from Barbour to—with reservations—Lyndsay *en bloc* if he had been to any serious extent acquainted with it.   That this argument is not purely intuitive is shown by his manifest admiration for Montgomerie, who is in his poetic assumptions and techniques the direct heir of the Makars.

James in his youthful zeal may indeed have seen himself as a poetic revolutionary in Scotland; but that he consciously rejected, on literary grounds, the work of his Scottish predecessors seems to me less likely than another possibility: that he was an early and illustrious victim of the Protestant syndrome memorably exposed and excoriated by Fionn MacColla: the unthinking and uninformed attribution of 'darkness and ignorance' to all periods between classical antiquity and the triumph of Protestantism.[12]   Barbour, James I as poet, Holland, Blind Harry, Henryson, Dunbar, Douglas: all these were representatives of the Christendom which, to James and his government—and, more importantly, to Buchanan and the king's other early mentors—was founded on superstition and idolatry; and therefore their works had probably never been allowed to form any part of James's education.   Lyndsay, because of his vigorous campaigning for reform at least from within the Church, would be the only one of the pre-Reformation poets who was not beyond the pale; but even in his case, James's use of the phrase 'of old' in reference to his work (*Phoenix*, 24)—if it has any importance other than as a rhyme tag—is rather oddly applied to a poet whose death preceded James's birth by less than a dozen years, and suggests that James perceived a gulf between himself and Lyndsay which the chronological gap is hardly sufficient to explain.   It is surely not without significance, too, that James's favourite among his contemporary French poets was a Huguenot.

If the argument of the preceding paragraph is correct, it is a striking instance in support of the theory that the Reformation has had a long-term effect of steadily and cumulatively weakening the Scots' awareness of their national culture and sense of national identity.

James's poetry is of considerable importance to students of his life and reign. No serious reader could regard it simply as evidence for his supposed vanity and pedantry: if those qualities are visible so too are humaneness, piety and, regarding his own poetic skill, an unmistakeably genuine modesty; and it is of course true that displays of learning are commonplace in mediaeval and Renaissance poetry, and that James's being one of the few monarchs to proclaim his Divine Right in print does not mean that the belief itself was his own idiosyncrasy. But his work deserves to be considered as literature too: in a period when the Scottish poetic scene gives, on the whole, the impression of a fair number of good or very good practitioners rather than a few great ones, he is fit to be mentioned in company with the Aytons, Fowlers and Alexanders of his court. James was clever and witty, he had ideas worthy of expression in verse, he had an ear for rhythm and sound-patterning, and his concept of poetry was high and serious. These qualities were not sufficient to make him a great poet or even a consistently good one; but the best work that can be salvaged from his poetic oeuvre show him to have been not only an effective patron, but a not unworthy practising member, of the Castalian Band.

NOTES

1   See Jenny Wormald, 'James VI and I: two kings or one?', *History*, LXVIII (1983), 187-209.

2   The edition of King James's poems used is that prepared for the Scottish Text Society by James Craigie, published as Numbers 22 (1955) and 26 (1958) of the Third Series, hereafter 'Craigie, 1955'. This edition presents different early texts of several of James's poems on facing pages. Since textual questions are not the concern of the present paper, quotations in such cases have been taken from the more standardised version: normally a printed as contrasted with a manuscript text. On the contemporary response to James's own poetry, see Craigie, 1955, 274-80.

3   See *The Works of Guillaume De Salluste Sieur du Bartas*, ed. U.T. Holmes, J.C. Lyons and R.W. Linker, 3 vols (Chapel Hill, 1935-40), III, 506.

4   Ibid., I, 203.

5   But see R.D.S. Jack's discussion and bibliography, 'Poetry under King James VI', in *The History of Scottish Literature. Volume I: Origins to 1660*, ed. R.D.S. Jack (Aberdeen, 1988), 125-40.

6   For example, see Caroline Bingham, *The Making of a King: The Early Years of James VI and I* (London, 1968), p.153, and Antonia Fraser, *King James VI of Scotland, I of England* (London, 1974), p.397.

7   *A Choice of Scottish Verse 1560-1660* (London, Sydney, Auckland and Toronto, 1978), p.173.

8   See Helena Mennie Shire, *Song, Dance and Poetry of the Court of Scotland under King James VI* (Cambridge, 1969).

9   *Thomas Hudson's Historie of Judith*, ed. W.A. Craigie, STS Third Ser. 14 (Edinburgh and London, 1941), 3.

10 Holmes et al., *The Works of du Bartas*, I, 203.

11 Craigie, 1955, xiii.

12 See his *At the Sign of the Clenched Fist* (Edinburgh, 1967), pp.130-2.

Dunbar in Paraphrase

Alasdair A. MacDonald

William Dunbar's modern reputation as one of the greatest poets of medieval Scotland seems so secure that it is strange to think that there was a time when he was well nigh forgotten. Although his contemporary prestige was such that several of his works were printed by Chepman and Myllar, Scotland's first printers, no other works of Dunbar's appeared in print before the *Ever Green* collection of Allan Ramsay[1]—a gap of over two centuries.[2] Only the fabliau, *The Freiris of Berwik,* was reprinted during this period, but that poem is now by general consensus excluded from the canon of Dunbar's works.[3] From the inclusion of poems by Dunbar in manuscript anthologies, however, one may deduce that he continued to be read throughout the sixteenth century and beyond; the latest witness is the Reidpeth MS (CUL MS Moore LL.v.10), dated 1622, which is a transcript from the Maitland Folio MS (Magdalene College Cambridge MS 2553) of c.1570.[4]

Dunbar returned to critical awareness as a result of the antiquarian labours first of Allan Ramsay, then of Lord Hailes and John Pinkerton.[5] In the nineteenth century there was a bifurcation in Dunbar studies, leading in directions either scholarly or popular. In the first category may be placed the editions by David Laing, John Small and Jakob Schipper;[6] in the second one may place the popular edition of James Paterson, which interspersed the poems with prose commentary, the selection by George Eyre-Todd, and the translation by William Mackean.[7] The subject of the following pages—the selection from Dunbar, 'adapted for modern readers', of James Logie Robertson[8]—may also be classed here. Although this work displays many unique features, it shares with the others already noted a patriotic pride in the poetry of the Scottish past, and a desire to spread this awareness among the reading public at large. A discussion of Logie Robertson's book may, therefore, be deemed not inappropriate in a Festschrift to honour Dr Helena Shire, who herself has done so much for the cause of the earlier literature of Scotland.

James Logie Robertson was born at Milnathort, Kinrossshire, on 18 September 1846, and stemmed, it is said, 'from the ranks of the people'.[9] After gaining his M.A. at Edinburgh he had several teaching posts, before his appointment as English master at Edinburgh Ladies College (later the Mary

Erskine School for Girls), where he remained until his retirement, in 1913. In October 1886 he applied—unsuccessfully—for the post of Librarian to the University of Edinburgh.[10] He died on 13 June 1922. From his wife's 'Memoir' of him, and from the writings of others, he emerges as a stimulating and humane teacher, who was regarded with evident respect and affection.[11] Logie Robertson had a prolific career in letters, under three aspects: he prepared editions of the works of Thomson, Burns, Scott, and Campbell; he produced guides to English literature and other works of pedagogical usefulness, not to mention a collection of original stories for children; and he was also a creative writer, publishing numerous essays on aspects of Scottish life and literature, besides collections of verse in both standard English and Scottish dialect.[12] The scholarly and educational works, together with some of the volumes of poetry, were published under his own name, but for the essays and some of the books of verse he employed the *nom de plume* of 'Hugh Haliburton'. *Horace in Homespun* has the distinction of having been published originally under the pseudonym, but later under the author's own name.[13] For reasons which will become apparent, the *Dunbar* is grouped among the original literary works of James Logie Robertson.

This is not the place for a detailed consideration of the total *oeuvre* of Logie Robertson, or for an assessment of his position among the writers of the late Victorian and Edwardian age. His contemporary success, however, and in particular that of the 'Hughie' pastoral poems in *Horace in Homespun*, was undeniable. Since the poet is—from a modern perspective—neither a perfect representative of the much execrated kailyard school nor an obvious harbinger of the modernists, he has received little critical attention. In a recent essay, however, Colin Milton has attempted something of a revaluation:

> But Logie Robertson is less important as a poetic precursor of MacDiarmid than for the part he played in recovering elements of the Scottish literary and cultural tradition which had been long neglected or ignored; he is an important figure in the general reinvigoration of Scottish intellectual life in the late nineteenth and early twentieth centuries which helped to create the conditions in which MacDiarmid's extraordinary achievement was possible.... [H]is championship of Dunbar in the *Scots Observer* and elsewhere did help to change the widely held view that Burns was the only really great poet that Scotland had produced—and if, in deference to the current idolatry of Burns he is fairly guarded in what he says about the relative merits of Dunbar and his eighteenth-century successor in 'Our Earlier Burns' the reader forms the distinct impression that he regards the Medieval Makar as the greater of the two.[14]

While MacDiarmid is famous *inter alia* for the dictum, 'Not Burns—Dunbar',[15] it would seem that in this regard he may actually have been following in the footsteps of his milder-mannered and most unrevolutionary predecessor. Indeed, in a letter to Professor Herbert Grierson of 30 April 1925 MacDiarmid speaks of 'the Scottish succession in which I am fain to have a part—Hugh Haliburton, Charles Murray, and Mrs Violet Jacob and others'.[16]   Logie Robertson's reversion from pseudo-Burnsian pastoral to the older manner of Dunbar precisely anticipates the new literary direction so stridently advocated by MacDiarmid in *Albyn*. It is interesting that after the *Dunbar* of 1895 Logie Robertson had little further to say in verse in the persona of Hugh Haliburton, and in his final collection of poetry, *Petition to the Deil*, he spoke in his own voice in an attempt—not a very successful one, it must be admitted—to come to terms with the challenging theme of the Great War.

Logie Robertson's interest in the tradition of Scottish literature is manifest from his many publications, and he had an almost unbounded admiration for the old ways and the old turns of expression. He was one of the first public figures to urge the establishment of a chair of Scottish literature within Scotland.[17] His earliest effort contained an essay in verse 'On the Decadence of the Scots Language, Manners, and Customs', later reissued (with some retouching) as the 'Lament for the Language'.[18] The final essay in *In Scottish Fields* is the 'Our Earlier Burns', already mentioned; in it Logie Robertson praises Dunbar, and for his illustrative quotations indulges in the creative rewriting which characterises his *Dunbar*.[19] One year later, in *Ochil Idylls*, he included the (standard English) poem, 'To William Dunbar', in which he declared his readiness to kneel at the 'neglected throne' of the earlier poet.[20] However, despite the remarks of Colin Milton quoted above, Logie Robertson was clear in his estimation of the relative merits of Dunbar and Burns. In his *History of English Literature* he wrote: 'The greatest poet of the period [1400-1580], and the greatest that Scotland has ever produced, Burns alone excepted, was William Dunbar...', and concerning Dunbar's *Dance of the Seven Deadly Sins* he comments:

> Its wild imagery, its power of characterisation, and its robust humour, touched with horror and sublimity, challenge comparison with the strongest of the humorous satires of Burns. It is indeed only on the lyrical side of his poetry that Dunbar is inferior to Burns.[21]

Later still, in a Petrarchan sonnet entitled 'Chaucer', the English master— 'Father of English verse!—Of Scottish too!'—Chaucer is favourably contrasted with his poetic heirs: King James I; Gavin Douglas, and Dunbar—'the bold Friar who stole behind the bower'.[22] Within the group of Middle Scots poets, however, the position of Dunbar was supreme.

Logie Robertson's *Dunbar* contains: the poem 'To William Dunbar' as Preface (pp.v-vi); a brief 'Chronological Table illustrative of the life and writings of William Dunbar' (pp.vii-viii); thirty poems (pp.9-109); a Glossary (pp.111-

120). The reader will immediately be struck by the extent to which the titles
given to the poems depart from the familiar wording of other editions:[23]

R		M	K
1	Sorrow on Himsel' (p.11)	2	70
2	The Use of Riches (p.13)	72	67
3	Contentment (p.16)	73	65
4	The True Philosophy of Life (p.19)	69	64
5	Hy-Jinks at Holyrood (p.22)	32	28
6	To the P.D. Demanding Copy (p.26)	3	21
7	The Priest (p.28)	12	40
8	Gnomic Verses (p.30)	41	77
9	This Warld's Vanitee (p.34)	7	62
10	Nothing Sure (p.37)	21	63
11	Prayer before the Sacrament (p.40)	83	6
12	A Meditation in Winter (p.42)	10	69
13	The Vanity O'T (p.45)	71	59
14	Easter Hymn (p.48)	81	4
15	The Makar's Complaint (p.51)	—	—
16	A Song of Rue (p.54)	49	8
17	The Greatest Gain (p.56)	70	66
18	To My Lords of 'Chacker (p.58)	25	46
19	On Change (p.60)	66	58
20	John Tamson's Man (p.62)	18	25
21	Discretion in Asking (p.64)	14	78
22	Change of Party (p.67)	11	41
23	Reign of Covetice (p.69)	67	68
24	The Thistle and the Rose (p.72)	55	50
25	Dunbar's Dream (p.83)	4	51
26	The Twa Cummers (p.87)	46	73
27	The Friars of Berwick (p.89)	93	—
28	Dunbar Flyting (p.103)	6	23
29	A Welcome to the Lord Treasurer (p.105)	24	47
30	To an Editor (p.108)	26	18

From the time of Allan Ramsay onwards, there has been not a little
fluctuation in the titles of Dunbar's poems; nevertheless, Logie Robertson's are
distinctive. Unlike many other editors, he eschews the use of incipits as
substitute titles, although he does give the opening lines of the relevant Dunbar
versions as mottos—this ensures that the original and the recreation will stand
in a quasicontrapuntal relationship to each other. Only two poems (Nos. 11 and
28) from his list have titles in the source texts, and both have been changed
(from 'The Tabill of Confessioun' and 'The Flyting of Dunbar and Kennedie');

this is itself an indication of Logie Robertson's individualistic treatment of the originals.

The titles have still further points of interest. Two of them (Nos. 6 and 30) reflect the new application which the poet—through his persona—has given them; the second of these is even equipped with a colophon in imitation of the early manuscripts: 'Quod Hugh Haliburton, on 31st December 1892'. Again, the 'sacrament' mentioned in No. 11 must have suggested to the poet's Calvinist readers Holy Communion (instead of Penance, as intended by Dunbar), and they might have conceived of the 'Easter Hymn' (No. 14) in the same way as they would the contents of *The Church Hymnary*. 'Hy-Jinks at Holyrood' (No. 5) is fair enough, if a trifle vulgar; here too we see modernising tendencies, since the word *Hy-jinks* is unrecorded before the early eighteenth century, and betrays Logie Robertson's debt to Allan Ramsay.[24]

There is no standard classification of Dunbar's poems according to subject-matter, but it is nonetheless interesting to relate Logie Robertson's selection to the groupings used by the two most recent editors. Mackay Mackenzie uses a nine-part division:[25] Personal 10 (6); Petitions 15 (7); Court Life 16 (3); Town Life 3 (0); Of Women 8 (2); Allegories and Addresses 13 (1); Moralisings 12 (7); Religious 7 (2); Some Attributions 9 (1). Kinsley, on the other hand, uses a five-part scheme: Divine Poems 7 (2); Poems of Love 10 (1); Poems of Court Life 32 (8); Visions and Nightmares 7 (3); Moralities 27 (14). From such lists Logie Robertson's preference for the short, personal, moralising lyric becomes abundantly clear. Gone is much that the modern critic is likely to esteem most highly in Dunbar: the *Tretis, The Goldyn Targe;* the *Dregy;* religious poems such as 'Rorate celi desuper' and 'Hale, sterne superne'; comic and satirical poems such as the 'Fenʒeit Freir' and the *Tesment of Maister Andro Kennedy;* the Bernard Stewart poems. Yet other works are represented in drastic abbreviation: the *Flyting* (three stanzas only); the *Freiris of Berwik*. Of the poems printed, twelve have the same amount of material (in terms of numbers of stanzas) as the originals, three have more, and fifteen have less. In a sense, therefore, Logie Robertson's selection from Dunbar is at least as much a deselection.

The art of paraphrase, as practised here, allows of considerable variation. Some of the versions closely resemble their models, others are similar in a more general way, some rearrange the order of the stanzas, while still others are so different as to amount to quite new poems.[26] Any combination is also possible, and several poems adhere to Dunbar in certain stanzas, only to make bold departures in others. In two poems (Nos. 6 and 30), Dunbar's relationship with his patron, the king, is replaced by Logie Robertson's relationship with his editor and P.D. (that is, Printer's Devil). The following composition, 'The Priest' (No. 7), may serve as an illustration of the later poet's free style of paraphrase, and should be compared with Dunbar's 'Off benefice, Sir, at everie feist' (K 40):

> To pick an' wale was for the priest;
> He aye was foremost at the feast,
>   And to forbid him was to wrang him;
> His crap was as the crap o' beast,
>   And lay-folk only lived to pang him.
>
> He flew at pheasant, flesh, an' fluke;
> He made collusion wi' the cook
>   For a' the choicest bits inside him;
> But, lord! how piteous a' did look
>   When to the haggis he applied him.
>
> So wags this blind auld warld yet,
> That to the greedy grants as debt
>   What never did by richt belang them;
> While he that naething tak's can get
>   Only a waiter's place amang them. (R 7, pp.28-9)

Logie Robertson's poem is an entertaining caricature, but it has little of the satire of Dunbar, whose humour is undergirded by a burning sense of social justice, founded upon the eternal verities of the Four Last Things. On the other hand, Logie Robertson's 'Thistle and the Rose' follows its model reasonably closely, albeit that it has a very different 'feel', as one can appreciate by comparing two versions of the stanza in which the dreaming poet, led by Aurora, enters the beautiful enclosed park, on the ninth of May:

> (a) Quhen this wes said, depairtit scho, this quene,
>   And enterit in a lusty gairding gent;
>   And than me thocht full hestely besene
>   In serk and mantill eftir hir I went
>   In to this garth, most dulce and redolent
>   Off herb and flour and tendir plantis sueit
>   And grene levis doing of dew doun fleit. (K 50, p.142)
>
> (b) She turned and went, and with her all the gleam
>   That such a glory to my chamber lent;
>   At which, methought, for it was still a dream,
>   In sark and mantle after her I went
>   Into a garden, fair and full of scent,
>   With herbs, and plants, and paths for naked feet,
>   Fragrant of breath and fresh with morning's weet. (R 24, pp.74-5)

Logie Robertson's version in this extract (though not throughout the poem) is a thoroughgoing translation: only 'sark' and the final word, 'weet', are recognisably

Scottish.   In the middle of the stanza he has been able to follow Dunbar *verbatim*, but not in most lines.   One can only guess at the reasons for the substitutions: was 'dulce and redolent' too archaic?; was 'tendir plantis sueit' felt to be tautologous, after 'herb and flour'?; was the phrase, 'Quhen this wes said', felt to be an episode marker fit for oral delivery only?; was one entry into the garden sufficient?   However this may be, one may have reservations about some of Logie Robertson's innovations: the bold rewriting in the opening lines surely repeats what has been said in other stanzas; the reminder that 'it was still a dream' is a shade heavy-handed; the 'paths for naked feet' (a pre-Raphaelitish touch?) interrupt a sequence of allusions to the garden scents.   A detailed scrutiny of the entire poem would reveal hundreds of such places, where the advantages of paraphrase are—to say the least— highly debatable.

While it is easy for the critic to carp, it is actually very difficult for a poet to produce a metrical paraphrase that will simultaneously closely follow its model and replace a superannuated with a modern idiom.   The versifications given in the essay 'Our Earlier Burns' (1890) afford a glimpse of the verbal tinkering which eventually resulted in the *Dunbar* of 1895:

> a) Thane had my dyt beine all in duill,
>   Had I my wage wantit quhill 3uill,
>   Quhair now I sing with heart onsair:
>   Welcum, my awin lord thesaurair!   (K 47, p.134)

> b) I had been deep in dumps and dool,
>   Had I wantit my wage till Yule;
>   But noo I sing with heart *un*-sair—
>   Welcome, my ain Lord Treasurér!   (1890, p.235)

> c) Nae doot but I'd been singin' dule
>   To gang without my wage till Yule;
>   Now I can sing, with heart unsair,
>   Welcome, my ain Lord Treasurér!   (1895, p.106)

One observes here Logie Robertson's early attempt—later reversed—to exaggerate the alliteration of the first line, his eventual success in avoiding the necessity of an awkward stress on the second syllable of 'wantit', his final decision to opt for a trochaic foot to provide a little prosodic variety at the beginning of the third line.   The end result, whatever one may think of it, is achieved with considerable craftsmanship, after a lengthy process of experimentation.

One of the interests of Logie Robertson's *Dunbar*, thus, is that it shows a modern poet's attempts to follow in the footsteps of an illustrious medieval predecessor.   Unfortunately for the later writer, he does not have the earlier poet's length of stride.   The Victorian paraphrase is today unlikely, perhaps, to win many new readers to Dunbar, but it nevertheless comprises an important cultural document in the history of the reception of the Middle Scots poet. With all its imperfections—its curious blend of literary piety, *aggiornamento* and *vulgarisation*—the selection still merits a certain attention. Just as the Augustan poets composed imitations of the ancient classics—an example which probably informed Logie Robertson's most popular collection, *Horace in Homespun*—so this scholarly minor poet turned to a classic of early Scottish verse for inspiration. Sadly, there were far too many aspects of Dunbar's work which he could not accommodate: the passionate, catholic christianity; the stock of mediaeval lore; the verbal pyrotechnics. For Logie Robertson it was possible—as it was not for MacDiarmid—to have a combination of Burns *and* Dunbar; that is at once both his strength and his weakness.

Appendix A

Provisional Bibliography of the Writings of James Logie Robertson.

(Note: No attempt has been made to give references to original publications in newspapers and magazines. Some of the books of essays listed under III(b) also contain verse.)

I.   SCHOLARLY WORKS

Allan Ramsay, *Poems* (London, 1887)
The Letters of Robert Burns (London, 1887)
Burns, Selected Poems (Oxford, 1889)
James Thomson, The Seasons and the Castle of Indolence (Oxford, 1891)
The Poetical Works of Sir Walter Scott (London, 1894)
The Complete Poetical Works of Robert Burns (London, 1896)
The Log of the 'Dutillet' (Inverness, 1904)
The Complete Poetical Works of Thomas Campbell (Oxford, 1907)

II.   PEDAGOGICAL WORKS

The White Angel of the Polly Ann and other stories (Edinburgh, 1886)
Tales and sketches by the Earl of Beaconsfield (London, 1891)
Tales by Douglas Jerrold (London, 1891)
A History of English Literature for secondary schools (Edinburgh, 1894)
English verse for junior classes (Edinburgh, 1896)
Outlines of English Literature for young scholars (Edinburgh and London, 1897)
English prose, for junior and senior classes (Edinburgh, 1898)
English drama for school and college (Edinburgh and London, 1900)
Milton: Paradise Lost I-IV (Edinburgh, 1900)
The Select Chaucer (London, 1902)
The Select Tennyson (London, 1903)
English exercises for junior and senior classes (Edinburgh and London, 1909)
Thackeray, The Virginians (London, 1911)
Nature in books (Oxford, 1914)

III.   ORIGINAL LITERARY WORKS

(a) as James Logie Robertson

POEMS

Poems (Dundee, 1878)
Orellana and other poems (Edinburgh, 1881)
With Janet Logie Robertson, *Our holiday among the hills* (Edinburgh, 1882)
Petition to the Deil and other War verses (Paisley, 1917)
Horace in Homespun and other Scots Poems, Memorial Volume (Edinburgh and London, 1925)

(b) as Hugh Haliburton

ESSAYS

'For Puir Old Scotland's Sake' (Edinburgh and London, 1887)
In Scottish Fields (London, 1890)
Furth in Field (London, 1894)
Excursions in Prose and Verse (Edinburgh and London, 1905)

POEMS

Horace in Homespun: A Series of Scottish Pastorals (Edinburgh, 1886), also as *Horace in Homespun* (Edinburgh and London, 1900)
Ochil Idylls and other poems (London 1891)
Dunbar: Being a selection from the poems of an old makar, adapted for modern readers (London, 1895)

Appendix B

'To William Dunbar'

(Note: The text is taken from the *Dunbar* of 1895, pp.v-vi. The earlier version in *Ochil Idylls* differs slightly in spelling and punctuation.)

From Scotland's later glory, Burns,
    The flower of Nature, fully blown,
My reverence instinctive turns
    To kneel at thy neglected throne,
Thou finer spirit, backward driven,
    Confined in priestly garments here,
Who found in Art a nearer heaven
    Wherein was neither sin nor fear.

With thee I tread the city ways,
    To wait at Royal James's court,
And watch with thine observant gaze
    Its pains, its follies, and its sport.
They welcome thee in bower and hall,
    The sprightly wits those chambers hold,
Thou alchemist, that turnest all
    In humour's crucible to gold.

Nor fails in thee the kindly heart
    That would thy brethren all embrace:
Beneath the friar's hood of Art
    Appears the thoughtful human face.
The mysteries of life and death
    Opprest thee, as they press us now;
Therefore is thine yet living breath—
    Our secret cares still speakest thou.

Thy fame, that waits in lingering bud,
    Had blossom'd long before our day,
But Flodden's red and raging flood
    Swept valour and thy voice away.
Alas, alas for Flodden yet,
    Heroic Scotland's early grave!
Can any after-growth forget
    The harvest sunk in Flodden's wave?

NOTES

1   *The Chepman and Myllar Prints* [facsimile], ed. William Beattie (Edinburgh, 1950); *The Ever Green*, ed. Allan Ramsay, 2 vols (Edinburgh 1724).

2   The catalogue of the National Library of Scotland lists the following among Dunbar's works: *Cogitations upon Death, or, The Mirror of Man's Misery*, 6th ed. (Edinburgh, 1688). At best, this work might be said to offer a rewriting of ideas found in one or two of Dunbar's poems, but the connection is tenuous.

3   *The Merrie Historie, of the Thrie Friers of Berwicke* (Aberdeen, 1622). Dickson and Edmond, quoting Pinkerton, refer to the advertisement of a printing of the poem by Robert Charteris, in (?)1603, but there seems to be no further trace of it: Robert Dickson and J.P. Edmond, *Annals of Scottish Printing* (1890; rpt Amsterdam, 1975), p.501.

4   For details of these manuscripts see: *The Poems of William Dunbar*, ed. James Kinsley (Oxford, 1979), pp.xiv-xv.

5   Ramsay's *Ever Green* (1724) has already been noted; *Ancient Scottish Poems*, ed. Sir David Dalrymple, Lord Hailes (Edinburgh, 1770); *Ancient Scotish Poems*, ed. John Pinkerton, 2 vols (London, 1786). One should also note the printing of *The Thistle and the Rose* by the Foulis brothers (Glasgow, 1750); nor should the *Select Poems of William Dunbar*, ed. R. Morison, Part I [all published] (Perth, 1788)—derived from the 1770 edition of Lord Hailes—be omitted from mention.

6   *The Poems of William Dunbar*, ed. David Laing, 2 vols (Edinburgh, 1834); *The Poems of William Dunbar*, ed. J. Schipper (Vienna, 1892-4); *The Poems of William Dunbar*, ed. John Small, 3 vols, STS First Ser. 2, 4, 16, 21, 29 (Edinburgh and London, 1893).

7   *The Works of William Dunbar, including his life 1465-1536*, ed. James Paterson (Edinburgh, 1860; reissued with new title page, 1863); *Mediaeval Scottish Poetry*, ed. George Eyre-Todd (Glasgow, 1892); *Poems by William Dunbar, from the obsolete*, trans. William Mackean (Paisley, 1890).

8   Hugh Haliburton [=James Logie Robertson], *Dunbar: Being a selection from the poems of an old makar, adapted for modern readers* (London, 1895). The book was given a thorough review by Rudolf Brotanek, *Anglia*, Beiblatt 6 (1895-6), 71-4.

9   Peter Smellie, *James Logie Robertson: the Poet of the Ochils* (Edinburgh, 1938), p.1.

10   See the pamphlet prepared for his candidature, with accompanying testimonials: NLS 5/112.(4).

11   Janet Logie Robertson, 'Memoir', in *Horace in Homespun* (Edinburgh and London, 1925), pp.v-x; *Centenary of James Logie Robertson* (Edinburgh, 1947)—this includes (pp.8-15) the text of John W. Oliver's celebratory address, 'James Logie Robertson'.

12   See Appendix A, above.

13   The 1886 edition contained a 'Preface, Notes, and Glossary by J. Logie Robertson, M.A.', as if from another person. These were dropped from the 1900 edition, which also replaced the original illustrations with new ones, by A.S. Boyd; the 1925 memorial edition has no illustrations.

14   Colin Milton, 'Modern Poetry in Scots Before MacDiarmid', in *The History of Scottish Literature*, IV, ed. Cairns Craig (Aberdeen, 1987), 11-36 (p.25).

15   C.M. Grieve[=Hugh MacDiarmid], *Albyn, or Scotland and the Future* (London and New York, 1927), p.35.

16   *The Letters of Hugh MacDiarmid*, ed. Alan Bold (London, 1984), p.307. One hopes that MacDiarmid was telling the truth. In the following year he was to write: '...I say that Charles Murray has not only never written a line of poetry in his life, but that he is constitutionally incapable of doing so—': C.M Grieve, *Contemporary Scottish Studies*, (London,[1926]), p.35.

17   *'For Puir Old Scotland's Sake'* (Edinburgh and London, 1887), pp.156-63: 'A Plea for Scottish Literature at the Universities'.

18   *Poems* (Dundee, 1878), pp.42-62; *'For Puir Old Scotland's Sake'*, pp.164-80.

19   *In Scottish Fields* (London, 1890), pp.200-46. The modernisations in this book are not identical with those given in the *Dunbar* of 1895; see further above.

20   *Ochil Idylls and Other Poems* (London, 1891), pp.97-8; for a text of this poem, see Appendix B, above.

21   *A History of English Literature*, with Introduction by Prof. Masson, 4th ed. (Edinburgh and London, 1903), pp.52 and 55.

22   *Excursions in Prose and Verse* (Edinburgh and London, 1905), p.126.

23   In the list, abbreviations R, M and K indicate respectively the editions of: Logie Robertson; *The Poems of William Dunbar*, ed. W. Mackay Mackenzie, revised by Bruce Dickins (London, 1960); *The Poems of William Dunbar*, ed. James Kinsley (Oxford, 1979). Poem No. 15, it may be noted, is based not upon a work of Dunbar's but upon an anonymous poem ('ffane wald I with all diligence') in the Maitland Folio MS—previously printed by Pinkerton under the title, 'The Danger of Wryting': *The Maitland Folio Manuscript*, ed. W.A. Craigie, 2 vols, STS New Ser. 7, 20 (Edinburgh and London, 1919-27), I, 237-8; II, 104, No. 27, *The Friars of Berwick* is not included by Kinsley.

24   See *SND*. Ramsay used the word in his 'Elegy on Maggy Johnston, who died Anno 1711': *The Works of Allan Ramsay*, ed. Burns Martin et al., 6 vols, STS, Third Ser. 19, 20, 29; Fourth Ser. 6, 7 (Edinburgh and London, 1945-74), I, 11 (line 21).

25   This is to include 'Some Attributions'. The numbers in brackets indicate the number of poems, per class, found in Logie Robertson's *Dunbar*.

26   One recent summary account—'Presents modernized paraphrases...usually abbreviated and bearing slight resemblance to the original'—requires considerably greater nuance: Walter Scheps and J. Anna Looney, *Middle Scots Poets* (Boston, Mass., 1986), p.142.

13

The Thre Prestis of Peblis in the Sixteenth Century

Sally Mapstone

The remains of MS RH 13/35 in the Scottish Record Office, Edinburgh, afford a tantalising glimpse of a compilation made within a few years of those famous sixteenth-century manuscripts, Bannatyne and Maitland.[1] Only fragments survive of a manuscript originally much larger, but constituting even in its depleted state a very interesting assembly of material. Unlike Bannatyne and Maitland, it has prose pieces as well as verse, interspersed with which is a sizeable amount of legal documentation. It was this material which enabled Marion Stewart, to whose work on the MS I am much indebted, to date it as copied between 1582 and 1586, a date which she found to be supported by the watermark.[2] Study of the legal memoranda also demonstrates that the MS was compiled and circulated among a group of East Lothian families, united through marriage and through religion. As Stewart has noted, the individuals whose names occur have in common a connection with the family of Cockburn of Ormiston, a family marked throughout the sixteenth century for its Reformist and pro-English sympathies.[3]

Its most prominent member during this period was the laird John Cockburn of Ormiston. An outline of his life gives some indication of the sort of milieu in which the MS was being circulated. During the 1540s John Knox was a tutor to his son, Alexander, and also to the sons of Hugh Douglas of Longniddry, who was married to John Cockburn of Ormiston's sister, Marion, and whose name is found among the legal matter in the MS.[4] It was at Ormiston Hall that George Wishart, later to be burned for heresy, was captured by Patrick, 3rd Earl of Bothwell in 1545; Ormiston was also taken and imprisoned in Edinburgh Castle, but escaped over the castle wall. Cockburn and Douglas of Longniddry assisted Somerset's English forces after the Pinkie campaign in 1547, and while Cockburn was later given by Edward VI lands in Northumberland and Durham for his services, he saw Ormiston Hall burnt in 1548 and other estates forfeited, some to the Bothwell family. Bad relations between the Cockburns and the Bothwells indeed continued: in 1559 John Cockburn of Ormiston was attacked and robbed by James, the 4th Earl, while on an envoy to Berwick; and William Sinclair of Hirdmanston, another of those named in a legal memorandum in the MS and husband of Cockburn's daughter, Sybil, was implicated in the murder of one of Bothwell's servants in 1565.[5] John Cockburn's activities from the 1560s to the 1580s continue to associate him with the radical side of the Reformist grouping. In 1566 he was one of those suspected of involvement in the murder of Riccio. One of his final political acts was participation, along with, among others, William Sinclair of Hirdmanston, in the so-called Ruthven Raid of 1582 in which the administration dominated by Lennox was overthrown and the young king James seized by the Reformist pro-English faction.[6]

There is no evidence that the manuscript was compiled for John Cockburn himself, and indeed it may well have been put together after his death in 1583, but it was certainly passing among his family and friends in and around Ormiston, Longniddry, and Haddington, and the connection between some of the material contained within it and the political and religious circumstances of the second half of the sixteenth century will be discussed below. Marion Stewart's researches show that its copyist was most likely one Thomas White, an elderly priest and notary public 'living and working in Haddington and probably closely involved with the family of Cockburn of Ormiston and their kin'.[7]

The literary tastes of this circle, as reflected in their MS, are pleasantly eclectic. They entertained themselves with the tales of *King Orphius* and *Sir Colling*, of which this MS preserves the only early copies.[8] They found more sober instruction in extracts from two of the *Gude and Godlie Ballatis*, material that bears out the link with the Reformed church.[9] Other vernacular pieces in the MS, almost entirely unstudied still, look at first sight of similarly moralistic character: two fragmentary prose pieces, 'A prayer off Salamon to obtein vysdome' and a 'history [which] makith mentioun how Issope excuissit him selffe beffoir his lord for eitting off þe fegis';[10] and parts of what has been described as 'an almost completely indecipherable poem on bishops'.[11] It is this work which concerns us, for it turns out to be 115 lines of the late fifteenth-century poem, *The Thre Prestis of Peblis*.

The textual history of the *Thre Prestis* is one, common to many Middle Scots pieces, of chance survivals and late or incomplete copies. The earliest surviving witness is the Asloan MS (c. 1515-30, hereafter A), but here only 359 lines have been preserved. Next now comes MS RH 13/35 (hereafter R), whose 115 lines correspond to 173/7-233/7 and 351/5-359/408 of the full poem, and which is now the poem's earliest witness for forty-five of them (364-408). The *Thre Prestis* is found complete, in 1344 lines, in the print made by Robert Charteris in 1603 (hereafter C), of which three copies are today extant: in the National Library of Scotland, the Folger Shakespeare Library, Washington, DC, and the Bodleian Library, Oxford (lacking about 200 lines).[12]

Despite its date, C is probably a reasonably reliable witness of a late fifteenth-century poem whose loose phrasing makes the assigning of more 'correct' readings a dubious business in any event.[13] Its reliability may be gauged by comparison of ll.1-359 in A and C. There are a host of minor variations, but these are for the most part small points of orthography, phrasing and word order. Of the significant variants, Protestant revision in C plays a part in two cases, but in the other instances the disposition of what look like better readings is fairly evenly spread between the two witnesses.[14] Thus, the large gap in years between A and C is not matched by major textual divergences, and C's dating does not make it a markedly inferior witness. This last point is now borne out by the additional collation of R. Its date, c. 1582-6, places it between A and C, though closer to the latter, and it is indeed more closely linked to C than A. For this reason, the 115 lines in R and C are given here in parallel. They all come from the early part of the poem, master John's tale of the three questions:[15]

R.

fol.4[r]

173/7   quhy burges barnis thrifis nocht to ye..... ...
    can neu.r thryffe bot off all bagis is ....[16]

175/9   and ewe. mair yat is forto say
    itt yatt yair elderis wan yai cast away
    yis questioun diclair full veill I can
    yai bigin nocht quhair yair fay....bigan
    bot with ane hilie hairt bayth derf and daft

180/4   yai ay bigin quhair yat yair fayairis left
    of yis matter lairglie to speik mair
    quhy yat yai thryve nocht to ye thrid air
    bicaus yair fayairis puirlie can bigin
    with hap and halfpenie and ane lamiskin

185/9   and puirelie ran fra toun to toun on feit[17]
    and yan rycht oft watschod vairie and veit
    quhill at ye last of mony smalis couthe mak
    yis bony pedder had ane guid fuit pak
    at ilkane fair yis chopmane ay was found

190/4   quhill yat his pak was worthe foutie pond[18]
    to beir his pak quhan yat he faillit force
    he bocht full sone ane mikill stalwart hors
    and at ye last sa vorthallie wp wan
    he coft ane cairt to carie pot and pan

195/9   bayth flanderis coffaris with co..teris and kist
    he wox a grund reche man .. .ny vist
    and syne into ye toun to sell and ..
    he held ane chop to sell his chaferie
    yan bocht he vow and wyslie c.uthe it ve

200/4   and efter yat sone sailit he ye sie[19]
    yan come he hame ane my..... ..che man
    ..d spousit syne ane mychtie .... rycht yan

C.

sig.A4^r

173/7 Quhy Burges bairnis thryuis not to the thrid air
       Can neuer thryue bot of al baggis is bair
175/9 And euer mair that is for to say,
       It that thair Eldars wan thay cast away:
       This questioun declair ful weill I can,
       Thay begin not quhair thair fathers began.
       Bot with ane hiely hart baith daft and derft,
180/4 Thay ay begin quhair that thair fathers left:
       Of this mater largelie to speik mair,
       Quhy that thay thryue not to the thrid air.
       Becaus thair fathers purelie can begin,
       With hap and halfpenny and a Lambs skin:
185/9 And purelie ran fra town to town on feit,
       And than richt oft wetshod werie and weit.
       Quhilk at the last of manie smals couth mak,
       This bonie pedder ane gude fute pak:
       At ilkane fair this chopman ay was fund'
190/4 Quhil that his pak was with fourtie pund.
       To beir his pak quhen that he faillit force,
       He bocht ful sone ane mekil stalwart hors:
       And at the last so worthelie vp wan'
       He bocht ane Cart to carie Pot and Pan:
195/9 Baith Flanders Coffers with Counters and Kist
       He wox a grund rich man or onie wist,
       And syne vnto the town to sel and by,
       He held a chop to sel his chaffery,
       Than bocht he wol and wyselie couth it wey,
200/4 And efter that sone saylit he the Sey:
       Than come he hame a verie potent man,
       And spousit syne a michtie wyfe richt than.

fol.4^V he saillit ouer ye sie sa oft and oft[20]

             .... shyp. .. cott

205/9   and wox sa full of warldis welth and vin

             his .andis he wesche in ane sillwer basin

             foroutin gold and sillwer into huird

             worthe thrie thousand pond was his copbuird

             reche was his gounis with wyair garmontis gay[21]

210/14   for Sunday silk for Ilk day grein and gray

             his wif was cumlie cled in scarllat reid

             scho had na dout of derthe of aill nor breid

             and efter yat with in ane twantie ȝeir

             his sone gat wp ane stalwart man and stere

215/19   and efter that yis burges we of reid

             diet as ve mon do all in deid

             and fra he was deid yan com his sone

             and enteritt in ye welthe yat he had von

             he step... nocht his step... on ye streit

220/4   to win his walthe nor for it vas he veit

             quhan he wald sleip he wantit nocht a vink

             to win his velth nor for it sweit nor svink[22]

             yairfor that lychtlie cumis will lychtlie ga[23]

             to win his walthe he had na vark nor wa

225/9   to win yis guid he had nocht ane ill houre

             quhy suld he haue ye sweit and nocht ye sour

             apone his fingeris with reche ringis on raw

             his moth.r nocht thollit ye reike on him to blaw

             and will nocht heir for werie schame and sin

230/4   that ewer his fayair sald ane scheip skin

             he wald yaim sane with benidicitie[24]

             quha spak of ony digrading of his digrie

             with twa men and ane varlat at his bak

fol.5^r

351/5   ad suos clericiis[25]

             Than to ye clairgie come yis nobill king

             off his questioun to heir ye obsoluing

             and yai as men off wisdome in all work

             had laid yair speiche vpone ane cunning clark

             ye quhilk in vain in scoill had nocht tain grie

355/60   in all syence sewin he was an apersie

             and in termis schort and sentence fair

             ye questioun bigan for to diclair

             yat is to say ye caus quhairfor and quhy

             in ald dayis and tymis of asistry

365   sa mony bischops war and men of kirk

             sa greit will had ay guid warkis to virk

             and yair prayaris maid to god of mycht

             ye dum men spak ye blind men gat yair sycht

He saylit ouer the Sey sa oft and oft,
Quhil at the last ane semelie ship he coft.
205/9 And wox sa ful of warldis welth and win,
His hands he wish in ane siluer Basin.
Foroutin gold or siluer into hurde,
With thrie thowsand pund was his Copburde:
Riche was his gownis with vther garments gay,
210/14 For Sonday silk, for ilk day grene and gray,
His wyfe was cumlie cled in Scarlet reid,
Scho had na dout of derth of Ail nor breid.
And efter that within a twentie ʒeir,
His Sone gat vp ane stalwart man and steir.
215/19 And efter that this Burges we of reid,
Deit as we mon do al indeid.
And fra he was deid than come his sone,
And enterit in the welth that he had wone:
He steppit not his steps in the streit,
220/4 To win this welth nor for it was he weit.
Quhen he wald sleip he wantit not a wink,
Sig. B To win this welth na for it swet na swink.
Thairfoir that lichtlie cums wil lichtlie ga,
To win this welth he had na work nor wa.
225/9 To win this gude he had not ane il houre,
Quhy sould he haue the sweit had not the soure.
Upon his fingers with riche rings on raw,
His Mother not tholit the reik on him to blaw:
And wil nocht heir for verie shame and sin,
230/4 That euer his Father sald ane sheip skin:
He wald him sayne with **Benedicite**,
Quha spak of onie degrading of his degrie,
With twa men and ane varlot at his bak,

Sig. B2ᵛ
351/5 THAN to the Clergie came this nobill King,
Of his questioun to heir the absoluing.
And thay as men of wisdome in al wark,
Had laid thair speich vpon ane cunning Clark,
The quhilk in vaine in scule had not tane grie,
356/60 In al science seuin he was ane A per se:
And in termes short and sentence fair,
The questioun began for to declair,
That is to say quhairfoir and quhy,
In auld tymes and dayes of ancestry.
365   Sa monie Bishops war and men of Kirk,
Sa grit wil had ay gude warkes to wirk:
And throw thair prayers maid to God of micht,
The dum men spak, the Blind men gat þair sicht,

ye deif heiring ye cruikeit gat yair feit
370   was naine in baill bot weill yai culd yaim beit
and quhairfor now all yat cuir can varie
me think ʒe mein quhairfoir sa may nocht ve
and yis is ʒour quodlibet and ʒour dout
and gif to ws to reid and gif it out

Solutio tertie questionis
375   This is ye caus rychtt mychttie king att schortt
to ʒour heines as we sall yis report
ye lawit folkis yis law wald neuer seis
bot *with* yair ws quhan bischopis var to cheis[26]
wnto ye kirk yai gaddarit alld and ʒing[27]
380   *with* meik hairt fasting and praying
fol.5ᵛ   and prayit god *with* wordys nocht in vaist
to send yame vitt doun be ye hally gaist
quhan yame amang wes ony bischope deid
to send to yame ane bischope in his steid
385   and ʒit amang ws ar fund ways thrie
to cheis ane bischop efter ane vyair die
yat is to say ye way of ye hallie gaist
quhilk taikin is of mycht and wertew maist
ye secund is be way of electioun
390   ane persone for to cheis of parfeccioun
in yat cathederall kirk and in yat sie
in place quhair yat bischop suld chosin be
and gif yair be nain abill yair yat can
yat office weill steir quhat sall yai yan
395   bot to ye thrid way to ga for yi
quhilke is callit wia scrutini
yat is to in all ye realme and land
ane man to gait for yair office gainand
bot thir thrie wayis foroutin ony pleid
400   ane suld we cheis efter ane vyairis deid
bot *sir* to yat ye contrair we find
quhilk putis all our hewines bihind
now sall yair nain of yir wayis thrie
be chosin now ane bischop for to be
405   bot yat ʒour mycht and maiestie will mak
quhat ewer he be to loue or ʒit to lak
yan heilie to sit on ye rainbow
.... cumis in at ye north windov[28]

The Deif men heiring, the Crukit gat thair feit,
370   Was nane in bail, bot weil thay could them beit,
And quhairfoir now al that cuir can warie,
Me think ȝe mene quhairfoir sa may not we:
And thus it is ȝour quodlibet and dout,
ȝe gaue to vs to reid and gif it out.

The ansvver to the thrid question.

375   THIS is the caus richt michtie King at short,
To ȝour Hienes as we sal thus report:
The Lawit folkes this Law wald neuer ceis,
Bot with thair vse quhen Bishops was to cheis.
Unto the Kirk thay gadred auld and ȝing,
380   With meik hart fasting and praying:
And prayit God with word not in waist,
To send them wit doun be the halie Gaist.
Quhan tham amang was onie Bishop deid,
To send to them ane Bishop in his steid.
385   And ȝit amang vs ar fund wayis thrie,
To cheis ane Bishope after ane vther die:
That is to say the way of the halie Gaist,
Quhilk takin is of micht and vertew maist.
The second is be way of Electioun,
390   Ane Persone for to cheis of perfectioun:
In that Cathedral Kirk and in that se,
In place quhair that Bishope suld chosen be.
And gif thair be nane abil thair that can,
That office weil steir, quhat sal thay than:
395   Bot to the thrid way to ga for thi,
Quhilk is callit (**via scrutiui.**)
That is to say in al the Realme and Land,
Ane man to get for that office gainand:
Bot thir thrie wayis withoutin ony pleid,
400   Ane should we cheis after ane vthers deid,
Bot sir now the contrair wee find,
Quhilk puts al our heauines behind:
Now sal thair nane of thir wayis thrie,
Be chosen now ane Bishope for to be.
405   Bot that ȝour micht and Majestie wil mak,
Quhat euer he be to loife or ȝit to lak:
Than heyly to sit on the Rayne-bow,
Thir Bishops cums in at the North window,

While R has its own distinctive orthographic features,[29] it agrees with C against A in a substantial number of places. By contrast, it is in agreement with A against C in only one major instance in the text (at 201/5) and in the preservation of the style of Latin rubrics that in C have been replaced by vernacular versions.[30] The handful of minor instances where R is also in agreement with A against C can all be explained either as printing errors in C or coincidental survival in R and A of small variations.[31] However, it is also true that many of the places in which R and C are agreeing against A are of a trivial nature, with little to suggest that they are always preserving a more accurate version. The places where R and C definitely look to be correct against A are 185/9, *feit* (for reasons of rhyme—A has *fut*); 208/12, *pond* (omitted in A); 214/18, *and* (A, *to*); and 355/9, *in vain* (A, *certane*).[32] But A has the better reading aginst R and C at 219/23, *thre* (RC, *his*) and probably at 228/32, *tholit nocht* (RC, *nocht thollit*). Of the other cases in this category, it is not possible conclusively to assign the authentic reading.[33]

Near as the relationship between R and C undoubtedly is, there is variation between them, some of which is of interest, particularly in the forty-five lines where R is now the earliest witness (364-408). C differs from R in thirteen places where C is the only other witness. Three of these are omissions by R, where C is clearly correct.[34] Five are small variations in phrasing.[35] But in three other instances, R's versions of 373-4 and 401 look at the least viable alternatives, and at 396 *wia scrutini* is definitely correct.[36] In addition, in those lines where A is also a witness, A and C agree together against R in seven cases, in one of which R is wrong, but in the others (though mostly very minor) it could in fact be right.[37] Its value as an independent textual witness is thus evident. In only one place, moreover, where R is at odds with both A and C, do they also disagree with each other.[38] Thus while analysis of R may demonstrate its greater connection with C, it also paradoxically serves as a reminder of the general concord between C and A.

It can be concluded that R cannot be the exemplar for C; but C must derive from a text of the poem closely related to R, while also retaining some readings which go back to A. R is related to A, but more distantly, indicating that there were probably a considerable number of intermediaries between them. Although it has had its fair share of slips, R is still a valuable witness, which will have to be taken into account in any future edition of the poem, especially for those lines in which it now precedes C as the earliest survivor. The relatively unimportant nature of its variants, moreover, also confirms the general reliability of C as the main witness for the poem, notwithstanding its late date.[39]

The inclusion of the *Thre Prestis* in this MS is also an interesting subject for consideration. A degree of popularity in the early sixteenth century is evinced by its presence in the Asloan MS, and the reference to it in the *Complaynt of Scotland* (1550) indicates that it continued to circulate.[40] Nevertheless, it was not included in either the Bannatyne or Maitland MSS. Why then should it have appealed to the compiler of R?

Chance would undoubtedly have contributed to the putting together of such a manuscript: one included what was to hand. And it is some indication of how much Scottish literature may have been lost to us that several of the items in R are unique to that collection. It is easy to see that the *Thre Prestis*, a specimen of the *speculum principis* tradition that offers moral advice to men as much as monarchs, would have an appeal as a piece serious but entertaining, a bridge between the lighter verse and the religious and moral works in R;[41] but there may be still more to its inclusion than this.

Doctrinally there is little in the *Thre Prestis* to offend the reformed religion, and certain things to commend it, such as the emphasis on the value of good deeds as well as faith in the final tale. But these are not the only aspects of the religious life dealt with in the poem. The content of some of the surviving fragments of R neatly draws the subject to our attention: the first tale has a considerable amount to say about bishops. The last of the king's three questions in John's tale is addressed to the third estate, his clergy. They are asked why they, and in particular the bishops, have fallen from the exemplary standards of the past. In his reply the wise clerk who speaks for the clergy acknowledges the disastrous effects of simony and avarice upon the spiritual estate, but attributes the decline in large part to the movement away from the past systems of selecting bishops through elections among the clergy to a situation where nomination has been appropriated by the crown:

> Now sal thair nane of thir wayis thrie,
> Be chosen now ane Bishope for to be.
> Bot that ʒour might and Majestie wil mak .... (403-5)

Recognising the justice of the criticism, the king agrees to remove himself from involvement in church affairs:

> With Kirk-gude sal I neuer have ado,
> It to dispone to lytil or to large,
> Kirk men to kirk, sen thay haue al the charge .... (434-6)

The account given here both does and does not have a bearing on the process of ecclesiastical appointments in late fifteenth-century Scotland. The three types of election open to a cathedral chapter in the choosing of a bishop are accurately set out, as is the charge that the crown's (often corrupt) intervention in elections had made a mockery of a system in which the approval of crown and Pope was intended to be sought only after the election had taken place.[42] Interestingly omitted, on the other hand, is any acknowledgement that not only the crown but also the papacy had long been challenging the electoral process by insisting on its own right to provision. Where papacy, crown, and cathedral chapter, after a judicious exercise of lobbying, were in agreement the outcome could be, and often was, an amicable one. But where they did not concur violent disputes, such as that in 1485 over the papal provision of George Browne to the see of Dunkeld could ensue.[43] Moreover, the second half of the fifteenth century saw an increase in the pressure put upon a papacy weakened by the schism and the conciliar movement to concede to the Scottish crown a greater say in the nominations of ecclesiastical appointments. A considerable concession was achieved in the papal indult of 1487, which gave the crown eight months in which to nominate appointees to benefices worth two hundred florins or more.[44] In this respect the *Thre Prestis* may give an emphasis that is quite deliberate. Though the papacy continued to exert its influence on appointments well into the sixteenth century, it was the role of the crown in ecclesiastical appointments that was the dominant issue in the last decades of the century.[45]

Where the poem entirely parts company with reality, affirming instead the simplistic and idealised mode of its genre, is in the king's agreeable withdrawal from church affairs. As the infamous appointments made by James IV and V showed, the reverse was true, and the continued engagement of the crown in the business of appointments undoubtedly justified some of the criticisms which the church received during the sixteenth century.[46]

This part of the *Thre Prestis*, however, had a rather different relation to the politics of the post-1560 church. The role of bishops was certainly not past history for the reformed kirk at the time of R's compilation in the early 1580s. The continued survival of the office despite the hostility of many Reformers, is one of the striking features of the Scottish Reformation. The factors behind the initial survival remained relevant throughout the rest of the century: the influential standing of many of the incumbents and the inability of the general assembly to shift them, constitutionally or otherwise; the willingness of some occupants to accord with the reformed religion; and the appreciation on the part of some reformers that there were things to be gained from having men of their own views in the bishoprics, albeit in restricted roles.[47] Following Mary's abdication and the establishment of the regency government in 1567, there was some movement towards a greater accommodation of the views of church and crown. In 1571-2 a settlement was arrived at by which the crown's nomination to a vacant bishopric would be followed by an election by chapters of ministers. Such bishops were intended to be:

> subject to the king and the general assembly *in spiritualibus* as they were to the king *in temporalibus* or, as the assembly phrased it 'subject to the discipline of the general assembly as superintendants have been heretofore in all sorts, as members thereof'.[48]

The battle between government and assembly continued nonetheless into the 1580s, fuelled by presbyterian advocates such as Andrew Melville, wholly opposed to the prolongation of bishoprics. The gap between what the assembly advocated (such as banning new elections to bishoprics and threatening excommunication to new archbishops) and what the government implemented remained a large one, despite the fact that the governmental administration was itself deeply divided and unstable, especially over religious interests.

Even the interim ascendancy of the Ruthven Raiders did not see the abolishing of bishops, and following James's escape in 1584 the administration headed by Arran brought in the 'Black Acts' affirming anew their authority.[49] Something of a compromise was achieved in 1586 whereby a presbyterian system was permitted with bishops in the position of moderators. But after James VI's assumption of power, the whole matter was revived again. As Donaldson writes, 'every time it seemed that the bishoprics would finally become extinct the issue had become a live one'.[50] In 1600 James contrived to appoint two 'parliamentary bishops', and by the end of the first decade of the seventeenth century parliament and general assembly had returned to the episcopate a greater degree of government over the presbyteries. Yet it is finally worth noting that the system was not necessarily disadvantageous to the reformed church: 'the evidence all suggests that the combination of bishops with presbyteries worked well and that under their joint direction kirk sessions operated more widely and more effectively than ever before'.[51]

The *Thre Prestis* was therefore put into MS R at the height of a very considerable controversy. Its sentiments on bishops in fact accord well with the moderate Reformist line of thinking in the 1570s and 1580s, and indeed into the next century: swingeing criticism of the corrupt practice of past holders of the office and the crown's tampering with appointments to it, and determination to bring both appointments and the exercise of episcopal power much more firmly under the kirk's control. Its emphasis on the value of an electoral system and the removal of the crown from church matters would certainly strike a chord with those prepared to countenance the perpetuation of the episcopate. John Cockburn of Ormiston is often described as a member of the more extreme Protestant faction among the nobility, but, as we have seen, even the Ruthven administration did not hurry to move conclusively against the bishops.

The appeal of the *Thre Prestis* to adherents of the reformed religion in the early seventeenth century is also more explicit in this light. Like his illustrious father, from whom he inherited his printing concern, Robert Charteris was a publisher of works sympathetic to or appropriated by Protestantism.[52] In the first decade of the century he printed some vernacular versions of the Psalms, *Ane Godlie Dreme* by Elizabeth Melville, the *Complaint of a Christian Soul* by George Muschet, and the immensely popular works of Sir David Lyndsay. Two years after the *Thre Prestis* he published in 1605 two lengthy poems by one James Cockburne, *Gabriels Salutation to Marie* and *Iudas Kisse to the Sonne of Marie*.[53] The dedication to 'Ieane Hamiltone, Ladie Skirling' makes it likely that the author was the James Cockburn who was brother of Sir William Cockburn of Skirling, who married his cousin Jean Hamilton in 1603.[54] This Charteris-Cockburn link is thus a rather interesting one, given C's affinities with R: that Charteris came by his copy-text from someone in that Reformist circle seems a distinct possibility.

The literary interests of the Cockburn family are almost a subject in themselves. One of the earliest important converts to the new religion, Patrick Cockburn, of the Choicelea branch, who became the first Protestant minister at Haddington, published abroad and in Scotland a series of Latin theological works, first Catholic and then Protestant.[55]   But the most intriguing literary connection comes through female members of the family. John Cockburn of Ormiston's daughter, Sybil, was married first, as we have noted, to William Sinclair of Hirdmanston. Her second marriage, in 1606, was to her relation John Cockburn of Clerklington, which is about seven miles from Ormiston.[56] He in turn had previously been married to Helen, daughter of Sir Richard Maitland, the poet, and sister of Mary, the woman closely associated with the copying of the Maitland Quarto MS. Helen Maitland herself at one point possessed the Maitland Folio MS, as an inscription within it confirms.[57] We can now see, therefore, that the compilations of the Maitland MSS and MS R were not only occurring around the same time but also among a circle of people likely to be well acquainted with each other. This new glimpse of such a literary milieu is yet another of the insights into sixteenth-century Scottish culture which this neglected MS offers us. There may well be still more to come.[58]

NOTES

1   The Bannatyne MSS (Draft and Main) are dated c. 1567-8. For recent discussion, arguing also for Bannatyne's earlier compilation of a collection of love poetry in 1565, A. A. MacDonald, 'The Bannatyne Manuscript: a Marian Anthology', *Innes Review*, XXXVII (1986), 36-47; also *The Bannatyne Manuscript*, Scolar facsimile (London, 1980), introd. by D. Fox and W. Ringler, pp.ix-xvi The Maitland Folio Manuscript was compiled between 1570 and Maitland's death in 1586; the Quarto Manuscript was copied c. 1585-6: *The Maitland Folio Manuscript*, ed. W.A. Craigie, 2 vols, Scottish Text Society, Second Ser. 7, 20 (Edinburgh and London, 1919-27), I, 1-6, 15-17; *The Maitland Quarto Manuscript*, ed. W.A. Craigie, STS, New Ser. 9 (Edinburgh and London, 1920).

2   See *King Orphius, Sir Colling, The brother's lament, Litel Musgray*, ed.
    Marion Stewart and Helena M. Shire, (Cambridge, The Ninth of May,
    1973); Marion Stewart, 'A Recently-Discovered Manuscript: "ane taill of
    Sir colling ye knyt"', *Scottish Studies*, XVI (1972, hereafter, 'Stewart
    1972'), 23-39; *'King Orphius'*, *Scottish Studies*, XVII (1973), 1-16.
    Stewart 1972, 23) matches the watermark (now impossible to examine) to
    Briquet no. 12814 (*Les Filigranes*, I, Geneva, 1907). This design (a
    crowned jug with a band round its middle with the initials TC) is, with
    small variations, quite common, cf. no. 12746 (c. 1557).

3   *King Orphius*, pp.18-19; Stewart 1972, 23. For details of the numerous
    branches of the Cockburn family: Sir Robert Cockburn, and Harry A.
    Cockburn, *The Records of the Cockburn Family*, (London and Edinburgh,
    1913, hereafter, 'Cockburn'). This volume criticises, as inaccurate and
    misleading, an earlier history by Thomas H. Cockburn-Hood, *The House of
    Cockburn of that Ilk*, (Edinburgh, 1888). The latter nevertheless provides
    much documentary detail not included in the later study, and, used
    judiciously, is a helpful source.

4   Cockburn-Hood, pp.125-6. Useful scene-setting is provided in Jasper
    Ridley, *John Knox* (Oxford, 1968), pp.27-73. Hugh Douglas of
    Longniddry died in 1555; see also note 6, below.

5   Cockburn, pp.115-21; Cockburn-Hood, p.135; *King Orphius*, pp.18-19.
    On Sinclair of Hirdmanston: *The Scots Peerage*, VII, ed. Sir James Balfour
    Paul (Edinburgh, 1910), 583.

6   Ridley, pp.448-9; Gordon Donaldson, *Scotland: James V to James VII*
    The Edinburgh History of Scotland III (Edinburgh and London, 1965,
    hereafter, 'Donaldson, 1965'), 178-82; on Sinclair of Hirdmanston's
    involvement in the Ruthven Raid, *Scots Peerage*, VIII, 583. Other
    individuals whose names occur in the MS include (1) Marion Cockburn,
    'relict of umquhyll Hew Douglas of Borg' (Stewart 1972, 23), a relationship
    confirmed by a document cited by Cockburn-Hood, p.126. (See also *The
    Register of the Great Seal of Scotland*, ed. James Balfour Paul and J.M.
    Thomson (Edinburgh 1883), III, no. 1846, for 1538.) Cockburn-Hood
    (pp.126, 229) claims that this Marion Cockburn was the daughter of Sir
    William Cockburn of the Skirling branch, to whom John Cockburn of
    Ormiston was related through his parents. (2) George and Francis Douglas
    of Borg, who were the sons of Hew and Marion. Cockburn-Hood, p.126,
    cites a document witnessed by George Douglas in 1557 for Marion, relict
    of Hugh Douglas of Longniddry, which further exemplifies the close
    connection between these families. For Francis see *Scots Peerage*, VIII,
    583. (3) John Sinclair, who was the father of William Sinclair of
    Hirdmanston.

7   *King Orphius*, p.20.

8   Their relation to later versions is discussed in Stewart's two articles cited
    in note 2, above.

9   For the stanzas, 'Our barnis now weill knawis how', and 'Remember man', see *The Gude and Godlie Ballatis*, ed. A.F. Mitchell, STS, 1st Ser. 39 (Edinburgh and London, 1897), pp.55 and 200. The earliest printed edition of the *Gude and Godlie Ballatis* is now known to have been produced in 1565. A new edition is being prepared by Professor A. A. MacDonald. Dr Helena Shire's apt comments on the mixed contents of the Bannatyne MS are also appropriate to MS RH 13/35: 'It resembles a two-way mirror, reflecting in one direction the courtly making of the past, in another the age of change', *Song, Dance and Poetry of the Court of Scotland under King James VI*, (Cambridge, 1969), p.12.

10   Stewart (*King Orphius*, p.18), reads 'segis'.

11   Ibid., p.18. Since Stewart first worked on the MS it has been repaired and restored. It is now easier to read, though still badly faded, eaten away and stained in places. Separate bifolios have been pasted onto large single sheets and, although some pages have catchwords, it is scarcely possible to recover the order of gatherings as so much material has been lost in between.

12   *STC* No. 19528. The most recent modern edition of the *Thre Prestis*, printing A and C in parallel is T.D. Robb's, STS, 2nd Ser. 8 (Edinburgh and London, 1920). Robb used the imperfect Oxford copy of C (Douce 527), supplementing its missing lines from the complete version available to him in Pinkerton's *Scotish Poems, Reprinted from Scarce Editions* (1792), and Francis Douce's handwritten insertions in his copy of C (Robb was unaware that the hand was Douce's). Robb's text of C (especially for these lines) is not entirely accurate. In this article quotation is taken from Robb's edition for A, but for C quotations are from the National Library of Scotland copy, of which there is also a facsimile reprint, *Thrie Tailes of the Thrie Priestis of Peblis*, The English Experience, no. 106 (Amsterdam and New York, 1969). After line 128, line numbering of A and C no longer accords; thus where line references to both A and C are given, the first reference is to A. The text in A is also printed in vol. II of *The Asloan Manuscript*, ed. W.A. Craigie, STS, New Ser. 16 (Edinburgh and London, 1925).

13   Robb (p.ix) assigned a *terminus ad quem* of 1492 for the poem, on the grounds that its reference to Granada as a heathen kingdom would be inappropriate after that date. A post-1490 dating has recently been proposed by Craig MacDonald, citing shared material between the *Thre Prestis* and John Ireland's *Meroure of Wyssdome*: 'The Thre Prestis of Peblis* and *The Meroure of Wyssdome*: a Possible Relationship', *Studies in Scottish Literature*, XVII (1982), 153-64. A dating of 1490-2 remains possible.

14   Protestant revision in C of references to the mass in A occurs at 129-30/129-32 (where C revises and adds two lines) and 161/5. Of the rest of the significant variants, A also looks correct at 67-8 (see Robb's note); 179/83; 219/23; 325/9; 346/50. C has two extra lines at 141-2, which

may well be authentic. It also looks correct at 44; 70; 102; 208/12; 214/18 (reference here is to *and steir* over A's *to stere*; C does not, as Robb claims, erroneously begin this line *He Sone*); 259/63; 323/7; 340/4; 355/9. Many others are far less easy to assign, for example, 2, 4, 13, 24, 25, 72, 117, 152/6, 166/70, 200/4, 201/5 (discussed below, note 30), 203/7, 213/17, 232/6, 234/8, 237/41, 265/9, 266/70, 271/5, 314/18, 322/6, 259/63. I have noted approximately sixty other minor discrepancies in phrasing or word order. I have not considered orthographical variants or variant forms such as *a/ane, at/þat, intill/into.*

15 The text of R is printed here with the approval of the Keeper of the Records of Scotland. Certain parts of R, notably 203/7 and 204/8, are almost obliterated. All abbreviation is expanded and signalled in italics. The scribe very often writes a dash over *u* or *v* when no abbreviation can be intended. No distinction is made between long and short *s* in this transcription. The scribe's form of *þ* is identical to that for *y*. Small differences between the text of C printed here and Robb's are given in notes 14 and 31. Two others are at 382, where C (as R) reads *doun* to Robb's *down* and 239 where C does correctly read *how sald he* (Robb was here consulting a modern witness).

16 *an.* This is scored through at the opening of the line.

17 *toun.* The first instance is inserted from the left-hand margin; insertion mark after *fra.*

18 *foutie.* A superscript mark near *u* is more likely the scribe's correction, to *fourtie*, than an abbreviation. My thanks to Dr Keith Williamson for this suggestion.

19 After this line, 203/7 has been wrongly inserted and scored through.

20 This line is obliterated at its correct point in the MS. The version here is that incorrectly inserted after 200/4.

21 *gounis.* As written there seems to be one minim too few here, and a long superscript dash probably indicates abbreviation.

22 *no.* This is scored through at opening of line; *velth* is inserted from left-hand margin: insertion mark is after *his.*

23 *yairfoir.* This is inserted from the left-hand margin.

24 *with.* This is scored through at the opening of the line.

25 [*sic*] A's version of the rubric here is *Ad Clericos.*

26 *var.* This is inserted above the line.

27 *sum.* This is scored through before *ȝing.*

28 The catchwords *and nocht* at the end of the page indicate the opening of 409.

29 Particularly, the disposition of *u*, *v*, and *w*; the tendency to *ai* spellings where A and C would have *e* (e.g. 184/8, *fayairis*, 386, vyair); *i* spellings where A and C would have *e* (e.g. 177/81, *diclair*, 180/4, *bigin*). These features are also found in *King Orphius* and *Sir Colling.*

30   At 201/5, despite obliteration of part of the line in R, it is clear that it has a version of A's *ane mychti riche man* rather than C's *a verie potent man*. It is possible that C here had the A and R reading in its exemplar, but changed it to avoid repetition in the next line with *a michtie wyfe richt þan* (202/6). Alternatively, C preserves a reading lost to A and R.

31   Of the six smaller instances, Robb's explanation for C's inversion of A and R's *derf and daft* (at 179/83) is obviously right: 'the words have been accidentally transposed and *t* has been added to *derf* to produce an apparent rhyme' (p.64); 190/4, A, *worth*, R, *worthe*, C, *with* (printed by Robb as *wirth*) is a simple printing error in C, repeated at 208/12. C errs again at 187/91, with *Quhilk* to A and R's *Quhill*. The two other cases are spelling variants: at 197/201, A and R have *into*, C *vnto*, and at 198/202, A and R have *ane*, C, *a*.

32   The form given for RC here and for note 33 is R's; C sometimes has slightly different spellings.

33   The others are as follows (A's form is given first): 174/8, *ar*; *is*; 175/9, *now*; omitted; 182/6, *quhy þai*; *quhy yat yai*; 186/90, *ofttymes*; *yan rycht oft*; 189/93, *ilk*; *ilkane*; 191/5, *þis*; *his*; 195/9, omitted; *with*; 199/203, *Thar*; *yan*; 200/4, *efter sone þan*; *efter yat sone*; 203/7, *And*; *he*; 207/11, *And*; *or*; 212/16, *for derth*; *of derthe*; 213/17, omitted; *ane*; 217/21, *fra þat*; *fra*; 232/6, *quhasa spak of*; *quha spak of ony*; 351/5, *his*; *ye*; 352/6, *assolʒeing*; *obsoluing*; 354/8, *cunnand*; *cunning*; 356/60, *þe*; omitted.

34   367, *throw* omitted in R; 369, *men* omitted in R (that C is right is indicated by 153/7); 397, *say* omitted in R.

35   (R's form is given first): 364, *in ald dayis and tymes*; *in auld tymes and dayes*; 373, *yis*; *thus*; 376, *yis*; *thus*; 398, *yair*; *that*; 399, *foroutin*; *withoutin*; (both forms are found elsewhere in the poem).

36   At 373, R's *ʒour quodlibet and ʒour dout* (C, *ʒour quodlibet and dout*) is a type of repeated phrasing found elsewhere in the poem (e.g. 101/5, 103/7; interesting is 145/9 where A has double phrasing and C does not). At 374 R's *and gif* (C, *ʒe gaue*) may look suspect given the use of *and gif* again later in the line, but the poet uses this sort of repetition elsewhere (e.g. 377). At 401, R's *bot sir to yat ye contrair* and C's *Bot Sir now the contrair*, are equally acceptable. For *wia scrutini*, see Robb's note, p.73.

37   At 188/92, R's *had* is intrusive. Its viable alternatives are (AC form is based on A's spelling): *coft* at 194/8 (AC *bocht*), where the usage is possible (cf. 204/8) and fits the alliteration; 219/23, *on* (AC, *in*); 222/6 and 224/8, *his* (AC *þis*); 226/30, *and* (AC, *had*), which is certainly possible as shown by the quotation cited in Robb, p.66; 231/5, *yaim* (AC, *him*).

38   359/63. The variations here are A, *That is to saye quharfor it is and quhy*; R, *yat is to say ye caus quhairfor and quhy*; C, *That is to say quhairfoir and quhy*. Comparison with one similar line, 147/51, gives

support to C's reading, but the variations between A and C at another, 271/5, divide equally in support for A and R at 359/63.

39   Collation of the full text of C with Robb's modern witnesses also shows that they are commonly pretty accurate. But the following more significant corrections might be noted: 239 read *With onie wald he be baith wod and wraith*; 240, *Quha at him speirit how sald he the claith*; 286, *man*; 1233, *wald be be* (i.e. here the mistake is also in C); 1289, *tymes*.

40   *The Complaynt of Scotland*, ed. A. M. Stewart, STS, 4th Ser. 11 (Edinburgh and London, 1979), p.112.

41   For the poem as a *speculum principis*, Sally Mapstone, 'The advice to princes tradition in Scottish literature, 1450-1500', Diss., Oxford, 1986, pp.317-54.

42   See John Dowden, *The Medieval Church in Scotland* (Glasgow, 1910), pp.19-52.

43   Ibid. See also A. Grant, *Independence and Nationhood: Scotland 1306-1469* The New History of Scotland III (Edinburgh, 1984),.92-3; Norman Macdougall, *James III: a Political Study* (Edinburgh, 1982), pp.222-5.

44   See Jenny Wormald, *Court, Kirk and Community: Scotland 1470-1625* The New History of Scotland IV (London 1981),.76-7; Macdougall, pp.229-30.

45   See D.E.R. Watt's conclusion: 'From the Scottish evidence at least the popes of the fifteenth century emerge more as followers than leaders', 'The Papacy and Scotland in the Fifteenth Century', in *The Church, Politics and Patronage in the Fifteenth Century*, ed. Barrie Dobson (Gloucester, 1984), p.129. On crown-papacy relations over appointments in the sixteenth century, Ian. B. Cowan, 'Patronage, Provision and Reservation: Pre-Reformation Appointments to Scottish Benefices', in *The Renaissance and Reformation in Scotland*, ed. I. B. Cowan and Duncan Shaw (Edinburgh, 1983), pp.75-92. On further gains in the crown's right to nomination, Donaldson, 1965, pp.135-6.

46   See Gordon Donaldson, *The Scottish Reformation* (Cambridge, 1960, hereafter, 'Donaldson, 1960'), pp.18-19, 102-5; I.B. Cowan, *The Scottish Reformation* (London, 1982), pp.51-2.

47   Donaldson, 1960, pp.55-9, 108-11, 158-9.

48   Ibid., p.164.

49   Ibid., pp.211-14; Donaldson, 1965, 198.

50   Donaldson, 1965, 201; Donaldson, 1960, pp.216-17.

51   Donaldson, 1965, 207.

52   See further, Robert Dickson and J.P. Edmond, *Annals of Scottish Printing* (Aberdeen, 1888), pp.490-508.

53   The only surviving copy of these poems is in the National Library of Scotland. They have never received detailed study. For brief comments:

David Irving, *The History of Scottish Poetry*, ed. John Aitken Carlyle (Edinburgh, 1861), pp.483-5; T. McCrie, *The Life of Andrew Melville*, 2 vols (Edinburgh, 1819), II, 325-6.

54   The dedicatory verses to *Gabriels Salutation* state that Jean Hamilton is 'eyghtene yeeres of age' (sig. A2). Regrettably little is known of James Cockburn. Cockburn (p.143) cites only one piece of documentary evidence, a marriage contract between James's sister, Margaret, and Thomas Bannatyne, minister of North Berwick, in 1614. Bannatyne's erratic career is recorded in Hew Scott (ed.) *Fasti Ecclesiae Scoticanae*, II, Parts 1-2 (1867-8), 324, 632-3. On Sir William and Lady Jean Cockburn of Skirling: Cockburn, pp.142-7.

55   See further, M.P. McDiarmid, '*The Complaynt of Scotlande:* Patrick Cockburn, Antonio De Guevera, Antonio De Fregoso', *Notes and Queries*, n.s. VI, No. 204 (1959), 245-8.

56   Cockburn, pp.165-6; see also *Scots Peerage*, V, 298.

57   Ibid.; *Maitland Folio MS*, II, 5: 'This buke pertenis to helyne m'.

58   I am most grateful to Mrs Priscilla Bawcutt for helpful advice and for saving me from one large error; to Dr Keith Williamson for checking and correcting the transcription of R; and to Professor Angus McIntosh for acting as a benevolent intermediary.

14

'A Sober and Peceable Deportment':
The Court and Council Books of Dumfries
1561-1661

Marion M. Stewart

On 19 August 1561, Mary Queen of Scots stepped ashore at the port of Leith to begin her short and troubled spell as Queen in her native country. The feuds and divisions that sundered her kingdom had their beginnings long years previously, in many cases before her birth, reaching from beyond the borders of Scotland. Her presence alone could not heal them. For the next hundred years her successors were to find their northern land a hard place to govern and Cromwell's Protectorate met with no easier task. Faction was rife, religious and political and, underlying all, were the old hostilities between rival and ambitious families ready to snatch every opportunity to enhance their own positions at the expense of their neighbours'.

The picture seems bleak and yet the period from 1561 to 1661 in Scotland is also one of vigour and excitement marked by dynamic change. From such a time of strong and conflicting opinions, much remains to us in journals, polemical writings, letters and literary works illuminating the issues of the day and the reactions to these of the more educated and articulate portions of society. But what of that elusive creature the contemporary equivalent of our 'man in the street'? The survival of the Court and Council Books of Dumfries from 1506 virtually without gap until the present day can, perhaps, answer that question for one particular town.

Dumfries has been a Royal Burgh since 1186. It lies amidst peat mosses for fuel and pastureland in the valleys of Nithsdale, Annandale, Eskdale and Galloway. The abundant archaeological remains in its vicinity from Iron Age forts to Roman camps, Neolithic burial grounds to centres of the Celtic Church of the Dark Ages show that this area has been richly and variously populated from the earliest times, and the central position of the town at the crossing of the river Nith has ensured its importance as 'Queen of the South'. For centuries, Dumfries was one of the most populous towns in Scotland with a flourishing trade promoted both by this strategic situation and by the seagoing ports within the confines of the burgh and nearby Glencaple, Kirkbean, Carsethorne, Annan and Kircudbright. Unlike Edinburgh, Perth, Linlithgow, Stirling, Falkland and Dunfermline, Dumfries was never the seat of the Scottish court though kings came and went on pilgrimage to Whithorn or on military expeditions against the English or the overmighty barons of the Border country. Dumfries had one unique feature, however, and that was its location so close to the border of England and at a position of such strategic importance as is recorded wearily in the Court and Council Books of December 1665 when the town's financial losses were being added up:

> Drumfries [is] lying in the roadway betwixt Glasgow, Ayr, Irvine, Galloway and Ingland so that all the forces which either went to England or came from England to any of these pairts came throw Drumfries and quartered thair...[1]

The Town Council of Dumfries comprised the provost and three bailies (the magistrates), the treasurer, the dean, twelve merchant councillors and seven craftsmen representing the seven incorporated trades, one of whom was convenor of trades. When the magistrates sat without the other councillors, their meeting constituted the Burgh Court. Until well into the seventeenth century, the proceedings of Court and Council were recorded continuously within the same minute books which therefore provide a remarkably full and detailed picture of the life and the inhabitants of the burgh and its landward area. Misdemeanours and disputes of all kinds came before the Burgh Court and all manner of deeds and contracts were registered in the Court Books. As for the Council, it sat usually once a week but sometimes met daily and its discussions ranged over every aspect of life in the community. All who wished to follow a craft or purvey goods within the burgh had to become burgesses or freemen on the payment of a burgess fee and the swearing of an oath of loyalty and all had to stand to watch and keep weapons always ready and at hand for the town's defence. All new burgesses were, of course, enrolled in the Court and Council Books. There could not have been much that happened within the town that did not find some echo in the pages of these books.

In the weeks around the time of Mary's arrival in Scotland in 1561, the Dumfries Court and Council Books are concerned only with the normal business of the burgh. Nine shillings is given to Herbert Stewart in alms;[2] Fergus McNaught is fined for having 'arranguslie withhald fra Robert Velche ane blak broun bakit kow the space of sex zeris';[3] the Council being 'ryiple advisit', choose Herbert Cunnyngham Court Clerk (and we have his Protocol Book from 1561 to 1574 surviving in fragments); and on the same date, John Adamson is chosen 'thoun mynstrall' for a year.[4] William Reid is found guilty of 'unressonable streikin David Curror sumtyme his presenteis [apprentice]... &...Roger Muirheid likwyis his prenteis & drawin thair bluids' for which he is fined and made to 'ask the gudton forgeifnes' as well as the unfortunate apprentices, and, at the same hearing, Herbert Maxwell denies the charge of

striking his servant Edward Brown.[5] The following week, the Council enacts
that no unmarried man may henceforth become a burgess:

> The quhilk day the Inqueist ryiplie advisit anent the makin of fremen nochtt
> havand houss land nor place to resaif as the burrow law requiris heirfoir thai
> ordane...that...thair be na freman maid in tyme cumyng quhill he be mariet
> & cled with ane vyif.[6]

The remaining weeks of the winter see the usual disputes over goods bought
and not paid for—'ane blak naig with tua quhit fuytt behynd' on 4 November;
'thre pund of blew vell brocht out of Edinburcht' on 3 December and 'thrie syids
of beiff' on 1 March 1561/2; of rent due; of inheritance denied—David Maxwell
seeking to prove that his brother John has 'vranguss withhald fra hym ane silver
ring & tua scheipskynnis'[7] amongst other items. A son undertakes to repair his
widowed mother's house 'to mak it lokfast and valtir fast';[8] the price of ale
within the town is fixed at 'auch pennies the quart';[9] Sir Patrick Vallace, now
calling himself 'minister of Drumfries' confirms that he has 'compleit
matrimony betuix Thomas Myll & Jonet McIlrewe'.[10] On 5 February 1561/2,
the Council enacts that 'na persone cutt doune & away tak his nychtbors
growand wod hege' or bear false witnes against him:

> na persone call ane uthir comond theif & speciafie ane criminale cryme to
> hym of the quhilk he beis fund cleine thairof and innocent undir the pane of
> xiss to the complenar without fauors & to ask the persone foirgevines in
> presens of the congregatioun...

Periodic inquests are held to determine right to inherit land and a protracted case
starts on 11 March 1561/2 with David Fell denying that he should be debarred
from his inheritance on the grounds of imputed 'bastardrie', calling for justice
from the magistrates 'as thai vald anser befoir God'.

The first indication of the wider world comes in a list of coins collected by the
burgh treasurer in feu duties which include 'empriors crounis', 'silver groitts',
'souss', 'half ane unicorne of gold', a 'dowbill dowikate', 'ane angell nobill', a
'Ross nobill', 'pestolatts', a 'frank', 'Ingliss crounis', a 'spanze riale', an 'abbay
croune' and 'crounis of the sone'—old and new money of Scotland, England,
France, Spain and beyond.[11]

On 7 October 1562, a new Council is sworn in and the language of the
Reformation echoes in their oaths of office—the provost 'as he vill anser to the
evirlasting lord on the extreym day', the scribes and clerks 'to tak the eternale
lord for thair...defence', the lynors (tasked to reaffirm the burgh boundaries) 'the
eternale god cumand betuene for vitnes'. And the next day we have mention of
John Knox preaching in the parish church when the witness in a debt case dates
his evidence 'this done the last day that John Knoks prechit in Drumfries kirk'.

Indications of the religious and political upheavals of the time are but feeble in Dumfries Court and Council Books which are only concerned with the daily business of the burgh at this period. Trade must be regulated and the monopoly of burgesses protected. Thus the setting up of a booth or loft by any unfreeman must be forbidden;[12] 'landwart...valkcars' [country cloth waulkers] may have a place reserved for them on the market day to sell 'claiths wrocht be thaim...providand that thai sett nocht up burd & verk within this burcht with thair lumis as fremen'[13] and new burgesses are sworn in as freemen, providing, along with their burgess fee, 'spice & vyne'[14]—perhaps to celebrate their new status. Stern warnings are issued against the stealing of peats[15] and public roups are held where, amongst such routine domestic and agricultural implements as 'quernis...ane hand ax...ane litill barrell, ane walter paill...ane feddir bed with ane bolster...ane spade...ane plew[t] with plew irnis...ane quheill barrow' and 'ane auld harrow' one finds the occasional reminder of the dangerous proximity of the Border—'ane sword' and 'ane steil bonat'.[16]

Lawlessness was never held at bay for long and the Court and Council Books are full of accounts of brawls and attacks. Indeed, probably the most common entry at this period is that recording the caution [surety] for such miscreants to keep the peace. This 'domestic' violence within the confines of the burgh is seen on a greater scale in the interfamily feuds throughout the Border country. When Thomas Roresone of Bardanoch and his kinsmen are summoned to Court in December 1580 for an alledged attack on Robert Fergusson of Craigdarroch and his kinsmen, they are said to have appeared 'boden in feir of weir with jakis...jeddart staifis lang culveringis and pistolettis'.[17]

By this time, Mary Queen of Scots had been a prisoner in England for more than a decade and the young James VI, having taken up the reins of government himself at the early age of twelve in 1578, was being pulled from faction to faction, being actually kidnapped by the pro-English party at the Raid of Ruthven in August 1582. For the whole of this period the Dumfries Court and Council Books reflect a scene of lawlessness in south west Scotland recording the Hornings [outlawry] and other forms of Diligence against one feuding family after another—Tyndings, Johnstons, Maxwells, Jardines, Carlisles and Irvings[18] —the fault of the latter being compounded, for their bandit gang included Englishmen—

> haveing consavit ane deidlie hatred & malise againis [John Carruthers younger of Holmend] tresonablie brocht in ye said english within our realme" [and having waylaid the unfortunate John] as he wes in sober and quyet maner doand his lefull affairis [and chased him] be ye space of thrie quarters of ane myle to john Tuidingis hous...hurt and woundit him with yair drawin swerds in the right scholder to ye effusioun of his bluid in greit quantitie and left him lyand for deid.[19]

The Horning of the Armstrongs recorded in December 1582 reads almost like a prose version of *The Ballad of Kinmont Willie* although that famous raid did not take place until April 1596. Heading the list of robbers are:

Sandiis Ringan Armstrang brother german to Will of Kinmont, Sandis Fergie Armstrang in Krtillheid, Sandis Jok Armstrang callit Wallis, Jok Armstrang callit Castells, Gerdie Armstrang, Francie and Thom Armstrang sonis to Will of Kinmont, Jhone Armstrang of Hollhous, Christie Armstrang of Barcleis his brother...Ringand Armstrang bastard sone to Will of Kinmont...young Christie Armstrang of Auchingabill...and Ronnie Armstrang in Carrentoun.

They, with about a hundred 'common theivis brokin men and out lawis' had stolen twelve score of sheep from Lanarkshire. Pursued for two days by the angry owners, a body of only seventeen men with a 'sleuth hound dog', the Armstrongs had turned on their pursuers and 'sot wpone and crewelie inwadit thaim for thair slauteris put violent hands in ther personis tuik tham captivis and presoners' holding them to ransom in 'strait firmance and captivitie'.[20] Unfortunately, although the rebellious Armstrongs were thus duly 'put to his heines horne be given of thrie blastis yrin',[21] it was not possible to serve warning on them at close quarters—'becaus the said persons duells vpon or borders qulks ar broken be thaim *ubi non est intus accessus* and or officars dar not repair to the perts qrin thai duell for fear of ther lyf'.[22]

It was not until after 1605 when James VI established a body of forty well-equipped horsemen to hunt down outlaws that some measure of law and order was imposed upon these turbulent families. Little wonder then, that the subject of keeping the watch is one which recurs so frequently in the Court and Council Books of Dumfries. On 2 November 1643 the Council decides that since 'thare is great burdans dayly...on ye baillies...qrby they cannot conveniently attend upon ye watchand of ye sd burghe', four 'serjantis' are to be appointed to oversee the nightly setting of the watch and to punish those who fail to appear to stand their turn. This is a recurring preoccupation. In March 1644 the Council complains of 'the slacknes in keiping the watche...therfore they ordane all these that have bein absent from the watche in tymes past this twelfmonth' to be fined and, in future, 'all men aither cum themselffs or send a sufficient sensable man provydet wt armes & conforme to ye wapinshaw'.[23]

By this time, the Civil War was under way, the first major royalist defeat taking place at Marston Moor in July 1644. Closer to Dumfries, nearby Caerlaverock Castle, held by the Earl of Nithsdale for the King, had fallen to the Covenanters in autumn 1640 as had Threave Castle a month later. In September 1643 the Scottish Covenanters signed the Solemn League and Covenant with the English Puritans under Cromwell. The landed interest in Annandale and Nithsdale was strongly for the Covenanting cause, but Montrose, supported by three local lairds, the Earl of Nithsdale, the Earl of Annandale and Sir John Charteris of Amisfield, attempting to turn the tide for the King, entered Dumfries on 14 April 1644 meeting no opposition from the prudent if unenthusiastic townsfolk.

During these years of civil war, the Court and Council Books still have as their staple fare the routine business of the town. Seven 'alewives' are fined for 'trangressing the townes actis the last yeare anent the aill pryce' in November 1643;[24] in December, Robert Stewart brings a complaint against George Stronge younger 'for abusing of him in his awin hous & striking of him & screwing his nose';[25] in the following May, two chapmen are causing a 'ryot' by brawling in the street;[26] in October 1645, John Gilly is fined twenty pounds for the shocking offence of 'abusing the magistrates behind yr baks & calling them scheipe'.[27]   In the spring of 1646, the Council, 'considering ye necessity of ane weill keipit schoole wtn yis burgh' sets aside 200 merks Scots yearly for the masters who are to teach 'the Latiners & yese who lairnis bot English' decreeing that 'all lads go to the high schoole' and 'ilk landwart barne' too and that 'no wemen keip scholis but such as are approvin be ye magistrates & counsall'.[28]   In the autumn it is found to be 'expedient that thare be visitors appoynted in ilk quarter of this burghe for visiting the seek'[29] and two months later, on 3 October 1646, a merchant who has dared to refuse to fill the vacancy in the Council to which he has been elected is fined one hundred pounds and has his 'booth closed up'.

But there are now increasingly frequent references to the war. On 21 May 1644, Bailie John Johnstoune produces for the Council's approbation 'the compt of the armes & ammunitione which was directed hym to buy for the touns use'. That October, two runaway soldiers appear before the Council, each promising to return 'to his colors at Newcastell within fyftein days under the pain of death'[30] and a proclamation goes round the town accompanied 'with touk of drum' on 28 January 1645 warning all who have sustained losses in the 'lait invasion' to make such known.   On 22 August 1645, 'the provest baillies & counsall with advyse of ye communitie of ye said burgh has concludet that in caice yis burghe be charget to capitulat wt Muntrose that they sall refuse to capitulat with him'—an unusually forthright statement of policy.

From now onwards, the presence of soldiers within the burgh is constantly mentioned whether they are being 'admittit burgesses gratis' as in the case of a colonel, six captains, three lieutenants, four cornets, three quartermasters and their servant on 15 February 1647, or whether the cost and inconvenience of quartering and provisioning them is the matter at issue.[31]   An additional tax on malt brewing has to be imposed on 16 March 1653 to deal with 'the manifold pressores and burdeines...vndirgone since the begineing of the wares by continewance of assessments and vthire publict burdeines especiallie for relief of poor orphanes and widowes'.[32]

These financial and other distresses are exacerbated by the need for the town to keep its own soldiers for its protection. In March 1648, the Council 'appyntit ane guard of 24 men and 3 serjants for the defens of the toun to be interteint vpoun ye tounes chairges at ane groat to ye souldars and vii to everie serjant',[33] James Young 'chyrurgiane' having petitioned successfully to be excused payment of stent that year because of 'his paynes in hireing of sojors'.[34] Warnings to increase the watch are issued regularly.[35]

A strong watch was needed for another reason. In 1645 and again in 1648 plague had swept the country and the repeated complaint of poverty and hardship in the Court and Council Books owes as much to this evil as to the scourge of war. On 25 February 1645 we find the Council instructing all inhabitants to keep very strict watch and to 'suffer nather personis nor goods to cum in to this toune qull they first acquent ye magistrates'. Further 'considering that yr is sundrie ostlers of this burgh who resetts strangers & runaway sojors preivilie...na persones ostlers or utheris resett ony strangers or runaway soiors...'. Beggars are also to be banished, the gates of the yards are to be strengthened to debar plague-bearing strangers, if need be at the town's expense, the owners being charged subsequently and all are warned not to 'use any bedding aithir in Edinburgh or the Eist borders and that no guids at all be broght from the eist border nor come from Edinburgh except confiscation of goods'. The 1648 outbreak coincided with the principal fair of Dumfries, the 'ruidfair' and it was decided to cancel this altogether lest packs of 'merchant wair' being carried into the burgh for the fair bring with them the plague of which the provost, visiting Edinburgh at the time, had written to the Council 'the greit feir and incres of the plague of pestilence in the Burghes of Edinburgh, Glasgow, Dundie and utheris pairtis'.[36]

After these several years of war, plague and financial distress, it is perhaps hardly surprising that 1649 and 1650 should be marked by a spate of witchcraft trials. These are recorded elsewhere than in the Court and Council Books of the burgh for the most part but it is noted in the Council minutes of 21 January 1650 that a councillor has been 'electit & choysin...to goe to Edinburgh to bring in ane commissioune anent the witches dittay'.

In the political upheavals of the early 1650s, the Council of Dumfries had no wish to become embroiled. On 11 August 1652, having received a letter from the Convention of Royal Burghs calling on Dumfries to send the usual representative to the forthcoming meeting in Edinburgh:

> the baillies and counsill finds it expedient that in respect that the sd conventioune is mainlie intendit for the unione betuixt this natione & England and they feiring that thair comissionar may aither be ensnared in that bussines or vtherweys be necessitat to protest agains the procedar of the convention and so irritat the burrowis and also the Inglish they have thoght gud to nominat no comissionar at this tyme.

An admirably frank piece of sitting on the fence.

An undated draft letter from the Council to General Monck (presumably written whilst he was 'ruling' Scotland (1650-51) after Cromwell had defeated the country), assures him 'how much we esteeme ourselves obliged to yor Lo. for yor wyse & sober deportment in your station & speciall care for maintanance of the publick peace of this natne the fruits wheroff we have hapillie enjoyit with our othirs countriemen & neighbors...', promising that:

> or deportment hes hitherto been sober & peceable under all these late revolutions so we resolve by the assistance of the Lord to carrie or selves quietlie & inoffencivlie and to preserve the publick peace acording to our power within the bowndes of our jurisdiction and to shunne all turbulent & seditios wayes and to doe everie thing for this effect that may consist wt the dutie of sober and peceable men and wt the freedome & saftie of or consciences.... [37]

Under the heavy pressure of finding the wherewithal to meet the town's financial obligations to the ever-present soldiers and to their 'widows & orphants', stress is laid on the strict exactment of traditional duties and customs and on the imposition of new ones.[38] Life must have been quite hard and real poverty common.

In the middle of the 1650s the Council seems to have been seized with a determination to purge the town of vice and immorality. From 1655 until 1660 there is a steady stream of single women being driven out of the burgh or, alternatively, being bound over to go into service or be married, their male kinsfolk standing caution that they will thus remove their tempting presence from the community.[39] On 20 March 1655, it is drunkenness that is at issue and several brewers are signing a pledge entered in the Council Book that:

> no vitious or scandalous persones sall be harboured or resett in our houses and that we nor none of our families sall be found drunk and that we sall resett no drunken persones qtsomevir in our houses and we sall not sell drink to any persone or persones within our houses vpoun the sabath....

In August, sexual laxity is the Council's target—'Johnne Burges younger weiver confest fornication with Helein Broune she being sleipie & in drink'[40] and was duly punished.

Strangers, always suspect, are now to be refused shelter within the burgh especially those who are paupers—

> Counsall considering the great hurt & inconvenience done to this burt by setting of houses to strangers athir scandalous or without testimoniallis or to these wha being of vther congregatiounes does burding the burt by thaimselffes and thair children whairas thair severall congregatiouns by the lawes of the natioune aucht to mantein thair awin poore.[41]

In 1657 the Council's onslaught on unruly behaviour intensifies. On 30 March, Margaret Maxwell is fined because 'she did cast ane cup at hir husband' and on 25 May, Will Hall 'is ordained to be whipped throw the most publict streit of this burt' and to promise 'to depairt himselffe wyffe & childreene' and 'giff ever he beis found within this burt that he sall be brunt on the cheik and suffer other punishment as the counsell think fitting...' a sentence being passed with increasing frequency at this time. Next month a shocking case of moral turpitude comes to light—'the counsell considering the filthiness committit be Robert Turner wt Agnes Harbertsone & Jannett Turner living all in one hous & lying altogither in one bed for a long space' all three are to be 'scourged instantly throw the cheif streits' and banished forthwith.[42] A few days later, on 20 June 1657, Agnes Rae, whose fault is not specified, is enjoined to keep the peace swearing 'to live and behave hirselffe civiley & christianlie vnder the paine of banishment'.

In July, the merrymaking at baptisms and weddings comes under attack:

> the counsell taking into thair consideratioun the great abuses comitted by too numerous conventions at brydles & baptisms...have restricted the samyn in tymes coming to the numbers efter specifeit viz every baptism not to exceid the number of twelf persons men & women...and that every brydle shall not exceid the number of twenty four persons & the pryce not to exceid aught s. scots & to continew our for one day.[43]

By September, the minister of Dumfries is so overwhelmed with work that the Council agree to find 'ane thowsand merks scots' for a salary for an assistant for him 'having befoir thair eyes the glorie of god the propagatioun of the gospell and the beiring doun of sinn & iniquitie in this place'.[44] So heavy is the emphasis at this period on the correction of morals that one could imagine the records to be those of the Kirk Session rather than the Burgh Court and Council Books.

In 1660 a new and ominous voice is heard in the deliberations of the council, that of Major Thomas Carruthers. His name had appeared a few times already in the sederunt list though there is no record of his having been elected to sit on the

Council and he was clearly not a burgess, for the record shows that he was admitted burgess, free, on 8 October along with Major James Grierson brother german to the Laird of Lag.   Nonetheless, on 4 October 1660, at the first meeting after the annual election of the Council when the magistrates and other officials are being chosen, 'Major Thomas Carruthers protestit that no man be put vpon the lists for magistracie or electit magistrats that are suspect of disloyaltie to his maitie [Majesty]'.   Such an unwarranted interference in the running of the Council is not to be ignored and 'James Muirheid protestit that the Counsall was dursed be Major Carruthers in the electione for voting of any man that wes cited'.   The Major's response is decisive; he 'producit ane order under the Chancellors hand to cite severall persones in Drumfreis to Edinburgh to anssr to what is laid to thair charge of qlk number James Muirheid is ane and thairfore protests he is no baillie'.   He follows this up by demanding the names of those 'that voted James muirheid to be baillzie'.   For the next twenty years the proceedings of the Court and Council are to be dominated by the presence of this or some other king's agent ever vigilant to report to higher authority any action or remark that did not seem to conform exactly in loyalty to Charles II or the religious establishment imposed by him upon his northern kingdom.   There are futile attempts at resistance but soon the independent voice and lively debate so marked a feature of these volumes in earlier times have quite disappeared. The tone is already set in the entry of 4 December 1660: 'the counsall is resolvit to bestow vpon Major Carrutheris ane silver cup worth ane hundreth merkis'.   In the event, it was to cost even more!

There is one final brave gesture of defiance.   In April 1661, just before Charles II's coronation, a special oath of allegiance is sent out over the country to which all those in positions of responsibility must swear.   The Council meets for this purpose in Dumfries on 9 April, but only the provost, one bailie and one councillor agree to do so, the other nineteen councillors present refusing to accept so absolute a statement of royal power in all aspects of church and state. They reconvene on 10 April and again the oath is put to the Council but only three more members agree to swear it.   On 11 April, the six who have taken the oath meet in the Tolbooth and 'having sittein abone halfe ane hor at the counsall table waiting for the apeirance of these magistrates & counsallors who the tua preceeding days did refuis to tak the oath...and naine apeiring & desyring to be admittit to the taking thairof' they cite the rebels to appear and once more administer the oath to them.   Finally, reluctantly, the dean, treasurer, deacon of trades and the town clerk swear the oath and there the matter rests.   On 16 April new councillors are sworn in to replace the fourteen who have steadfastly refused to accept the royal edict.

And so the century ends with Charles II back on his throne as it had begun with the return of his great-grandmother, Mary Queen of Scots, to hers.   The Court and Council Books of Dumfries are only one source amongst many even for their own town that reflect the ebb and flow of affairs of state and give, as well, a glimpse of the lives of the townsfolk going about their daily business. The magistrates and Council on the whole served their town faithfully according to their own lights. Ever jealous of their own and the burgh's privileges, they kept an eye to its prosperity and future security. Above all, throughout a hundred years of constant and dangerous political and religious tumult, their shrewd and prudent management kept Dumfries on a reasonably calm and steady course: perhaps not heroic but no mean achievement nonetheless.

NOTES

1   All references (unless otherwise specified) are to the Court and Council Books of Dumfries and are by date of entry. Where this is stated in the text, it is not repeated in a footnote. Alfred E. Truckell, the former Curator of Dumfries Museum, has transcribed long passages from these records and his voluminous notes and transcripts are an invaluable starting point.

2   25 July 1561.

3   31 July 1561.

4   1 October 1561.

5   7 October 1561

6   15 October 1561.

7   17 December 1561.

8   21 January 1561/2.

9   5 February 1561/2.

10   21 January 1561/2.

11   1 October 1562.

12   28 October 1562.

13   25 November 1562.

14   3 November 1562.

15   21 April 1563.

16   22 April 1563.

17   10 December 1588.

18   5 April 1581 (Tyndings); 25 April 1581 (Johnstons); 31 December 1582 (Maxwells); 17 June 1583 (Jardines), and 6 June 1583 (Carlisles and Irvings.

19   6 June 1583.

20   5 December 1582; transcribed by G.W. Shirley, *Transactions and Journal of Proceedings of the Dumfriesshire and Galloway Natural History and Antiquarian Society* (1910-11), pp.298-302.

21   20 June 1581.
22   5 December 1582, transcribed by Shirley, loc. cit.
23   14 March 1644.
24   30 November 1643.
25   8 December 1643.
26   15 May 1644.
27   15 October 1645.
28   30 May 1646.
29   8 August 1646.
30   18 and 19 October 1644.
31   See also 1 November 1651.
32   See also 1 November 1651; 22 June 1653, and 4 November 1653.
33   27 March 1648; see also 8 November 1648.
34   28 February 1648.
35   18 February 1650.
36   1 September 1648.
37   Council Book 1651-61, fol.iii.
38   4 November 1653; 1 March 1653, and 12 April 1656.
39   13 August 1655 et seq.
40   17 August 1655.
41   28 July 1656.
42   11 June 1657.
43   6 July 1657.
44   21 September 1657.

15

David Lyndsay's 'Antique' and 'Plesand' Stories

Janet H. Williams

David Lyndsay opened his *Dreme* with an epistle to James V that is a charming though late example of the formal petition. It is also, undeniably, one man's 'personal reminiscences'.[1] Lyndsay's epistle lists facts—his devoted offices since the prince's birth, and the former activities shared by himself as familiar servitor and the 'our ʒong' king. That these details have not been considered more closely is surprising: the *Dreme* is Lyndsay's first work for the sixteen-year-old James as King of Scots in person as well as name. It is without question a literary and historical landmark of the reign, the formal beginning of a conscious shaping of James V's attitudes to monarchy and to the allied political, social, and religious issues he would face as leader. Those details of the past Lyndsay selected for recall at such a moment are surely important.

Prominent among these is Lyndsay's list, in three of the epistle's eight stanzas, of the 'antique' and 'amiabyll' stories, fables, and 'Prophiseis' that he has told his young charge:

> I haue, at lenth, the storeis done discryue
> Off Hectour, Arthour, and gentyll Iulyus,
> Off Alexander, and worthy Pompeyus,
>
> Off Iasone, and Media, all at lenth,
> Off Hercules the actis honorabyll,
> And of Sampsone the supernaturall strenth,
> And of leill Luffaris storeis amiabyll;
> And oft tymes haue I feinʒeit mony fabyll,
> Off Troylus the sorrow and the Ioye,
> And Seigis all, of Tyir, Thebes, and Troye;
>
> The Prophiseis of Rymour, Beid, & Marlyng,
> And of mony vther plesand storye,
> Off the reid Etin, and the gyir carlyng,
> Confortand the, quhen that I sawe the sorye. (33-46)

Scottish Text Society editor, Douglas Hamer, has envisaged these stories as lost works by Lyndsay himself, and interprets accordingly: 'Most were probably written for the King's benefit, and as part of his education, athough Lindsay was never the King's tutor'.[2]   More recently, Sandra Cairns has assumed that Lyndsay told these same stories 'purely for [James's] amusement and pleasure'.[3] Lyndsay does indeed say: 'More plesandlie the tyme for tyll ouerdryue,/ I haue…the storeis done discryue' (32-3). The exact nature of these stories, and of Lyndsay's attitude towards them, becomes of even greater significance when, at the end of his catalogue, Lyndsay links his own forthcoming poem to them, as 'a storye…new' (48). The catalogue of stories may thus provide the way to a better understanding of Lyndsay's purposes for his poem, and help to resolve critical interpretations.

Lyndsay refers first to the heroic histories, chronicles and romances he has told the prince. James has been, Lyndsay says, 'rycht Inquisityue' (30) to know them.   Such gatherings of exemplary material, their presentation to the monarch, and even the flattering recall of the monarch's eagerness to be so entertained, are aspects of the long-established occupation of those close to the king's person and within his court. The monarch's familiar servitors, it is now well documented, were expected to offer him political and moral advice, and to encourage him to study the ancient and modern histories for the practical lessons and examples they provided.[4]

Surviving records give ample demonstration of this particular young king's awareness of the tradition and its benefits. In July 1527, he awarded Hector Boece a generous pension for his *Historia Scotorum*.[5]   Soon after, certainly before August or September 1531, James commissioned John Bellenden to produce a prose translation of Boece's Latin text.[6] Similarly, William Stewart, probably a servant of James's mother, Queen Margaret, began his commissioned metrical translation of Boece by 1531.[7]   Both Bellenden and Stewart appended to their translations more intimate poems, in which James and his hoped-for conduct are referred to either obliquely or directly. In Bellenden's 'Proheme apon the Cosmographe', for example, a 'crounit King…/ With tender dounis riseing on his beird' is introduced (stanza 8).[8] That the young James was expected to identify with this figure, taking personally the moral instructions that follow, is not lessened when, in the penultimate stanza, the king in the poem is tactfully named as 'val3eant Hercules'. William Stewart, describing his translated book as 'mony nobill storie,/ … / Of eldaris deidis (22, 24), uses an allegorical figure— cousin to 'Discretioun' (12)—to instruct the king. James is to 'considder the rycht ay as he reidis,/ Thair nobilnes and als thair douchty deidis' (30-1), and 'How that he wes predestinat to ring,/ Siclike as tha…' (35-6).[9]

In this company, Lyndsay's first-listed stories in the *Dreme*'s epistle are plainly orthodox choices, though it can also be said that they were especially appropriate to the circumstances of the fatherless and captive young man. But their orthodoxy as examples of advice literature colours Lyndsay's assertion to

James that he told these stories simply '[m]ore plesandlie the tyme for tyll ouerdryue' (32). This is also the diplomatic wording of an intimate, the careful description of the 'Yschare' (23) and 'cheiffe Cubiculare' (24) of the boy who had now become king.

Accounts of noble role models and their 'actis honorabyll' (37) are not, however, all Lyndsay remembers telling James. Neither the next-listed 'Prophiseis of Rymour, Beid, & Marlyng' (43), nor the two following tales of the 'reid Etin' and the 'gyir carlyng' (45), could be classified in this way. What do these works contribute to Lyndsay's catalogue?

Looking first at the prophecies, it is not clear from the wording in the *Dreme*'s epistle whether Lyndsay is referring to one poem entitled 'The Prophiseis of Rymour, Beid, & Marlyng' perhaps of his own authorship,[10] to separate prophecies, or to these three names as representative of those writings that could be defined as political prophecy.[11] Versions of the prophecies attributed to these figures, like those of others often associated with them—Bertlington, Waldhave, Gildas[12]—existed long before the early sixteenth century. (Thomas the Rhymer's forecasts, for example, are said to date from the late thirteenth century, while references to Merlin's are found from at least the twelfth century.)[13] Similarly, sixteenth-century offical records of both Scotland and England are like those of earlier centuries: all contain evidence of the strength of popular belief in these ancient prophecies, or in contemporary re-interpretations of them. These records show also that such beliefs were taken seriously by the authorities, who dealt harshly with those whose interpretations threatened political stability.[14]

By Lyndsay's day, however, educated commentators were often openly sceptical. One such was John Major, whose *History of Greater Britain* was published with a dedication to James V six years before Lyndsay wrote the *Dreme*. He refers frequently to the role in Scotland's past that his source chroniclers gave to prophecy, but he does not agree either with them or with popular attitude:

> Our writers assure us that Thomas often foretold this thing and the other, and the common people throughout Britain give no little credence to such stories, which for the most part—and indeed they merit nothing else—I smile at. For that such persons foretold things purely contingent before they came to pass I cannot admit ....[15]

Though likewise emphatic in expressing his opinion, the learned 'actor' of the later *Complaynt of Scotland* (c. 1550) is less sure that prophecy has no power at all. He also seeks to discredit the 'vane credens' given to the 'propheseis of merlyne' by the 'vulgar ingnorans'. Notwithstanding, he expresses the hope that the prophecy he discusses, and condemns Englishmen for believing—'that ingland and scotland sall be baitht vndir ane prince'—will be fulfilled, though by the conquest of England by Scotland, rather than *vice versa*.[16]

Several of these differing attitudes to prophecy are used to good effect by David Lyndsay. Much later than the *Dreme*'s reference to prophecy as 'plesand storye', Lyndsay's prologue-proclamation for the Cupar performance of the *Satyre of the Thrie Estaitis* (1552) refers to the subject again, but this time the figures associated with prophecy are grouped with other representatives of superstitious nonsense. In these Cupar Banns, the braggart soldier Fyndlaw of the Futeband is made to reveal his real cowardice by the Fool, who is able to frighten him with a simple sheep's head on a stick. Fyndlaw capitulates at once, with these entertainingly ignorant words:

> I[n] nomine patris et filij,
> I trow ʒone be the spreit of gy.
> Na, faith, it is the spreit of marling,
> Or sum scho gaist, or gyrgarling,
> Allace for evir, how sall I gyd me?
> God sen I had ane hoill till hyd me.
> Bot dowt my deid ʒone man hes sworne;
> I trow ʒone be grit gowmakmorne.
> He gaippis, he glowris; howt welloway;
> Tak all my geir and lat me gay.   (250-9)

In the *Satyre*, on the other hand, Lyndsay's reference to Merlin's prophecy—from the wisely-foolish mouth of Foly—is more equivocal. Foly's jumbled text is condemned by the herald Diligence as 'ane evill faird mess' (1690). Yet the few lines Foly quotes are part of a prophecy known from the fifteenth century, which foretold England's defeat by various opponents, usually including Flanders, France, Spain, Norway, Germany, and Scotland.[17]   And so when Foly refers to the then-contemporary wars of Scotland and England, of the Emperor and the king of France, the princes of Germany, Spain, Flanders, and Italy, and of the Pope (1653-68), to show that Merlin's prophecy 'beis compleit this ʒeir' (1680), the so-called 'mess' seems likely to be proven otherwise; Foly's theme, the numberless infinity of fools, seems wisely demonstrated, and Lyndsay makes a point, indirectly, yet with striking force, about the current need for religious and secular heads of government to take stock of their policies.

Lyndsay's varied treatments of prophecy and the figures associated with it—as either 'plesand', as superstitious nonsense, or as an exercise in cynical ambiguity—span and reflect the political changes of thirty to forty years. By the 1550s, when Foly is preaching, James V was dead, and Scotland, its young Queen absent in France, was disunited within its own borders on religious and political issues.[18]   During the minority (1513-24), conversely, there had been fervent hopes for a return to stability and the renewal of the 'glore of princelie gouernyng' (*Papyngo*, 504). The timely return of James IV, whose death at Flodden had come, in these troubled times, to be questioned, was looked for by some—a contemporary reading of Thomas's prophecies of the return of Arthur.[19] After 1515, the regent John Duke of Albany was associated with the figure of deliverance in the political prophecies of Bertlington.[20] By 1524, however, the conditions of the regency could no longer be an inspiration for such thoughts: on 26 July of that year, James was invested in person with the symbols, though not yet the reality, of sovereignty.[21]

This is the time when readings from the 'Prophiseis of Rymour, Beid, & Marlyng' might well have cheered the 'sorye' and powerless young king, even 'confortand' him (to use Lyndsay's exact wording in the *Dreme*, 46). For were they not reminders to James that he was now becoming the focus of such hopes for both the country's future stability and the end to the wars against England?[22] By 1538-9, evidence of such a climate of opinion is found in an exchange of letters between James and the Bishop of Llandaff at York. The Bishop reports the fears of Sir Thomas Wharton, warden of the English western marches, that he, James, had sanctioned the Scots composition and circulation of 'dispitfull and sclandarus ballattis' and 'vane and fantastik prophecyis'. James, stating that it must be the work of English subjects or Scottish rebels in England trying to make trouble between Henry and himself, adds that, as to the prophecies, 'we nevir tuk ne sall tak regard to thame, as thingis proceding without foundment and aganis the gude cristin faith quharintill we leif assuritlie'.[23] Whether in 1538 he could admit this openly, in 1528, at the beginning of James's personal rule, the recall of these prophecies in the *Dreme*'s innocent context of reminiscences, would indeed have been both 'plesand' and adroit.

Of the 'mony vther plesand storye' (44) Lyndsay recalls, the next named is the tale of the 'reid Etin'. Lyndsay's allusion to it is now the earliest recorded,[24] but he implies, by his reference to the tale in a list of otherwise more familiar pieces, that in 1528 the story was known at least within the court. A reference made twenty-two years later, in the *Complaynt of Scotland*, supports this, and indeed suggests that the tale's possible audience was even wider, at least by that later time. The reference is in the writer's 'Monolog', within a summary of the 'storeis' and 'flet taylis' told by the shepherds, their wives, and the servants, for 'recreatioune'.[25] This pastoral setting, underlining the *Complaynt's* implied dispraise of court and city life, indicates also that the stories told in this setting should be a representative sample of writing then popular in Scotland without the court.[26]

Contemporary versions of the Red Etin tale itself have not survived, though the *Complaynt of Scotland*'s descriptive title—'the taiyl of the reyde eyttyn vitht the thre heydis'—indicates the sixteenth-century tale's fabulous subject matter.

Further possible evidence may be sought, however, in versions recorded in later centuries. These, as Professor David Buchan and others have noted, have affinities with Aarne-Thompson 303, 'a wonder tale with an extensive European spread'.[27] Together with the pieces of early evidence already mentioned here, therefore, these later Scottish versions, fruits of the nineteenth-century antiquarian revival of interest in a subject previously uncharted, support the argument that the tale was being told from at least the sixteenth century onward in Scotland.

The version collected by Peter Buchan in the early nineteenth century tells of three young men, two of whom are brothers, who set out in turn to seek their fortunes. In the course of difficult journeys, in which magic tokens and grotesque beasts play important parts, each man is confronted by the Red Etin, in this Englished version, 'a horrid monster, who spared no man, having three frightful heads'.[28] In a dénouement that is apposite to James V's own newly-favourable situation, the youngest man, receiving and heeding the magic tokens along his way, is able to behead severally the Red Etin, free the king of Scotland's daughter, and restore his brother and neighbour to life. Lyndsay groups this tale of the Red Etin monster appropriately, it would seem, with the prophecies and with the story of the powerful giant-witch of Scotland, the 'gyir carling'.

Lyndsay's reference to the story of this fabulous creature is again the earliest recorded,[29] but in this case her tale, or a version of it, is also preserved. It is found in the Bannatyne Manuscript (fols 136b-137a),[30] in a three-stanza poem full of alliterative verve and mock-heroic skill. Dr Helena Shire first drew attention to it as a possible devising for the young Scots king, and suggested that it may have been written by David Lyndsay himself.[31] She noted in evidence Lyndsay's clear mastery of its alliterative metre in the *Satyre of the Thrie Estaitis*; the poem's overall energy yet absence of bawdry, and the nursery-joke outcome of the gyre carling's forceful blow to her would-be lover, Blasour:

> behind the heill scho hatt him sic ane blaw
> Quhill blasour bled ane quart
> off milk pottage Inwart....   (9-11)

Whether or not Lyndsay is the author of the Bannatyne poem, he has declared in the *Dreme*'s catalogue that he told 'Seigis all' (42) to the young king, so it is interesting that the *Gyre Carling* begins thus:

> In Tiberus tyme the trew Imperiour
> Quhen tynto hillis fra skraiping of toun henis wes keipit ....

This has long been recognised as a parody of the opening to the popular late fourteenth century English alliterative work known as the *Siege of Jerusalem:*

> In Tiberyus tyme þe trew emperour,
> Sir Sesar hym sulf seysed in Rome ....[32]

With the child king as audience, the Scots parody acquires specific meaning; the youthful James undoubtedly would have recognised the jesting allusion.

In stylistic matters, the *Gyre Carling* is clearly related to the several other comic poems recorded in the Bannatyne and Asloan Manuscripts: 'Quha douttis dremis is bot phantasye?' (*Lichtoun's Dream*, Bann. MS fols 101a-102a); 'Hiry, hary hubbilschow' (*The Maner of ye crying of ane playe*, Bann. MS fols 118b-120b; Asloan MS fols 240a-242b); 'Sym of lyntoun be þe ramis horn' (*King Berdok*, Bann. MS fols 142b-143a); 'My guddame wes ane gay wyfe' (*Kind Kittock*, Bann. MS fols 135b-136a) and 'Listis lordis I sall ȝow tell' (*The Laying of Lord Fergus's Ghost*, Bann. MS fols 114a-115a), the latter also, like the *Gyre Carling*, featuring 'beittokis bour' (5). Like these, the *Gyre Carling's* verse, though seemingly relaxed and colloquial in the manner of the natural storyteller,[33] is highly patterned,[34] apparently recalling for satiric 'antique' effect, an alliterative mode that had flourished much earlier as a vehicle for serious work.[35] Above all the *Gyre Carling's* sense and presentation of the comic is shared. As in other pieces, in the *Gyre Carling* this takes the form of the interaction of fabulous and otherworldly characters with creatures from the familiar domestic world—a shepherd, moles, dogs, wives, and hens mingle with the king of faery and the gyre carling herself. Part of this comic sense is also conveyed by the use of various incongruities, of subject and activity, of function, or size. The task of Blasour's moles—to 'warp doun' (cast, throw or fling down)[36] the 'grit' gyre carling's surely equally immense tower—has the same quality of madness about it that puts whales in 'ane medow grene' (*Lichtoun's Dream*, 59), or supplies the gun turned on King Berdok with bullets of radishes. Follies of landmark origin are also sometimes associated with these discrepancies in size, and the *Gyre Carling* has its own example. Just as, in *The Maner of ye crying of ane playe*, the giantess-wife of Gog Magog 'spatt lochlomound' (45), so the gyre carling, laughing at Blasour's demise, 'lut fart / North berwick law' (12-13).

All the same, the *Gyre Carling* is notably different from these other poems in its treatment of setting. Initially, the Bannatyne poet changes only this element of the *Siege of Jerusalem* opening. It remains the same far-off time of Roman imperial rule, but the place is lowland Scotland, and at first, is specifically Lanarkshire. Though strict chronology is somewhat wanting, this is based on fact: Roman traces are still to be found near Tinto Hills, and also at Cramond, mentioned in stanza three. The *Gyre Carling's* locations, moreover, if wonderfully bathetic in context, are in themselves and as a group not disorienting in the expected manner. This contrasts with *Kind Kittock*'s guddame, who 'dwellt far furth in france, on falkland fell' (2), a description that delivers the mild shock of an impossibility (even if a French colony of craftsmen near Falkland may have inspired it); in *Lichtoun's Dream*, and several other poems, alternatively, odd associations are created by the linking of places by alliterative relationship alone, as in 'poill, pertik, peblis and portiafe' [Poland, Pertik, Peblis and Port Jaffa] (33). By contrast, the area covered in the *Gyre Carling* is coherent and well-defined. The 'defensable bestes' of the *Gyre Carling*'s king of faery, for example, are recruited from an area between Dunbar and Dunblane. These are likely alliterative companions, but also define a stretch of country that would be looked to naturally for extra troops to resolve a siege to the south. What is more, they in turn are sensibly supplemented (given the initial joke that the force is canine), by 'all the tykis'(17) from the more northerly—and more wild and bellicose?—Perth town of Tarvey.[37] Haddington, where the gyre carling has 'widlit sa & wareit' (29) the laying hens, is near to both North Berwick (13) and Dunbar (16).

All the Scottish locations in the *Gyre Carling* are therefore within an area very likely to be familiar to James V, who we know moved between the various royal residences during his minority.[38] Assumptions of his familiarity with the poem's landscape consequently need not depend upon the fact, perhaps only co-incidental, that James's step-father, the Earl of Angus, who had custody of the king from July 1525, held among his baronies lands in both Lanarkshire, country of the Tinto Hills, and East Lothian, where the Douglas stronghold of Tantallon Castle looked inland to the landmark 'created' by the gyre carling, North Berwick Law.[39] That one of James's first acts, on attaining power in 1528, was to 'sett ane sege' on Tantallon's 'mony grit stane' (18) is a nice distortion of the literary plot that could not have been foreseen by its creator.

If the Bannatyne poem was indeed the version of the gyre carling's story told to James, then Lyndsay presented to him a tale in which a younger, but still recognisable, country was a stage—to comic scenes played by that traditional progenitor, the giant; to marvels and curses, and to delightful topographic and historical nonsense. The tale, in its lively alliterative style, was certainly set out to entertain and amuse. Equally, it might have been designed to extend a young king's mental landscape of his kingdom, to overlay the harsh experience of the destructive factionalism of its power-seeking nobles with a sense of the country's wondrous origins.

Returning to the epistle and to Lyndsay's catalogue within it, what has been discovered? Lyndsay's care for the young king's 'amusement and pleasure' in the previous powerless years is emphasised by the balanced yet varied nature of his selection of remembered stories (just as, in the poem's final 'exhortatioun',

Lyndsay's concern for the reigning king as responsible to his people is behind the more direct admonition he there offers). It is equally plain that each story or group of stories in this catalogue has been chosen to make its own contribution to a well-devised educational scheme, which offered James exemplary counsel, inspiring forecasts of his own future role, and jocular portraits of his kingdom in ancient times. More important than both is the less straightforward finding: that the link made by Lyndsay between these stories and his own poem as a new story, declares his own interest. For if part of what Lyndsay has been suggesting to James in the epistle is that he can now be—like the heroes of his 'antique storeis' or King Arthur in the 'plesand' 'Prophiseis of Rymour, Beid, & Marlyng'—saviour to his divided realm, then the complement must be the suggestion that Lyndsay himself can assume, indeed has assumed a role, similar to that of those earlier prophets, of the king's spokesman and guardian. So what follows the *Dreme*'s epistle—of Lyndsay, rather than the king himself, falling asleep in his seashore cave while awaiting the real and metaphorical return of spring to a blighted Scotland, and thereafter, of Lyndsay, on James's behalf, experiencing the instructive dream-vision in which Scotland's welfare is examined from every point of view—seems apt indeed.

NOTES

1   See T.F. Henderson, *Scottish Vernacular Literature* (1898, 3rd rev. ed. Edinburgh, 1910), p.208; C.S. Lewis, *English Literature in the Sixteenth Century*, (Oxford, 1954), p.101.

2   *The Works of Sir David Lindsay*, III, Scottish Text Society 3rd Ser. 6 (Edinburgh and London, 1934), 12. All quotations of are from this edition, STS 3rd Ser. 1, 2, 6, 8 (1931-6).

3   S. Cairns, 'Sir David Lindsay's *Dreme*: Poetry, Propaganda and Encomium in the Scottish Court', in *The Spirit of the Court*, ed. G.S. Burgess and R.A. Taylor (Cambridge, 1985), pp.110-11.

4   See, for example, R. Firth Greene's *Poets and Princepleasers* (Toronto, Buffalo, London, 1980), especially pp.135-67; S.L. Mapstone, 'The Advice to Princes Tradition in Scottish Literature, 1450-1500', Diss. Oxford, 1986.

5   See the full discussion, *The Chronicles of Scotland Compiled by Hector Boece. Translated into Scots by John Bellenden 1531*, ed. E.C. Batho and H.W. Husbands, STS 3rd Ser. 15 (Edinburgh and London, 1941), p.436.

6   Ibid., p.437.

7   See J.M. Sanderson, 'Two Stewarts of the Sixteenth Century. Mr William
        Stewart, poet, and William Stewart, elder depute clerk of Edinburgh', *The
        Stewarts*, XVII, No. 1 (1984), 25-30.

8   *The Mar Lodge Translation of the History of Scotland by Hector Boece*,
        ed. G. Watson, STS 3rd Ser. 17 (Edinburgh and London, 1946), p.5.

9   William Stewart, *The Buik of the Croniclis of Scotland, or a Metrical
        Version of the History of Hector Boece*, ed. W.B. Turnbull, 3 vols
        (London, 1858).

10   Murray, ibid., pp.52-61, appends the prophecy found in BL MS
        Landsdowne 762, fols 75a-88a and Bodleian, Oxford MS 12653 (Rawlinson
        C. 813) fols 72b-88a. *He* gave it the title, 'The Prophisies [*sic*] of
        Rymour, Beid, and Marlyng', alluding to Lyndsay's *Dreme*, l. 43. See also
        Sharon L. Jansen Jaech's discussion of this, '"The Prophisies of Rymour,
        Beid, and Marlyng": Henry VIII and a Sixteenth-Century Politcal
        Prophecy', *Sixteenth Century Journal*, XVI, No. 3 (1985), 291-9.

11   R. Taylor, *The Political Prophecy in England* (1911, rpt New York, 1967),
        p.2ff, gives a succinct definition of the term 'political prophecy'.

12   See *A Collection of Ancient Scottish Prophecies in Alliterative Verse:
        Reprinted from Waldegrave's Edition MDCIII*, Bannatyne Club (Edinburgh,
        1833).

13   *The Romance and Prophecies of Thomas of Erceldoune*, ed. J.A.H. Murray,
        Eary English Text Society Orig. Ser. 61 (London, 1875), pp.ix-xvii; E.B.
        Lyle, 'Thomas of Erceldoune: the Prophet and the Prophesied', *Folklore*,
        LXXIX (1968), 111-21; Geoffrey of Monmouth, *The History of the Kings
        of Britain*, trans. L. Thorpe (Harmondsworth, 1966); J. Wood, 'A Celtic
        Sorcerer's Apprentice: the Magician Figure in Scottish Tradition',
        *Proceedings of the Third International Conference of Scottish Language and
        Literature*, ed. R. Lyall and F. Riddy (Stirling/Glasgow, 1981), pp.127-42.

14   For examples, see M.H. Dodds, 'Political Prophecy in the Reign of Henry
        VIII', *Modern Language Review* XI (1916), 276-84; K. Thomas, *Religion
        and the Decline of Magic*, (London, 1971), pp.396-415.

15   *A History of Greater Britain as well England as Scotland*, trans. A.
        Constable, Scottish History Society X (Edinburgh and London, 1892),
        190-1.

16   Robert Wedderburn, *The Complaynt of Scotland*, ed. A.M. Stewart, STS 4th
        Ser. 11 (Edinburgh, 1979), 64, 65, 66-7. All quotations are from this
        edition.

17   See C.W. Previté-Orton, 'An Elizabethan Prophecy', *History*, II (1918),
        210-11.

18   Lyndsay's acute awareness of the change is evident in his 'Epistil to the
        Redar' (actually addressed to his book), attached to *The Monarche*, ll. 1-
        117.

19   Taylor, ibid., p.77.

20   Murray, ibid., pp.xxxiv-vi.

21   *The Letters of James V*, ed. R.K. Hannay, and D. Hay (Edinburgh, 1954), pp.110-13; Gordon Donaldson, *Scotland: James V to James VII*, (Edinburgh, 1965), p.38.

22   Dodds, ibid., p.281.

23   *James V Letters*, p.365.

24   See *DOST* and *SND*, s.v. 'etin'. ('Etin' is recorded from c. 1515 and 'reid etin' from 1528.)

25   A.J. Aitken, 'Oral Narrative Style in Middle Scots', *Actes du 2e Colloque de Langue et de Littérature Ecossaises (Moyen Age et Renaissance)*, ed. J.-J. Blanchot and C. Graf (Strasbourg, 1978), p.109, suggests that the author of the *Complaynt* 'seems to oppose' 'flet taylis' and 'storeis'. Lyndsay, though he uses 'storeis' to refer to all of his pieces, is possibly making a similar distinction: his own 'flet taylis' (the prophecies and the folk tales) are carefully grouped together.

26   *Complaynt of Scotland*, p.xl.

27   David Buchan, 'Folk Tradition and Literature till 1603', *Bryght Lanternis: Essays on the Language and Literature of Medieval and Renaissance Scotland*, ed. J. Derrick McClure and Michael R.G. Spiller (Aberdeen, 1989), p.7. I am most grateful to Professor Buchan for his patient explanations and invaluable references.

28   'Ancient Scottish Tales: An Unpublished Collection Made by Peter Buchan', ed. J.A. Fairley, in *Transactions of the Buchan Field Club*, IX (1908), 143-7. See also Robert Chambers, *Popular Rhymes of Scotland* (4th ed. Edinburgh, 1870; rpt Detroit, 1969), pp.89-94; Joseph Jacobs, *English Fairy Tales* (3rd ed. London, 1897; rpt New York, 1967).

29   *DOST*, s.v. 'gyre-carling'; *SND* s.v. 'Gyre', I, senses 1 and 3.

30   All quotations are from *The Bannatyne Manuscript*, Scolar facsimile, introd. by D. Fox and W. Ringler (London, 1980). The text of the poem is incomplete: stanza 2 lacks line 6; stanza 3 line 7.

31   'Style King James V', an unpublished paper delivered at the Second International Conference on Scottish Language and Literature (Medieval and Renaissance), Strasbourg, 1978.

32   In *Early Popular Poetry of Scotland*, ed. D. Laing, revised by W.C. Hazlitt (London, 1895), II, 18-19, Laing refers to John Leyden's note of this in his edition of the *Complaynt of Scotland* (Edinburgh, 1801), pp.221-2. *The Siege of Jerusalem*, ed. E Kölbing and M. Day, EETS, Orig. Ser. 188 (London, 1932).

33   See A.J. Aitken, 'Variation and Variety in Written Middle Scots', in *Edinburgh Studies in English and Scots*, ed. A.J. Aitken, A. McIntosh and H. Palsson (London, 1971), pp.178, 195-6.

34   See the full discussion by M.A. Mackay, 'The Alliterative Tradition in Middle Scots Verse', Diss. Edinburgh, 1975, pp.413-8.

35   See W.A. Craigie, 'The Scottish Alliterative Poems', *Proceedings of the British Academy*, XXVIII (1942), 217-36; J.P. Oakden, *Alliterative Poetry in Middle English*, II (Manchester, 1935), 84; T. Turville-Petre, *The Alliterative Revival* (Cambridge, 1977), p.117.

36   *CSD*, s.v. sense 2.

37   Compare Major, *History*, p.49, on the Wild Scots, who 'dwell more towards the north' and for whom 'war rather than peace is their normal condition'.

38   Attempts to free the king, for example, were made near Melrose, and Linlithgow (both 1526) and were finally successful (1528) when the king escaped from Edinburgh and rode to Stirling.

39   *An Historical Atlas of Scotland c. 400-c. 1600*, ed. P. McNeill and R. Nicholson (1975; rpt St Andrews, 1976), pp.71 and 182 (Map 79).

I acknowledge gratefully the help of Dr E.B. Lyle.

POEMS

16

My Grandmama

She teaches me
the little patterns, the maps
of poetry.
But, stupid student, words
and tags are lost
so easily they evade, finding
definition distasteful
and escape my mind.
I cannot dance
and think alone of my feet
cannot live and remember always how to breathe
--detracting from the beauty--sinful vagrancy.

What I dare to learn
is better than many label-handfuls:
what delicate paces,
furious stilnesses
please the eye and ear
of many Men, writing
patterns before I
And you--
with own patterns of your mind,
what pictures your dancing makes,
the music of your breaths
for the pattern--magic
dear Grandmama of mine
I thank you with love
And simple rhyme.

Helen Bromwich

17

A Gift from Helena

You find them in the corner of a drawer,
at the back of a shelf,
taking up space, gathering dust,
presents—useless, ludicrous,
but affection-prompted,
and guilt forbids their throwing-out.

And there are treasures—
sparkling, gleaming—
precious in themselves,
value-added-to by love,
but burdened.
Suppose them lost, broken, stolen?
Then grief, then consternation.

I have a gift,
bolted and barred beyond all robbery,
safe from time's tarnishing,
accessible at a switch's click
for gloating, for clutching:
the chapel of King's glowing
in the reverence of candles;
music mounting, dying in the vaulting
raised at the Royal Saint's expense;
the long-dreamed-of become here-and-now—
Helena's gift.

Janet Caird

18

The Antagonism

to Helena Shire

The Makers did not make
The muddy winter hardening to privation,
Or cholera in the keep, or frost's long ache
Afflicting every mortal nation
From lord to villagers in their fading dyes
—Those who like oxen strained
On stony clearings of the ground
From church to sties.

They sought an utterance,
Or sunshine soluble in institution,
An orthodoxy justified, at once
The dream and dreamer warmed in fusion,
As in the great Rose Window, pieced from duty
Where through Christ's crimson, sun
Shines on your clothes till they take on
Value and beauty.

But carved on a high beam
Far in the vault from the official version
Gape gnarled unChristian heads out of whom stream
Long stems of contrary assertion,
Shaped leaf ridging their scalps in place of hair.
Their origins lost to sight,
As they are too, cast out from light.
They should despair.

What stays for its own sake,
Occulted in the dark, may slip an ending,
Recalcitrant, and strengthened by the ache
Of winter not for transcending.
Ice and snow pile the gables of the roof
Within whose shade they hold,
Intimate with its slaty cold,
To Christ aloof.

Thom Gunn

INDEX

Addison, Joseph, 82
Advocates Manuscript 18.1.2, 64
Albany, Duke of, *see* Stewart, John
Albyn (MacDiarmid), 114
Alexander I, 81
Alexander, Sir William, 27, 100, 110
Alnwick, 82
Amatoria, 100, 101
Amicus certus in re incerta cernitur
    (Ennius), 62
Anderson, M.L., 60, 61, 62-3, 65-6
Andrewes, Lancelot, 57
Aneau, Barthélemy, French
    Calvinist, 37
Angus, Earl of, *see* Douglas,
    Archibald
*Answere to the Libell called the
    Comons teares*, 107, 108
Antiquae Lectiones (Canisius), 50,
    51
Arthur (King), 159, 163
Ariosto, 40
Asloan Manuscript NLS 4233, 125-
    6, 131-2
Ayton, Sir Robert, 110

Bald, R.C., 50
Ballade of Barnard Stewart (Dunbar),
    116
ballads
    Child collection, 82, 85-8, 89-
        90, 91, 92, 93, 94, 147
    as folksong, 82, 84, 85, 91, 93, 94
    and historical fact, 82, 83, 84, 89-
        90, 93, 94
    oral transmission of, 89, 90, 92,
        93

    recorded in Scotland from 18th c.,
        85, 90, 94
    Sidney's response to, 82
    traditional, 90, 91, 92, 93
Balliol MS 354 (Hill), 59
Bamburgh, 82
Bannatyne, George, 21, 22, 29, 59
Bannatyne Manuscript NLS
    MS.1.1.6, 21, 22, 24, 29, 59,
        63, 67, 124, 133
Barbour, John, 109
Basilikon Doron, 100-1, 108
Bassandyne, Thomas, Scottish
    bookseller and printer, 61
Battle of Harlaw (Child 163), 85
Battle of Otterburn (Child 161), 82,
        85-8, 89-90, 91, 92, 93, 94
Bell, Thomas, *The downfall of
    poperie*, 29
Bellenden, John, 156
Berners, Lord *see* Bourchier
Bertlington, prophet, 157, 159
Biathanatos (Donne), 50
Bible
    Charteris stock, 26, 27
    Geneva, 60
    Latin (Adv. MS 18.1.2), 64
black-letter type, 22, 25, 27, 28, 30
Blind Harry, 109
Boece, Hector, *Historia Scotorum*,
    156
Borders
    as ballad source, 82, 89
    boundaries agreed upon, early
        14th c., 81
    routes across, 82-3

Borders—*contd*
  strategic importance of Dumfries
    in, 144
  see also Wardens of the Marches
Bothwell family
  feud with Cockburns, 124
Bourchier, John, Lord Berners, 81,
    89, 93
Brahe, Tycho, 101
Bronson, Bertrand, *Traditional Tunes
    of the Child Ballads*, 94
Buchan, David, 160
Buchan, Peter, 160
Buchanan, George, 77, 109
Burghley, Lord *see* Cecil
Burns, Robert, 113, 114, 118, 119
Butter, Nathaniel, English stationer,
    23, 28-9
Bynneman, Henry, English printer,
    27

Caerlaverock Castle, 147
Cairns, Sandra, 156
Caldwell, George, Scottish publisher,
    70
Campaspe (Lyly), 27
Campbell, Colin, 3rd Earl of Argyll,
    64
'Can goldin Titan' (Montgomerie),
    60, 97
Canisius, Henricus, *Antiquae
    Lectiones*, 50, 51
Carr, Robert, Viscount Rochester, 31
Carruthers, Thomas, 151-2
Castalian Band, 22, 96, 106, 110
Catholic Appeal for Protestants, A
    (Morton), 50, 51
Cecil, William, Lord Burghley, 43
chapbooks
  authenticity, 71
  decline in popularity of, 71
  dialogue in, 71-2
  nature of, 70-71
  see also Graham, Dougal
Charles II, 94, 152

Charteris, Henry, Scottish bookseller
    and printer, 21, 25, 26-7, 135
Charteris, Margaret (Wallace), 26, 27
Charteris, Robert, bookseller and
    printer, son of Henry, 21, 22,
    23, 24, 25, 26, 29, 30, 32, 125,
    135-6
Chaucer, Geoffrey
  and Logie Robertson, 114
  and Spenser, 46, 47
  Wife of Bath's Prologue, 64
Chepman and Myllar (Scottish
    printers), 112
Cheviot Hills, 82, 101
Chevy Chase (Child 162), 82
Child, F.J., *English and Scottish
    Popular Ballads*, 82, 85, 89, 90,
    91, 92
Churchyard, Thomas, *A discourse on
    the queenes maiesties
    entertainment in Suffolk and
    Norfolk*, 27
Cicero, 62
Civil War (1642-9), 147, 148, 149
classics, the
  James VI's interest in, 98-9, 100,
    101
Cockburn, John, of Ormiston, 124-5,
    135
Cockburn of Ormiston family, 124;
  feud with Bothwells, 124
  literary tastes, 125, 136
  pro-English sympathies, 124-5
  property, 124
  Reformist beliefs, 124-5, 135
  relations with Charteris family,
    135-6
Cockburn, James, 136
Cockburn, Marion, 124
Cockburn, Patrick, 136
Cockburn, Sybil, 124, 136
coinage
  collected by Dumfries burgh, 145
  English and Scots differences, 31,
    145

Colin Clout's Come Home Again, 38-9

commonplace books, 59, 61, 64
  see also Maxwell MS

Complaint of a Christian Soul (Muschet), 135

Complaint of his mistressis absence from Court (James VI), 106

Complaynt of Scotland
  ballads listed in, 85
  and prophecy, 157-8
  Red Etin in, 159-60
  Thre Prestis of Peblis in, 132

Convention of Royal Burghs (1652), 149

Court and Council Books of Dumfries
  alms, 144, 148-9
  burgess enrolments, 144, 145, 146, 148, 151-2
  Civil War, 148, 149
  contracts, 144, 145
  disputes, 144, 145, 146, 148
  education, 148
  feu duties, 145
  fines, 144, 148, 151
  hornings, 146, 147
  kirk, 145, 151
  laws, 145, 146, 147, 149
  misdemeanours, 144, 145, 148, 150, 151
  officers of Court and Council, 144, 145, 147, 148, 152
  plague, 149
  price fixing, 145
  trade regulation, 146, 148, 149
  witchcraft, 149

Covenanters, 147

Craig, David, 71

Craig, Thomas, 28

Craigie, W.A., 109

Cramond, 161

Cromwell, Oliver, 143, 147, 150

Cunningham, William, 6th Earl of Glencairn, 61

Cupar, 21, 29, 158

Cupar Banns (Lyndsay), 158

Dalrymple, Sir David (Lord Hailes), 112

De Amicitia (Cicero), 62

De Regimine Principum, 63

Dennistoun, James, 59

Derwentwater's Farewell, Jacobite song, 94

Desportes, Philippe, 101

Discourse on the queenes maiesties entertainment in Suffolk and Norfolk, A (Churchyard), 27

Doctor Faustus (Marlowe), 28

Donaldson, Gordon, 135

Donne, John
  attitudes to liturgy, 48-9, 50, 51, 52-5, 56-7
  conversion to Anglicanism, 48-9, 51, 57
  and Council of Trent, 49
  and Sir Henry Goodyer, 50, 51
  Biathanatos, 50
  'Goodfriday, 1613. Riding Westward', 49
  'Hymne to Christ, at the Authors last going into Germany', 49
  'Hymne to God my God, in my sicknesse', 49
  'Hymne to God the Father', 49, 51
  Ignatius his Conclave, 49
  Pseudo-Martyr, 57
  'Satire III', 49
  Sermons, 48, 49
  see also 'Litanie'

Douglas, Archibald, 6th Earl of Angus, 162

Douglas, Gavin, 103;
  and Logie Robertson, 114
  response of later poets to, 108-9
  Eneados, 62, 109

Douglas, Hugh, of Longniddry, 124

Douglas, James, 2nd Earl of, 81, 82, 83-4, 89-90, 91, 92, 93, 94

Downfall of poperie, The (Bell), 29

Dreame on his Mistris my Ladie Glammis (James VI), 107
Dregy (Dunbar), 65, 116
Dreme (Lyndsay), 22, 155-66
Drummond, William, 98
du Bartas, Guillaume de Saluste, 97, 102-3, 109
Dumfries
    Burgh Court, 144
    Court and Council Books, 143, 144-54
    Royal Burgh, 143, 149
    strategic importance, 143, 144
    Town Council, 144, 145, 147, 148, 152
Dunbar, William
    and Chepman and Myllar, 112
    editions of his works, 112, 116
    in manuscript anthologies, 112
    and Logie Robertson, 112-23
    and Ramsay, 112, 115, 116
    reputation, 112
    response of later poets to, 108-9
    Ballade of Barnard Stewart, 116
    Dregy, 65, 116
    Elegy on Bernard Stewart, 116
    'Fenʒeit Freir', 116
    Flyting of Dunbar and Kennedie, 115, 116
    Goldyn Targe, 116
    'Hale, sterne superne', 116
    'Off benefice, Sir, at everie feist', 117
    'Rorate celi desuper', 116
    'Tabill of Confessioun', 115
    Tesment of Maister Andro Kennedy, 116
    Thrissil and the Rois, 117-18
    Tretis of the Tua Mariit Wemen and the Wedo, 116
Dunbar (E. Lothian), 162
Dunbar (Logie Robertson), 112, 113, 114, 118
Dunblane, 162
Dunfermline, 143

Edinburgh, 21, 22, 23, 25, 27, 29, 77, 143, 152
Elegie written by the King concerning his counsell for Ladies & gentlemen (James VI), 107
Elizabeth I, 27, 32, 40
Elizabethan Proverb Lore in Lyly's Euphues and in Pettie's Petite Pallace (Tilley), 61, 62
Eneados, 62, 109
Ennius, 62
Essayes of a Prentise (James VI), 60, 66, 98
Ettrick Forest, 89
Euphues (Lyly), 61, 66
euphuism, 61-2
Ever Green (Ramsay), 112
Eyre-Todd, George, 112

Fabricius, George, *Poetarum Veterum Ecclesiasticorum Opera Christiani* (1564), 51
Faerie Queene, The, 35-47;
    Book III, 35-6, 40, 41, 43, 44, 46, 47
    Book IV, 38, 43, 44, 45
    Book V, 42
    Book VII ('Mutabilitie'), 39
    Cupid in, 35, 46
    edition of 1590, 35
    edition of 1596, 35, 43
    eroticism in, 43
    Orpheus and Eurydice myth in, 46, 47
    reversal of sexual roles in, 40-2
    revisions, 35, 43-4, 46
    Venus in, 38-9, 40-1, 46
    see also Spenser, Edmund
Falkland, 97, 143, 162
'Fenʒeit Freir' (Dunbar), 116
Flodden, battle of (1513), 159
flyting, 65-6, 116
Flyting (Montgomery), 65

Flyting of Dunbar and Kennedie, 115, 116
Fortress of Perfect Beauty (Sidney), 27
Fowler, Alastair, 39
Fowler, William, 110
Fox, Denton, 63
Francis I, 40
Frazer, John, *Humorous Chap-Books of Scotland* (1873), 71
Freiris of Berwik, 112, 116
Froissart, Jean, 81, 83-4, 89, 90, 93
Furies (James VI), 102-3

Gabriels Salutation to Marie (Cockburn), 136
Gaelic borrowings in Scots, 66-7
Glasgow, 69, 70, 72-3, 74, 76, 77
Glencairn, Earl of *see* Cunningham
Godlie dream, Ane (Elizabeth Melville), 28, 135
Golding, Arthur, translator of Ovid, 37
Goldyn Targe (Dunbar), 116
'Goodfriday, 1613. Riding Westward' (Donne), 49
Goodyer, Sir Henry, 50, 51
Gourlaw, Robert, Scottish bookseller and printer, 61
Gowreis Conspiracie (1600), 28
Graham, Dougal, chapbook writer, 69-70
  authenticity of his writing, 72, 79;
  food, 76-9
  goods and gear, 74-5
  homes, 72-3
  sanitation, 74
  sleeping, 73-4
  textiles, 75-6
  Haverel Wives, 75, 79
  History of John Cheap the Chapman, 69, 73, 74, 75, 77, 78
  History of the Rebellion, 69, 70, 72, 73, 76

Jockey and Maggie's Courtship, 73, 74-5, 77, 78-9
Leper the Taylor, 73, 74, 76, 78, 79
Young Coalman's Courtship, 77
Graham, James, 6th Earl and 1st Marquis of Montrose, 94, 147-8
Gray Manuscript Adv. MS 34.7.3, 64
Grierson, Herbert, 114
Gude and Godlie Ballatis, 125
Guido delle Colonne, *Historia Troiana* (1494), 64
Gyre Carling, The (Bannatyne MS 136b-137a)
  attribution to Lyndsay, 160, 162
  earliest reference by Lyndsay, 160
  parody of *Siege of Jerusalem*, 160-1
  setting, 161-2
  style, 161

Haddington, 125, 136, 162
Hailes, Lord *see* Dalrymple
'Hale, sterne superne' (Dunbar), 116
'Haliburton, Hugh' *see* Logie Robertson
Hamer, Douglas, editor of Lyndsay, 21-2, 155-6
Hamilton, Jean, 136
Haverel Wives (Graham), 75, 79
Hecyra (Terence), 63
Hedgeley Moor, battle of (1464), 82
Henderson, Andrew, *Scottish Proverbs* (1832), 61
Henry III, 81
Henry IV Part I, 61
Henry IV Part II, 83
Henry VIII, 81, 89, 93, 96
Henryson, Robert, 108, 109;
  Preaching of the Swallow, 63, 108
  Testament of Cresseid, 108
Herd, David, 85, 89, 91

Heywood, Thomas, *If you know not me or the troubles of Queen Elizabeth*, 29

Hill, Richard, 59, 64

His Majesty's Poeticall Exercises (James VI), 101

Historia Scotorum (Boece), 156

Historia Troiana (Guido), 64

History of English Literature (Logie Robertson), 114

History of Greater Britain (Major), 157

History of John Cheap the Chapman (Graham), 69, 73, 74, 75, 77, 78

History of the Rebellion (Graham), 69, 70, 72, 73, 76

Holland, Richard, 109

Homildon Hill, battle of (1402), 81, 82, 83

Horace, 62

Horace in Homespun (Logie Robertson), 113, 119

Howard, Frances, Countess of Essex, 31

Hudson, Thomas, 109

Hume of Godscroft, David, 91, 92

Humorous Chap-Books of Scotland (Frazer), 71

Hunting of the Cheviot (Child 162), 82, 85

'Hymne to Christ, at the Authors last going into Germany' (Donne), 49

'Hymne to God my God, in my sicknesse' (Donne), 49

'Hymne to God the Father' (Donne), 49, 51

If you know not me or the troubles of Queen Elizabeth (Heywood), 29

Ignatius his Conclave (Donne), 49

In Scottish Fields (Logie Robertson), 114

'inkhorn' terms, 66

Iudas Kiss to the Sonne of Marie (Cockburn), 136

Jack, R.D.S., 101

Jacob, Violet, 114

James I, 109

James III, 103

James IV, 103, 134, 159

James V
    church appointments, 134
    minority, 155, 156, 158-9, 160-1, 162
    personal reign, 155, 159, 160, 162
    and regency of Albany, 159
    relations with England, 159
    relations with Lyndsay, 22, 32, 155, 156, 157, 160-1, 162-3
    works dedicated to, 157

James VI and I
    arms, 23
    classics, interest in, 98-9, 100, 101
    contemporary evaluation of, 97
    and du Bartas, 97, 102-3, 109
    and flyting, 66
    and Hudson, 109
    influence of earlier Scots poets on, 97, 108-9
    and Logie Robertson, 114
    and Lyndsay, 22, 23, 32, 108-9
    and Montgomerie, 26, 97, 98, 108, 109
    patron of the arts, 21-2, 96, 97
    physical features, 96
    poet, 96-111
    political achievements, 96, 135, 147
    Protestant religion, 21-2, 102, 104, 105-6, 109
    publishing, interest in, 22, 23, 24-5, 26, 27
    and Ruthven Raid, 125, 135, 146
    and Saint Gelais, 101
    and (Esmé) Stewart, 103
    Amatoria, 100, 101

James VI—*contd*
  Answere to the Libell called the
    Comons teares, 107, 108
  Basilikon Doron, 100-1, 108
  Complaint of his mistressis
    absence from Court, 106
  Dreame on his Mistris my Ladie
    Glammis, 107
  Elegie written by the King
    concerning his counsell for
    Ladies & gentlemen, 107
  Essayes of a Prentise, 60, 66, 97,
    98, 109
  Furies, 102-3
  His Majesty's Poeticall Exercises,
    101
  Lepanto, 97, 103, 104-6
  Phoenix, 103-4, 109
  Reulis and cautelis (Ane Schort
    Treatise), 66, 96-7, 109
  Satire against Woemen, A, 107
  Schort Poem of Tyme, 108
  'Sen thocht is frie', 98
  Sonnet 2 ('Apollo nixt'), 99
  Sonnet 6 ('But let them think'), 99
  Sonnet 7 ('And when I do
    descriue'), 99
  Sonnet 8 ('And graunt the lyke'),
    99
  Sonnet 9 ('O Dreidfull Pluto'), 99
  Sonnet 12 ('In short, you all
    forenamed gods'), 99, 109
  Sonnet to Chanceller Maitlane, 99
  Uranie, 102
James Carmichaell Collection of
  Proverbs, The, 60
Jockey and Maggie's Courtship
  (Graham), 73, 74-5, 77, 78-9
Johnie Armstrong (Child 169), 91
Jonson, Ben, 28, 36

Kennedy, Quintin, *Ane Litil Breif*
  Tracteit, 63
Kind Kittock, 161, 162
King, Adam, 28

King Berdok, 161
King Lear, 29
King Orphius, 125
Kinmont Willie (Child 186), 147
Kinsley, James, 116
Knox, John, 21, 124, 145

Laing, David, 59, 112
'Lament for the Language' (Logie
  Robertson), 114
Lanarkshire, 147, 162
Laying of Lord Fergus's Ghost, The,
  161
Lennox, Earls of *see* Stewart
Lepanto, 97, 103, 104-6
Leper the Taylor (Graham), 73, 74,
  76, 78, 79
Lévi-Strauss, Claude, 37
Lewis, C.S., 38, 39, 42-3
Lichtoun's Dream, 161, 162
Lines (Montrose), 94
Linlithgow, 143
'Litanie, A' (1608), 48;
  canonical form, 50, 51, 52, 56
  and Cranmer's litany, 51, 52, 53,
    56
  precedents (Notker, Ratpertus),
    50-1
  Purgatory omitted from, 55
  saints in, 52, 53, 54-5, 56, 57
  see also Donne, John
Litil Breif Tracteit, Ane (Kennedy),
  63
Lives (Walton), 51
Logie Robertson, James, 112-23
  advocate of Scottish literature, 114
  bibliography of his works, 119-20
  and Burns, 114, 118
  and Dunbar, 112, 113, 114-23
  'Hugh Haliburton', 113, 114, 116
  and Ramsay, 116
  reputation, 113-4
  Dunbar: Being a selection...adapted
    for modern readers (1895), 112,
    113, 114, 118

Logie Robertson—*contd*
History of English Literature, 114
Horace in Homespun, 113, 119
In Scottish Fields, 114
'Lament for the Language', 114
Ochil Idylls, 114
'Our Earlier Burns', 114, 118
Petition to the Deil, 114
London, 22, 23, 27, 28, 31, 32
London prodigall, The, 29
Louis XIV, 96
Lydgate, John, *Temple of Glass*, 45
Lyfe and actis of Wm Wallace
 (1600), 28
Lyly, John, 62, 67;
 Campaspe, 27
 Euphues, 61, 66
 Sapho and Phao, 27
Lyndsay, Sir David
 and church reform, 21, 23, 32,
  109, 135
 familiar servitor to James V, 22,
  32, 155, 156, 157, 159, 162-3
 Lyon King of Arms, 22, 23
 poet, 21, 22, 108, 135, 155-66
 Cupar Banns, 158
 Dreme, 22, 155
 'Epistil' to the *Dreme*, 155-66
 and 'gyir carling', 157, 158, 160-2
 and heroic histories, 155, 156-7,
  163
 Papyngo, 159
 and 'Prophiseis of Rymour, Beid
  and Marlyng', 155, 157-9, 163
 and 'Siegis', 155, 161
 Warkis (1568), 21, 22
  see also *Satyre of the Thrie
  Estaitis*

Macbeth, 56
MacColla, Fionn, 109
MacDiarmid, Hugh, 103, 113-14,
 119
MacGregor, George, editor of Dougal
 Graham, 69, 70, 71

Mackay Mackenzie, William, 116
Mackean, William, 112
McKerrow R.B., 23
Maitland, Helen, 136
Maitland, Mary, 136
Maitland, Sir Richard, 59, 136
Maitland Folio Manuscript Mag-
 dalene College Cambridge
 MS 2553, 59, 112, 124, 133,
 136
Maitland Quarto Manuscript, 136
Major, John, *History of Greater
 Britain*, 157
Mallis, Andrew, 64, 65
Malory, Sir Thomas, 94
Maner of ye crying of ane playe, The,
 161
Margaret Tudor, 156
Marston Moor, battle of (1644), 147
Mary, Queen of Scots, 23, 85, 134,
 143, 144, 146, 152, 158
Maxwell, John, 59, 60, 65, 67
 see also Maxwell MS
Maxwell Manuscript EUL Laing
 III.467, 59-68;
 Anderson transcript, 60, 62-3, 65
 flyting in, 65-6
 Gaelic in, 66-7
 Geneva Bible quoted in, 60
 handwriting in, 60, 61
 'inkhorn' terms in, 66
 linguistic value, 66, 67
 Motherwell transcript, 59
 owners, 59
 proverb collection in, 59, 61, 62,
  64, 66, 67
 'rowndales' (triolets) in, 65-6
 sources, 61-7
Melville, Andrew, 135
Melville, Elizabeth (Lady Culross),
 Ane godlie dream (1603), 28,
 135
Merlin, 157, 158
Metamorphoses (Ovid), 36-7, 41
Meun, Jean de, 45

Milton, Colin, 113-4
Minstrelsy of the Scottish Border (Scott), 88-9, 90, 91, 93, 94
Monck, George, 150
Montgomerie, Alexander, 26, 60, 65, 67, 98, 108, 109
  'Can goldin Titan', 60, 97
  Flyting, 65
Montgomery, Sir Hugh, 84, 85, 91
Montrose *see* Graham, James
Morton, Thomas, *A Catholic Appeal for Protestants* (1609), 50, 51, 57
Motherwell, William, 59, 61, 63, 66, 67, 70-1
Mure, William, of Rowallan, 60
Murray, Charles, 114
Muschet, George, *Complaint of a Christian Soul*, 135

New Inn, The (Jonson), 36
Newcastle, 81, 83, 84, 89, 90
North Berwick Law, 161, 162
Northumbrian Minstrelsy (Collingwood Bruce and Stokoe), 94

Ochil Idylls (Logie Robertson), 114
Ode IV (Horace), 62
'Off benefice, Sir, at everie feist' (Dunbar), 117
Otterburn, battle of (1338)
  Froissart's account of, 81, 83, 84, 89-90, 93
  traditional site of, 82
  see also *Battle of Otterburn*
'Our Earlier Burns' (Logie Robertson), 114, 118
Ovid, 36-7, 41, 46, 62
Palinod of John Colvill (1660), 28
paper in the 16th c.
  English, 24, 25
  French, 25
  prices, 25
  Scottish, 24, 25

Percy, Henry, Earl of Northumberland ('Hotspur'), 81, 82, 83-4, 85, 89-90, 91, 93
Perth, 143
Petite Pallace of Pettie his Pleasure, A (Pettie), 61, 62, 66, 67
Petition to the Deil (Logie Robertson), 114
Pettie, George, *A Petite Pallace of Pettie his Pleasure* (1576), 61, 62, 66, 67
Philotus, 26, 27, 28, 30
Phoenix (James VI), 103-4, 109
Picta Poesis (Aneau), 37
Pinkerton, John, 112
Pinkie, battle of (1548), 124
Plato, 36
plays, in England, 22;
  printers' devices in, 23
  printing traditions of, 23-4, 27
  types used, 27-8
plays, in Scotland
  printers' devices in, 23, 26, 27
  printing traditions, lack of, 22, 27
  types used, 27
Plutarch, 36
Poetarum Veterum Ecclesiasticorum Opera Christiani (Fabricius), 51
Ponsonbie, William, printer, 40
'Prayer off Salamon to obtein vysdome', 125
Preaching of the Swallow (Henryson), 63, 108
'Proheme apon the Cosmographe' (Bellenden), 156
Propertius, 62
prophecy, political, 157-9
proverbs, 31, 59, 61, 62, 64, 66, 67
Psalms...in meter (1603), 28
Pseudo-Martyr (Donne), 57
Puritans, 147

Ramsay, Allan, 112, 115
Red Etin, The
  affinities with Aarne-Thompson
    303, 160
  Complaynt of Scotland reference,
    159
  fabulous subject matter, 159-60
  earliest reference by Lyndsay, 159
  Peter Buchan, version of, 160
Redpeith Manuscript CUL MS
  Moore LL.v.10, 112
Reformation
  effect on drama, 21-3, 32
  and language, in Council oaths of
    office, 145
  and Lyndsay, 21-2, 23, 31-2, 108,
    109
  and Scottish national culture, 110
  and *Thre Prestis of Peblis*, 133-6
Renaissance
  attitudes to classical world, 36-8
*Reulis and cautelis...in Scottish
    Poesie (Ane Schort Treatise)*,
    66, 96-7, 109
Reynes, Robert, 59, 64
Riccio, David, 125
Richard II, 81
Rolland, John, *The Sevin Seages*,
    62, 67
roman type, 22, 27, 28, 29, 30
Romans in Britain, 82, 161
Romeo and Juliet, 92
'Rorate celi desuper' (Dunbar), 116
Rowley, S., *When you see me you
    know me...the historie of Henry
    VIII*, 29
royal arms of Scotland
  motto, 64-5
  red lion device, 22
*Royal entertainment of the earl of
    Nottingham, The* (1605), 28
Russell, Gideon, and Mungo, Scots
    millers and paper makers, 25
Ruthven Raid, 125, 135, 146

Sandys, Edwin, 57
Saint-Gelais, Mellin de, 101
Sapho and Phao (Lyly), 27
Satire against Woemen, A (James
    VI), 107
'Satire III' (Donne), 49
Satyre of the Thrie Estaitis, Ane
  alliterative metre in, 160
  Bannatyne MS text, 24, 29
  Bodleian (Gough 221) copy, 24,
  cast list, 1602 omission of, 30
  Cupar performance, 21, 158
  Cupar text (1552), 29
  Edinburgh text (1554), 29
  edition of 1602, 21, 22, 23, 24
  English readership, 22, 23, 28,
    30-2
  language, Scots and English
    differences in, 30-2
  Lincoln Cathedral copy, 25
  paper, of 1604 title page, 24
  price in 1599, 25
  printers' devices in, 23
  prophecy in, 158
  proverbs in, 31
  sales, in 1597, 25; in 1599-1603,
    26
  stage directions in, 29
  title-page of 1604 (BL copy), 22,
    23-4
  Warkis (1568), omission in, 21
  watermarks in, 24-5
  see also Lyndsay, Sir David
Schipper, Jacob, 112
Schort Poem of Tyme (James VI),
    108
Scott, Sir Walter, 89, 90, 91, 93,
    94
Scottish Proverbs (Henderson), 61
Scottish Record Office Manuscript
    RH 13/35
  circulation, 125
  contents:
    Gude and Godlie Ballatis, 125

SRO MS RH 13/35—*contd*
  'history [which mentions] how
    Issope excussit him selffe...',
    125
  King Orphius, 125
  'Prayer off Salamon to obtein
    vysdome', 125
  Sir Colling, 125
  Thre Prestis of Peblis, 125, 126,
    128, 130, 132-3
  copyist, Thomas White, 125
  earliest witness for *Thre Prestis*
    ll.364-408, 125-6, 128, 130,
    131-2
  Reformist links, 125
'Sen thocht is frie' (James VI), 98
Seneca, 62
Sermons (Donne), 48, 49
Sevin Seages, The (Rolland), 62, 67
Shakespeare, William
  King Henry IV Part I, 61
  King Henry IV Part II, 83
  King Lear, 29
  Macbeth, 56
  Romeo and Juliet, 92
Sharpe, C.K., 92, 94
Sheath and the Knife, The (Child 16),
  92
Shire, Helena Mennie, 3-12, 15-17,
  22, 26, 38, 112, 160, 170, 171
Sidney, Sir Philip
  and chivalry, 94
  Fortress of Perfect Beauty, The, 27
  response to ballads, 82
Siege of Jerusalem, 161
Sim, Adam, of Coulter, 59
Sinclair, Sir William, of
  Hirdmanston, 124, 125, 136
Sir Colling, 125
Small, John, 112
Solemn League and Covenant (1643),
  147
Sonnets (James VI), 99, 100, 101,
  109

speculum principis tradition, 133,
  156-7
Spenser, Edmund, 35-47, 94;
  and Chaucer, 46, 47
  epic theory, 47
  hermaphrodite emblem, use of, 35,
    36-9, 40, 44, 46
  Letter to Ralegh, 47
  Ovid, indebtedness to, 36-7
  Colin Clout's Come Home Again,
    38-9
  see also *Faerie Queene*
Staple of news, The (Jonson), 28
Stewart, Esmé, Lord d'Aubigny and
  1st Duke of Lennox, 103
Stewart, John, Duke of Albany,
  regent, 159
Stewart, Marion, 64, 124, 125
Stewart, Matthew, 4th Earl of
  Lennox, 125
Stewart, William, 156
Stirling, 143
Stokoe, John, 94
Symposium (Plato), 36

'Tabill of Confessioun' (Dunbar), 115
Tantallon Castle, 162
Tanner MS 407 (Reynes), 59
Tasso, 40
Temple of Glass (Lydgate), 45
Terence, 63, 67
'Tesment of Maister Andro Kennedy'
  (Dunbar), 116
Testament of Cresseid (Henryson),
  108
Thomas the Rhymer, 157, 159
Thre Prestis of Peblis, 124-42;
  circulation, 132
  Complaynt of Scotland reference,
    132
  popularity, 132-3, 135
  textual history, 125-6;
    Asloan MS, 125, 132
    Charteris print, 125-6, 127, 129,
      131-2, 136

Thre Prestis—contd
   SRO MS RH 13/35, 124, 125-
   6, 128, 130, 131-2, 136
   theological position, 133-6
   see also SRO MS RH 13/35
Threave Castle, 147
Thrissil and the Rois, 117-18
Tilley, M.P., 59;
   *Elizabethan Proverb Lore in
   Lyly's Euphues and Pettie's
   Petite Pallace*, 61, 62
Tinto Hills, 160, 161, 162
*Traditional Tunes of the Child
   Ballads* (Bronson), 94
Tragedy of Darius (Alexander), 27
*Tretis of the Tua Mariit Wemen and
   the Wedo*, 116
triolets ('rowndales'), 65-6
'True Report of the Baptism of the
   Prince of Scotland' (Butter), 28-9

*Vnione Britanniae seu de regnorum
   Angliae et Scotie, De* (1604), 28
Uranie (James VI), 102

Vautroullier, Thomas, printer, 27

Waldegrave, Robert, printer, 27, 32
Wallace, Margaret (Charteris), 26, 27
Walton, Izaak, 51
Wardens of the Marches, 81, 159
Warkworth, 82
watermarks, 24-5, 124
Waterston, Robert, 25
Wharton, Thomas, 159
When you see me you know me
   (Rowley), 29
White, Thomas, copyist of SRO MS
   RH 13/35, 125
Whiting, B.J., 59, 62, 64
Wife of Bath's Prologue, 64
Wishart, George, 124

Yeavering, battle of (1414), 82
Young Coalman's Courtship
   (Graham), 77

◊